HUMANITY: TEXTS AND CONTEXTS

Humanity: Texts and Contexts

Christian and Muslim Perspectives

A record of the sixth Building Bridges seminar
Convened by the Archbishop of Canterbury
National University of Singapore, December 2007

MICHAEL IPGRAVE
and
DAVID MARSHALL, EDITORS

GEORGETOWN UNIVERSITY PRESS
Washington, D.C.

Library of Congress Cataloging-in-Publication Data

Humanity : texts and contexts : Christian and Muslim perspectives : a record of the sixth Building Bridges seminar, convened by the Archbishop of Canterbury, National University of Singapore, December 2007 / Michael Ipgrave and David Marshall, editors.
p. cm.
Includes bibliographical references and index.
ISBN 978-1-58901-716-0 (pbk. : alk. paper)
1. Theological anthropology—Christianity—Congresses. 2. Theological anthropology—Islam—Congresses. 3. Human beings—Congresses. 4. Christianity and other religions—Islam—Congresses. 5. Islam—Relations—Christianity—Congresses. I. Ipgrave, Michael. II. Marshall, David.
BT701.3.H86 2010
233—dc22

2010012462

♾This book is printed on acid-free paper meeting the requirements of the American National Standard for Permanence in Paper for Printed Library Materials.

15 14 13 12 11 9 8 7 6 5 4 3 2
First printing

Printed in the United States of America

CONTENTS

PARTICIPANTS

Muhammad Abdel Haleem

King Fahd Professor of Islamic Studies, School of Oriental and African Studies, University of London

Amin Abdullah

Rector, State Islamic University (Universitas Islam Negeri), Yogyakarta, Indonesia

Asma Afsaruddin

Associate Professor, Department of Classics, University of Notre Dame, Indiana

Albakri Ahmad

Dean of Majlis Ugama Islam Singapura (Islamic Religious Council of Singapore) Academy, Singapore

Seyed Amir Akrami

Lecturer, al-Mahdi Institute, Birmingham, U.K.

Syed Farid Alatas

Associate Professor, Department of Sociology, National University of Singapore

Clare Amos

Director of Theological Studies, Anglican Communion, London

John Azumah

Senior Research Fellow, Akrofi-Christaller Memorial Centre, Akropong-Akuapem, Ghana

Azizan Baharuddin

Director, Centre for Civilisational Dialogue, University of Malaya, Kuala Lumpur

Osman Bakar

Professor of Islamic Thought and Civilization, International Institute of Islamic Thought and Civilization (ISTAC), Kuala Lumpur

Mark Chan

Centre for the Study of Christianity in Asia, Trinity Theological College, Singapore

Roland Chia

Dean of the School of Postgraduate Studies, Trinity Theological College, Singapore

Vincent Cornell

Asa Griggs Candler Professor of Middle East and Islamic Studies, Emory University, Atlanta, Georgia

Ellen Davis

Amos Ragan Kearns Distinguished Professor of Bible and Practical Theology, Duke University, Durham, North Carolina

Hugh Goddard

Professor of Christian-Muslim Relations, University of Nottingham, U.K.

Michael Ipgrave

Archdeacon of Southwark, Church of England

John Langan

Rose Kennedy Professor of Christian Ethics, Georgetown University, Washington, D.C.

Daniel Madigan

Director, Institute for the Study of Religions and Cultures, Pontifical Gregorian University, Rome

Jane Dammen McAuliffe

Currently, president of Bryn Mawr College; formerly Dean of the College of Arts and Sciences, Georgetown University, Washington, D.C.

Esther Mombo

Academic Dean, St Paul's United Theological College, Limuru, Kenya

Ustaz Nazirudin Mohd Nasir

Head, Office of the Mufti, Majlis Ugama Islam Singapura (Islamic Religious Council of Singapore), Singapore

Ng Kam Weng

Research Director, Kairos Research Centre, Kuala Lumpur

Michael Northcott

Professor of Ethics, School of Divinity, University of Edinburgh, U.K.

Michael Nai-Chiu Poon

Director, Centre for the Study of Christianity in Asia, Trinity Theological College, Singapore

JOHN PRIOR
Lecturer, Ledalero Institute of Philosophy, Maumere, Indonesia

RECEP ŞENTÜRK
Professor of Sociology, İslâm Araştirmalari Merkezi (Centre for Islamic Studies), Istanbul

MONA SIDDIQUI
Professor of Islamic Studies and Public Understanding, University of Glasgow, U.K.

MUHAMMAD SUHEYL UMAR
Director, Iqbal Academy, Lahore, Pakistan

ROWAN WILLIAMS
Archbishop of Canterbury, Church of England

TIMOTHY WINTER
Lecturer in Islamic Studies, University of Cambridge, U.K.

MOHAMED YUNUS YASIN
National University of Malaysia, Petaling Jaya, Selangor, Malaysia

ACKNOWLEDGMENTS

MANY THANKS are due to the president of Georgetown University, Dr. John J. DeGioia, for generous and essential support for the 2007 Building Bridges seminar, and for assistance in making possible the publication of this record. We also wish to acknowledge the assistance and partnership of Syed Dr. Farid Alatas and colleagues in the National University of Singapore in hosting the event, and the kind hospitality of Tan Sri Francis Yeoh, CBE, in providing accommodation for participants. We appreciate the cooperation of the Anglican Diocese of Singapore and of the Majlis Ugama Islam Singapura (Islamic Religious Council of Singapore), who were closely involved in arrangements for the seminar.

INTRODUCTION

Humanity in Context

Michael Ipgrave

THIS VOLUME PROVIDES a record of the papers delivered and the texts discussed at the sixth annual Building Bridges seminar of Christian and Muslim scholars, convened by the Archbishop of Canterbury at the National University of Singapore in December 2007 on the theme "Humanity in Context."[1] As in previous seminars in the series, an overarching subject of central interest to both Christians and Muslims was addressed by using the resources that each faith had to offer out of its own integrity, and formal and informal dialogue between the participants grew out of the structured presentations that are recorded here. This volume does not attempt to capture the richness and variety of those exchanges, but we hope that the wealth of material presented here will stimulate a like dialogical engagement among and between the book's readers. If this mirrors the experience of Singapore, that dialogue will often be as intense between Christian and Christian, or Muslim and Muslim, as between those of different faiths.

The first lecture of the seminar appropriately began by quoting Hamlet's famous exclamation: "What a piece of work is man!" for this seminar took as its starting point the prince's sense of both awe and puzzlement at what it means to be a human, "the beauty of the world, the paragon of animals," and at no point did it share his subsequent disillusionment: "And yet, to me, what is this quintessence of dust? Man delights not me." The theme chosen, "Humanity in context: Christian and Muslim Perspectives on Being Human," was indeed daunting in its breadth and depth.

Out of the vast possibilities offered for reflection, three questions in particular were singled out for attention: What does it mean to be human? What is the significance of the diversity that is evident among human beings? What are the challenges that humans face in living within the natural world? The seminar sought to focus on theological responses to each of these questions, drawing on the wealth of material found in both Christian and Islamic scriptures and traditions, and recognizing also the way in which all questions relating to humanity have been made both more complex and more urgent through the rapid changes that have affected our societies and our world. In a pattern slightly different to that of earlier seminars, the three major themes of "Being human," "Living with difference," and "Guardians of the environment" were all introduced first through individual lectures delivered in the public part of the seminar. More detailed engagement with six particular dimensions of these themes was then undertaken by closed sessions of the seminars reading and discussing together coupled biblical and Qur'ānic texts. What is presented here are edited versions of the three pairs of public lectures together with the twelve sets of scriptural texts and the introductions to those texts provided by the scholars; the Archbishop of Canterbury has also added his own concluding reflections.

The three themes of human identity, human diversity, and human stewardship raise questions of different kinds from one another, yet it became apparent at the seminar that for Christians and Muslims they have two features in common. In the first place, these are issues that believers in both faiths face side by side. The resources that Islam and Christianity have to offer for understanding humanity in context are in many ways quite different from one another, yet it is certain that we are seeking to understand one common humanity, and that one common humanity lives its life in the one common context of a shared earth. While previous Building Bridges seminars have shown how it is possible to model dialogue creatively around issues that are contested between Christians and Muslims, the focus in Singapore was rather on a sense of common purpose in addressing issues that affect us equally and inseparably.

This sense was perhaps enhanced by the fact that, although a considerable part of the seminar was devoted to looking at issues of human diversity, it was agreed that this would not include the issue of religious diversity, touched on in earlier seminars; in this seminar, race, culture, and gender were the indices of difference being addressed. Moreover, for the first time in the seminar series, some Qur'ānic texts were introduced by Christian scholars, and some biblical texts were introduced by Muslim scholars. This "cross-reading" of texts can be seen as a sign of the collegiality that is possible when faithful believers who have grown to trust and respect one another meet in openness in the presence of their respective scriptures.

Second, this does not mean that the three themes explored here are in themselves anodyne, or that the dialogue around them would proceed based on an easy consensus. On the contrary, all three, in different ways, raise highly topical and massively controversial issues for both Christians and Muslims, and much of the discussion within the seminar was correspondingly robust.

This is perhaps most obvious in relation to the theme of diversity, where gender issues are among the challenges that most sharply divide Christians of differing views and Muslims of differing views. Although it was not addressed in a structured way, the seminar discussion was also conducted with an awareness of the even more contentious issue of differing attitudes to human sexuality. In relation to the environmental theme of guardianship or stewardship, the urgent argument lies perhaps not so much within either Christianity or Islam as in the relation of faiths to the current ecological crisis: how can either faith establish its credibility in offering hope for a sustainable future through the account that it gives of humanity's place in the world? Underlying that account, of course, is the still more primary question, of who humans are designed to be, or whether their being is not in any sense designed. Both Christians and Muslims recognize that an adequate answer to the question of who we are is the key to knowing how we should live, and both believe that there can be no adequate answer without reference to a good and purposeful God. For many today, that message is greeted with incredulous rejection even as for others it brings purpose and hope.

Note

1. Records of previous Building Bridges seminars have been published as follows, all edited by Michael Ipgrave: *The Road Ahead: A Christian–Muslim Dialogue* (London: Church House, 2002); *Scriptures in Dialogue: Christians and Muslims Studying the Bible and the Qur'ān Together* (London: Church House, 2004); *Bearing the Word: Prophecy in Biblical and Qur'ānic Perspective* (London: Church House, 2005); *Building a Better Bridge: Muslims, Christians, and the Common Good* (Washington, D.C.: Georgetown University Press, 2008); and *Justice and Rights: Christian and Muslim Perspectives* (Washington, D.C.: Georgetown University Press, 2009). For further information on the Building Bridges seminars, see http://berkleycenter.georgetown.edu/networks/building_bridges.

PART ONE

Human Identity, Difference, and Guardianship

The six contributions in this part are in three pairs, each comprising a Christian and an Islamic perspective, and each contribution addresses aspects of three questions: What does it mean to be human? What is the significance of the diversity that is evident among human beings? What are the challenges that humans face in living within the natural world? In each case, although in different ways and from different theological and geographical places within the two faiths, the contributions seek to draw out of scripture and tradition perspectives that speak to humanity's contemporary situation.

Ng Kam Weng, drawing primarily on a Reformed understanding of Christianity, emphasizes both the misery and the glory of humanity, and relates both aspects to the controlling gospel story of fall and redemption; he emphasises the role, both functional and ontological, of the doctrine of the "image of God" in shaping Christian anthropology. This is a point taken up by Mona Siddiqui who, as she develops the three motifs of human nature, human alienation, and human vocation in Islam, does so with conscious reference also to Christian views, pointing out both points of convergence and significant differences.

Michael Ipgrave traces some of the ways in which the Christian community has responded to the challenges of racial, cultural, and gender diversity by drawing on the history of earlier responses to the distinction of slave and free; he discerns a Trinitarian dynamic in the evolution of the Church's response. Vincent Cornell, in his careful analysis of what the Qur'ān has to say about human difference, stresses the need to recognize the context in which the scriptural texts were revealed, the ways in which they have been interpreted in history, and the reality of vernacular traditions in shaping the Islamic tradition as a whole.

Azizan Baharuddin's presentation of an Islamic perspective on "guardianship of the environment" draws on central themes of the Islamic spiritual tradition, such as unity (*tawḥīd*), gratitude to God, and the paradoxical freedom of servitude, setting these within a holistic philosophical and theological approach that calls for a civilizational dialogue bringing commitment to sustainable development. Michael Northcott, recognizing the ambiguity of Christianity's historical record in relation to the environment, points to the richness of the concept of guardianship embedded in traditional Christian faith and sharply poses the question whether we are to be stewards or slayers of the earth.

CHAPTER ONE

Being Human

1.1 The Image of God, Human Dignity, and Vocation

Ng Kam Weng

> What a piece of work is man! How noble in reason! How infinite in faculty! In form and moving how express and admirable! In action how like an angel! In apprehension how like a god! The beauty of the world! The paragon of animals!
>
> *Hamlet*, Act 2, Scene 2

The Contemporary Crisis of Humanity

The human race has reason to be proud. It sends space probes beyond the solar system. It shatters the atom to capture the most elusive subatomic particles. It constructs mathematical models of the universe at its birth. Yet ironically, the very success of the modern knowledge enterprise has become a stumbling block to humankind's quest for self-knowledge in the modern world.

With its prowess in unlocking the secrets of nature and its technological power, the human race is convinced that it is master of its own destiny. It sees no relevance for religion. It prefers Prozac to priests. Why rely on faith to move mountains when bulldozers will do the job? If human fulfillment comes through technological advancement, why be distracted by heavenly promises? After all, we can create heaven on earth.

It was not too long ago that we heard the optimistic slogan: "My grandfather preached the gospel of religion; my father preached the gospel of socialism; I preach the gospel of science." Such optimism was shattered by two world wars, the tyranny of dictatorship exemplified by Hitler's Holocaust and Stalin's Gulag, and the genocides in Africa. To be sure, the world community found consensus for human rights for the first time with the United Nations Declaration of Human Rights (1948) based on the inherent dignity possessed by every individual. Unfortunately, the only thing that seems universal arising from the declaration is the universal abuse of human beings.

One may assume that developed nations are not spared the trauma of war and violence that plague poor countries. Still, social analysts worry about the loss of democracy through mass media manipulation and the vulnerability of modern civilization with the proliferation of weapons of mass destruction. Science itself has become an ecological time bomb. T. S. Eliot's words resonate with us:

> Where is the Life we have lost in living?
> Where is the wisdom we have lost in knowledge?
> Where is the knowledge we have lost in information?

In the early 1970s a French philosopher declared, "God is dead, Marx is dead, I am not feeling well myself." Indeed "not feeling well" is the pervasive mood of contemporary modern man. This cry expresses the melancholy that is symptomatic of a modern life that has lost its meaning, coherence, and depth.

Robert Bellah, an outstanding sociologist, observes how traditional moral and religious communities seem unable to provide stable anchors in the avalanche of change: "A lifestyle enclave is formed by people who share some feature of private life. Members of a lifestyle enclave express their identity through shared patterns of appearance, consumption, and leisure activities, which often serve to differentiate them sharply from those with other lifestyles. They are not interdependent, do not act together politically, and do not share a history."[1] The scenario is most aptly captured by Marshall Berman's description of contemporary societies:

> To be modern is to find ourselves in an environment that promises us adventure, power, joy, growth, transformation of ourselves and the world—and, at the same time, that threatens to destroy everything we have, everything we know, everything we are . . . modernity can be said to unite all mankind. But it is a paradoxical unity, a unity of disunity: it pours us all into a maelstrom of perpetual disintegration and renewal, of struggle and contradiction, of ambiguity and anguish. To be modern is to be part of a universe in which, as Marx said, "all that is solid melts into air."[2]

It is ironic if not tragic when human beings finally conclude that life, if not the world, is devoid of meaning in the midst of the knowledge explosion in the scientific disciplines. In the words of one writer, "At the heart of modern media is a vacuum of meaning." We may try to fill the void with entertainment to the extent of amusing ourselves to death—to borrow Neil Postman's words.

Others, nevertheless, may question why we should so easily surrender to passivity or escapism. It seems that the pervasive sense of meaninglessness is unprecedented in contemporary society. True, there have always been nihilists in human history. But the norm seems to be for human beings to believe in a moral universe that is historically sustained by religious traditions. Perhaps it is timely to revisit such traditions in general and Christianity in particular to unravel the mystery of the human race, its misery, and its majesty.

If my depiction of the sensibilities of contemporary humanity is correct, perhaps I should eschew—at least for present purposes—the temptation to wax eloquent about the traditional rhetoric of religious discourse that often centers on the human soul. Perhaps, if only for the purpose of gaining a hearing from the modern world for the abiding relevance of the teachings of Christianity, I may engage in a concrete analysis of the human condition. I hope this modest enterprise will lead to the discovery of pointers suggesting that human glory and dignity has a transcendental source and that the final happiness of humankind includes something more than its material needs. More importantly, despite the upbeat rhetoric of the priests of modernity (represented by naturalistic scientists such as Richard Dawkins), the reality that cannot be ignored is that scientific progress exacts a terrible price on humanity. In other words, perhaps the human race today should take more seriously the dark side of modernity that is acutely exposed by the analysis of the Christian faith.

The Mystery of Humankind

It is right that we begin our analysis with a phenomenological reading of the human race that is concretely rooted in its experience of social relations and historical processes. This approach ensures that we do not fall into abstract and arguably irrelevant theorizing about an abstract deity dealing with an abstract humanity. Nevertheless, we cannot be satisfied with any fragmented perspective characteristic of the specialized domains of specific disciplines, whether in the sciences or the humanities. We must press beyond to gain a sense of the wholeness that comes from a theological analysis of humanity. In effect, this demands an integration of theology and social analysis. In the celebrated words of John Calvin, "man never achieves a clear knowledge of himself unless he has first looked upon God's face, and then descends from contemplating him to scrutinize himself."[3] We cannot truly know ourselves if we ignore the light of God's revelation, which illuminates our whole life to uncover our true nature within the concrete realities of life.

The Majesty and Misery of Humankind

In the light of revelation, humankind's true nature is seen to be characterized by both majesty and misery. We turn now to explore these two aspects of the human condition.

The Misery of Humankind

There is little dispute over the fact that the human race exists in a fallible and faulty condition. Psychologists and therapists diagnose the human condition using various categories of neurosis, but the success of these professionals in restoring human wholeness is increasingly questioned. Recognizing that psychotherapy can only achieve partial success will hopefully persuade the helping profession to reconsider the neglected category of sin to diagnose and remedy psychological disorder. The theological category of sin may be unpopular to secular therapists, but it provides a cogent explanation for the pervasive moral failure of human beings. If correct diagnosis is the essential prerequisite for a cure, then surely the category of sin ought to be included as a diagnostic tool in the restoration of human wholeness.

There is no single definition for sin because the category is used to describe a complex set of pathological forms of human behavior conveniently grouped under the "Seven Deadly Sins": pride (*superbia*), envy (*invidia*), anger (*ira*), sloth (*acedia*), avarice (*avaritia*), gluttony (*gula*), and lust (*luxuria*).

The sin of pride (*superbia*) or the tragedy of being excessively ambitious (*hubris*) and the sin of desire (*concupiscentia*) played a pivotal role in humankind's fall from innocence to sin as described in the book of Genesis. Adam and Eve wanted to be as God even though it meant disobeying—indeed, outwitting—God, whom they suspected of selfishness in keeping good things from them in order to keep them from growing toward moral autonomy. It was desire that consumed Eve (and Adam), who found the fruit of the knowledge of good and evil pleasing to the eye and desirable for eating.

More importantly, we must not miss the most radical (i.e., going to the root) or profound significance of sin epitomized by Adam and Eve's act of defiance against God. The tragedy is that their fall into sin led to uncontrollable passion and mutual estrangement between humans. Love and reciprocity was lost between Adam and Eve: "To love and to cherish" became "To desire and to dominate." Finally, the fall ruptured the relationship between God and humanity and resulted in the banishment of humankind from the presence of God.

The complex phenomenon of sin is also confirmed elsewhere in the Bible. For instance, 1 John 2:15–17 says, "Do not love the world or the things in the world. If anyone loves the world, the love of the Father is not in him. For all that is in the world—the desires of the flesh and the desires of the eyes and pride in possessions—is not from the Father but is from the world. And the world is passing away along with its desires, but whoever does the will of God abides forever."

The Christian view of sin is based not just on some ancient traditions. It is premised on the evident phenomena of universal moral failure that betrays a prior corruption of human nature. G. K. Chesterton once quipped that "Original Sin" was one doctrine that is truly confirmed by human experience. Sinful acts are merely manifestations of a sinful nature, sinful nature itself being a primordial event (the fall or innate moral corruption) that left humankind bereft of God's gracious presence and power. Consequently, human beings existing in a spiritually and morally deprived condition are unable to please God or to prevent themselves from falling into sin.

The Christian insistence on the universality of sin cannot be attributed to some external or impersonal force. All human beings remain responsible for their own moral acts because they willingly choose to follow the tendency of their inborn moral corruption leading to personal acts of sin. These twin assertions are the thrust of the Christian formulation of the doctrine of original sin viewed as a rupture in humankind's relationship with God.

Reinhold Niebuhr gives one of the most eloquent and persuasive discussions of original sin in modern times. In his book *The Nature and Destiny of Man*, Niebuhr asserts:

> Man is a sinner. His sin is defined as rebellion against God. The Christian estimate of human evil is so serious precisely because it places evil at the very centre of human personality: in the will. This evil cannot be regarded complacently as the inevitable consequence of his finiteness or the fruit of his involvement in the contingencies and necessities of nature. Sin is occasioned precisely by the fact that man refuses to admit his "creatureliness" and to acknowledge himself as merely a member of a total unity of life. He pretends to be more than he is. . . . His sin is the wrong use of his freedom and its consequent destruction.[4]

Precisely because human beings want autonomy from God, they will not subject themselves to God's moral demands; they always operate from inordinate self-love. Niebuhr suggests that such autonomy (or unbelief) is concomitant with pride or an attitude of self-sufficiency and defiance against God. Original sin is a complex package of unbelief (lack of trust), rebellion, and idolatry; it ends up with human beings replacing God with the self—in effect, replacing the Creator with the creature. The Christian tradition associates original sin with Adam's historical act of defiance, but the doctrine of original sin also accurately describes the fundamental relation of every human being to God. Every person is as immediately involved with original sin as Adam and Eve were.

In summary, the primary source of moral failure is not intellectual defect. It is rather humankind's inability or unwillingness to accommodate itself to God's moral demands. Still, although we remain cognizant of the disruptive effect of sin, we cannot deny that in principle human beings are moral creatures. Their moral failures only highlight their moral tragedy that is so aptly pictured by Blaise Pascal, "Man is neither angel nor beast. When he tries to be an angel, he acts like a beast."

It is important that we recognize the ambiguity of human existence and the human historical enterprise. That being the case, the balanced approach is neither to judge human beings for their shortcomings nor to approve their hubris. We cannot lose sight of humankind's moral vocation or its hope of moral restoration. Unlike gnostic religions that enjoin flight from this evil world to gain mystical union with God, Christianity maintains that the destiny of humanity includes stewardship, and the ordering of this earth entails a moral enterprise that requires purposive moral decisions and communal action.

The Majesty of Humankind

We must avoid two errors in our reflection on humanity. First, we must ignore the naturalistic philosophers who argue that human beings remain merely animals, albeit the highest beings in the animal kingdom. To be sure, such a devaluation may be softened by qualifications such as "*homo faber*" (tool maker) or "*homo sapiens*" (intelligent creature). Nevertheless, such labels fail to do justice to the uniqueness—indeed, the distinctiveness—of humanity, which stands out with special characteristics that include the use of complex language and symbolic thought, the production of culture and technological innovations, and fostering community based on moral values. It is surely significant that only human beings display religious longings.

Second, our analysis must do justice both to the majesty and misery of the human race.[5] The Psalmist exclaimed with a sense of wonderment, "When I look at your heavens, the work of your fingers, the moon and the stars, which you have set in place, what is man that you are mindful of him, and the son of man that you care for him?"[6] Human beings may be made lower than heavenly beings, but they are entrusted with dominion over all creation. They are under God's rule but rule over creation.

The Creation story emphasizes several aspects of the dignity and high calling of the human race. First, the Bible affirms the original goodness of creation that includes human beings. As such, all humans are potentially redeemable from the present corruption of nature. That is to say, the Bible does not think of the human race apart from the original goodness and aim of God's creation. Conversely, the goodness of creation emphasizes that the predicaments of human existence are not due to the inadequacy of God's law and structuring of the world. God created the cosmos and not chaos. He intends human beings to flourish and enjoy the benefits of his creation.

Second, we are struck by the special qualities of human beings. To be sure, humans exist as creatures among other creatures in the natural world, but it is precisely their moral freedom or their ability to transcend their physical existence that marks them as unique among all created things. In particular, freedom is the ability to become what God intended human beings to be. It should be stressed that freedom is not a matter of liberty or indifference. On the contrary, freedom is the ability to orient life toward moral excellence that contributes to the development and flourishing of social and cultural life. One may even go so far as to say that morality is the participation of human beings in the ordering of nature. Christian moral action is about our joyful response to the duty God has entrusted to us. God made the world a dynamic system, a historical process that continually challenges us to grow to our full potential.

Such a positive attitude toward humanity and creation is well expressed by John Calvin, who speaks of God's "common or general grace" endowed on human beings and creation that becomes evident in the great human achievements in earthly matters. That is to say, God has endowed his gracious gifts to everyone. These "natural" gifts or "light of nature" are possessed by all, godly and ungodly alike.[7] We will do well to emulate Calvin, who marveled at the intellectual and artistic achievements of unbelievers and attributed such achievements to the common grace that God makes available to all people: "Whenever we come upon these matters in secular writers, let that admirable light of truth shining in them teach us that the mind of man, though fallen and perverted from its wholeness, is nevertheless clothed and ornamented with God's excellent gifts. If we regard the Spirit of God as the sole fountain of truth, we shall neither reject the truth itself, nor despise it wherever it shall appear, unless we wish to dishonor the Spirit of God."[8]

Human achievements through "natural" gifts or "common grace" should not be confused with other gifts that God may endow through special grace, which for the Christian includes the blessings of God's special revelation and work of redemption.

Nevertheless, it should not be surprising that the "goodness" of fallen human beings and their "conformity" to the will of God in a limited fashion displays some parallels to the life of believers in their sanctification exemplified by their obedience to God's commands and in their doing of God's will. G. C. Berkouwer writes, "This approach wished to acknowledge the fact that in real life we do not encounter an absolute antithesis between complete holiness and complete evil, but that we find, in the concrete experiences of our existence, deeds in the lives of unbelievers which are unmistakably similar to the good works of the believers."[9]

These good deeds presume that God is actively holding back the full power and corruption of sin so that, even where hearts have not been spiritually renewed, human beings are nevertheless able to conform to God's will to relative degrees. In practical terms, people may exhibit morality as well as perform righteous deeds that work for the benefit of the common good.[10]

Third, the uniqueness of the human race is preeminently manifested in the relationship of human beings with God as creatures addressed by God. Only human beings are called to prayer. The corollary is that human beings fully recognize and achieve their potential in a living and dynamic relationship with God; they do not exist as completely self-enclosed beings. The essential and constitutive nature of humankind is fully comprehended only in its relationship with God. Human beings find their greatest joy and attain their fullest potential when they experience grace in a living and responsive relationship with God. As the Westminster Shorter Catechism declares, "Man's chief end is to glorify God, and to enjoy him forever." That being the case, God, the *summum bonum*, is the end that brings human fulfillment and perfection. Robert Louis Wilken aptly elaborates:

> As we grow in virtue we delight in the good that is God. Hence freedom is never set forth in its own terms; it is always seen in relation to God. Because human beings were made in the image of God our lives will be fully human only as our face is turned toward God and our actions formed by his love. Freedom is as much a matter of seeing, of vision, as it is of doing. We know ourselves as we transcend ourselves, and we find ourselves as we find fellowship with God. Happiness, the happiness that gives fullness to life, will be ours only as our will conforms to God's will.[11]

The Mandate Given to Humankind

Reference to the ordering of life brings our discussion to what is called the cultural mandate. In traditional theology, the cultural mandate applies to duties such as work, marriage, government, and culture. Note, however, that human beings are still held responsible to God regardless of their fall into sin. Indeed, despite sin, God maintains his common grace of preserving goodness in human society so that there remains the possibility of redemption or new beginnings for human beings.

The original mandate given in Genesis 1:28–30 remains in effect despite human sin. Gordon Spykman elaborates:

> God mandates mankind, as his "junior partners," to join him as co-workers in carrying on the work of the world. The original creation was good, but not yet perfect. It stood poised at the threshold of its historical development. God's creating work was finished. Nothing good was lacking. Both structurally and directionally, everything was in state of readiness, laden with potentiality. All these very promising potentials were eagerly awaiting their intended realization. To this end God enlists the services of his imagers, male and female, as his co-workers. Made in the divine likeness, we are called to exercise our office by continuing his work in the midst of his world. This original mandate still stands as a direction-setting cultural signpost along the roadway of world history.[12]

The cultural mandate commands us to use our rich talents and gifts to order the world. The mandate begins with agrarian activities in the Garden of Eden. It undoubtedly legitimizes the flourishing of technology. The cultural mandate will find its full flourishing in the heavenly city that God intends to display with full magnificence when he eventually redeems and uplifts humankind.[13]

The cultural mandate is not to be celebrated as the achievement of human autonomy. In the final analysis, we exercise our gifts and talents as we wish but in conformity to the norms built into creation (creation order and subsequently the covenant demands of God). Humans are to be responsible in exercising their talents whether in creative arts or technology or commerce, not to exploit but to create resources to be shared for the common good. Ours is not an initiating but a responsive and responsible freedom. The abiding framework for human freedom is faith in God, love toward our neighbors, and care for the earth.[14]

The Image of God

A full discussion of the image of God should consider the image of God as both ontological (structural) and functional (directional), although Christian discussion of the image of God has historically tended to focus on ontology. The image of God is something every human being possesses. There is no consensus as to what the image of God is ontologically, but it has been associated with the human capacity for reason, morality, and spirituality.[15]

From the structural or relational perspective, respect and regard for human life arises from the dignity that God endowed on the human race by giving it dominion over all things.[16] Each person is unique and precious because every individual is made in the image of God. "Whoever sheds the blood of a human, by a human shall that person's blood be shed; for in his own image God made humankind."[17] These verses demand that every human being be treated as equal regardless of race, gender, or social position. Concomitant with human equality must be protection from harm and along with it the range of inalienable human rights including the right to respect, the right to life, and the right to certain freedoms upheld by the United Nations Declaration of Human Rights.[18]

By way of comparison we note how a secular perspective will, if informed by Marxist historical ideology, ground human rights on the equality of the proletariat on its path of historical fulfillment, or, if informed by evolutionary theory, suggest rights come along with membership of the human race as a successful evolving species. Surely, to ground human rights on changing processes will result only in uncertainty and subjectivism. In contrast, the biblical emphasis is that the promotion of human rights is not dependent on a shifting and subjective assessment of what some people deserve compared to others. The promise that human beings are created in the image of God ensures the nonnegotiable conferment of dignity and human rights on every person.

Such an awareness of the inalienable nature of human rights was already evident among the earliest Christian writers. Wilken, citing the early Christian theologian Lactantius, argues that

> freedom of religion is necessary because of the nature of God. Religion, says Lactantius, has to do with love of God and purity of mind, neither of which can be compelled. "Why should a god love a person who does not feel love in return?" he asks. Religion cannot be imposed on someone, it can only be promoted by "words," that is, by persuasion, for it has to do with an interior disposition, and must be "voluntary." "Nothing," he writes, "requires freedom of will as religion."[19]

The Christian concept of humankind as made in the image of God has proved to be a rich source for reflection on morality and the legitimation of human freedom. Still, given the enigma of humankind's present condition, some Christian thinkers are hesitant to equate the image of God with any ontological or essential human qualities (be they related to the human capacity for language, reason, or relationship). These thinkers instead focus on how to relate the image to the office or calling God has entrusted to human beings. That is to say, the image of God is viewed in its functional aspect that is preeminently expressed in the covenant relationship between God and humankind.

Perhaps the dichotomy between ontological and functional aspects of the image of God is unnecessary since it may be precisely because human beings are endowed with specific ontological qualities that they are capable of discharging functional or vocational tasks entrusted by God. In particular, it is the quality of being endowed with covenantal personhood that most aptly equips humans to discharge their covenantal commission.

Michael Horton draws on the insights of Meredith Kline for a fuller appreciation of the image of God. In particular, it is the character of royalty that qualifies human beings to rule over creation: temple (dominion, kingship); the ethical dimension (the foundations of the temple are justice, equity, truth, righteousness, holiness, goodness); and glory (physical beauty). "To be the image of God is to be the son of God."

As such, Horton emphasizes that the glory of the royal son is ethical-official, rather than corresponding to a particular essence in the human constitution. "As image of God," Kline writes, "man is a royal son with the judicial function appertaining to kingly office. The renewal of the divine image in men is an impartation to them of the likeness of the archetypal glory of Christ."[20]

Humankind in its kingly office is entrusted with the duty to keep the covenant with God. What is a covenant? Sometimes it is understood as a treaty or an alliance between two parties ratified by treaty documents. The Bible indicates that the all-sufficient God took the initiative to establish a covenant that includes special favors and protection to the people of the covenant. The covenant described in the Bible goes beyond legal requirements because the two parties enter into a special relationship, pledging a mutual commitment of an intensely personal kind. Hence, loyalty and faithfulness are the central qualities of the biblical covenant.

We cannot miss the graciousness of God in taking the initiative to set up a covenant with sinful humanity. The covenant is indeed God's gracious provision whereby people who deserve to be banished from his presence are offered a new relationship with him. As 1 Peter 2:9–10 says, "You are a chosen people, a royal priesthood, a holy nation, a people belonging to God that you may declare the praises of him who called you out of darkness into his marvelous light. Once you were not a people, but now you are the people of God; once you had not received mercy, but now you have received the mercy of God."

It is evident that divine revelation goes beyond transmission of information. It has a more inclusive role of establishing a covenant relationship. The relationship is ratified by the ritual of atoning sacrifice that emphasizes that sinful people can enjoy the benefits of this covenant only because God has provided the means to overcome and cover sin that had earlier caused estrangement between God and the human race. Finally, the covenant includes the provision of authoritative scriptures that spell out in detail the obligations entailed in keeping this relationship, which is a way of life characterized by utmost loyalty, trust, and obedience to God.

From the covenant point of view, God's covenant word becomes the normative benchmark of our duty to our neighbor. According to Micah 6:8, "He has told you, O man, what is good; and what does the Lord require of you but to do justice, and to love kindness, and to walk humbly with your God?"

Human vocation—that is, the fulfillment of the cultural mandate—gains a depth and dimension with the covenantal requirement exemplified by the love command. Moral duty to one's neighbors is now informed by respect for personhood and obedience to the love command of God (vertical dimension). How we treat others especially in matters of human rights and fundamental liberties is not determined by the subjective judgment of some people about others but in accordance to the abiding claim of God's comprehensive love command to us all.

Imitation of God requires the implementation of a legal system that protects the powerless and shows compassion toward the vulnerable.[21] Exaction of interest from the poor is prohibited and the poor hired servant must not be oppressed.[22] Kindness is to be extended even to the resident alien who must be treated with justice.[23] In sum, "You shall not pervert the justice due to the sojourner or to the fatherless, or take a widow's garment in pledge."[24]

Nevertheless, such laws require a sense of social responsibility and compassion for the welfare of the needy and weak rather than a set of demands enforced legalistically. That is to say, the covenant assumes a social order held together by habits of neighborliness.

That the covenant demands of God intensify and extend moral duty is clear from the provisions found in the book of Deuteronomy, the covenant book par excellence of the Bible. In contrast to the normal human instinct to restrict rights and privileges only to members of one's community, the covenant assumes justice will be extended to aliens: "The Lord your God is God of gods and Lord of lords, the great God, mighty and awesome, who is not partial and takes no bribe, who executes justice for the orphan and the widow, and who loves the strangers, providing them food and clothing."[25]

Elsewhere we read that aliens must be allowed Sabbath rest, and that they must not be oppressed.[26] Aliens are even permitted to benefit from the law of gleaning.[27] Significantly, this command came immediately after the giving of the Ten Commandments. Finally, and supremely, we have the command to love our neighbors as ourselves.[28] The rationale for these commands is expressed in Leviticus 19: 34, which says: "The alien who resides with you shall be to you as the citizen among you; you shall love the alien as yourself, for you were aliens in the land of Egypt."

Covenant Renewal

Like creation, the biblical covenant possesses a dynamic quality. God continues to intensify his offer of covenant and extends the scope of the covenant that he offers in working out his redemption of humankind. Hence one may speak of the history of the covenant (taking the backward perspective) or even covenant eschatology (taking the future perspective). In this regard, human history is seen as the unfolding of God's covenant promises. Concomitantly, the original creation mandate will be fulfilled in history as humankind builds a renewed civilization premised on God's love command and develops creation to its highest level of glory.

In particular, the fulfillment of God's covenant promise is found in the redemption of human history and the renewal of creation through Jesus Christ. The whole earth is cleansed and will be glorified under the dominion of Jesus Christ. The great book of Romans declares that a new humanity will be constituted "to be conformed to the image of his Son, in order that he [Jesus] might be the firstborn among many brothers."[29] Christ infuses his glory to restore fallen humanity so that the *imago dei* of those who are united with him will be restored and "uplifted" into a new humanity.[30] Elsewhere, Paul highlights that assimilation to Christ as the image of God results in a renewed person who exhibits a Christ-like character and life to the watching world.[31] Stanley Grenz, however, emphasizes: "Yet envisioned here is no mere private beholding, leading to an individualistic 'me-and-Jesus'" understanding of transformation. Rather, the metamorphosis involves the reformation of relationships and the creation of a new community of those who share together in the transforming presence of the Spirit and who thereby are, as A. M. Ramsey notes, "realising the meaning of their original status as creatures in God's image."[32]

In short, conforming to Christ who is the image of the invisible God has become the new eschatological goal (*telos*) for renewed humanity. The covenant life as God originally intended is now possible with humanity renewed in the image of God. Michael Horton explains: "Only by being reconciled to God in Jesus Christ by the power of the Spirit working through the means of grace in the church can covenant-breakers be constituted covenant-keepers and be kept in that covenant until one day the image of God is finally not only perfectly restored but confirmed in everlasting righteousness."[33]

It is unfortunate that so much reflection on humanity seems so mesmerized by the past, encapsulated by the event of the fall of humanity into sin, that we lose sight of the future. Indeed, Christians envisage both a restoration and uplift through the recreation of the earth. In the words of the Bible, there will be a "new heaven and a new earth." The new creation will be glorified and will stand both in continuity (it is the same earth) and discontinuity (it will be cleansed from sin and corruption and glorified) with present creation.

Nevertheless, creation is not subsumed under the new creation of God; it retains its integrity as the present sphere of human stewardship and the sacramental reminder of the hope of glory. In Paul's words, "For the creation was subjected to futility, not willingly, but because of him who subjected it, in hope that the creation itself will be set free from its bondage to decay and obtain the freedom of the glory of the children of God. For we know that the whole creation has been groaning together in the pains of childbirth until now. And not only the creation, but we ourselves, who have the first fruits of the Spirit, groan inwardly as we wait eagerly for adoption as sons, the redemption of our bodies."[34]

The book of Isaiah portrays life in restored creation (the new city of God). It is a place where "the kings of the earth shall bring their glory and nothing unclean shall enter it, but only the glory and honor of the nations."[35] Richard Mouw elaborates: "The Holy City is not wholly discontinuous with present conditions. The biblical glimpses of this City give us reason to think that its contents will not be completely unfamiliar to people like us. In fact, the contents of the City will be more akin to our present cultural patterns than is usually acknowledged."[36]

I can do no better than to summarize the glorious vision of human destiny with the words of Anthony Hoekema: "The Bible assures us that God will create a new earth on which we shall live to God's praise in glorified, resurrected bodies. On the new earth, therefore, we hope to spend eternity, enjoying its beauties, exploring its resources, and using its treasures to the glory of God."[37]

1.2 Being Human in Islam

Mona Siddiqui

I place this discussion of being human in the dual reality of the Qur'ānic world, the eternity and permanence of God, and the mortality and finitude of humankind. This is a world where creation does not begin with human beings but where humanity's role within the created order becomes central to the whole story of God, creation, and the afterlife. The whole process of creation is not described in detail although there are several words that are used to convey a sense of creation, such as *khalaqa*, *bara'a*, *ansha'a*, *dhara'a* and *faṭara*. All things are created with a purpose, the heavens and the earth have been created with the truth (*ḥaqq*) or in wisdom (*ḥikma*), and all of nature is a sign (*āya*) from God, going forth from the Divine and returning to the Divine. Here, humankind is one part of created being among others. Among the variety of themes connected with God's creative powers and the creation of humanity, it is possible to detect three scriptural themes that unfold as the defining aspects of human existence: the nature of human beings, human alienation, and human destiny. These themes give us some insight into the essence of humankind, the complex nature of our relationship with God and the rest of his creation, and our ultimate return to God.

The focus on humanity lies both in the biological makeup of humankind and in its inherent distinctiveness in relation to the rest of God's physical and natural creation. This distinctiveness has been seen in terms of dignity and nobility: for the Islamic tradition, human beings are created in the best of forms (*fī aḥsani taqwīm*) and are the noblest of creation (*ashraf al-makhlūqāt*). But this dignity is a complex term tying humanity to God and nature in physical and metaphysical ways. Human dignity in general has been a widely used term in religious scholarship with significant implications for human life, yet the concept is open to a variety of meanings. The word dignity, rooted in the Latin *dignus* and *dignitas*, both meaning "worthy of esteem or honor," has come down to us from the classical tradition. But both in Greek and Roman thought, the concept of universal human dignity did not exist; the concept was applicable to particular human beings but not to all. The Greeks identified the person of *aretê*, virtue or excellence, as one who could merit dignity. The Stoics leaned toward a more humanitarian brotherhood of all and claimed that because all human beings had reason, they could all have an intrinsic dignity if they lived a life that was essentially rational, self-reflective, and in accordance with their natural surroundings. But intrinsic human worth could not be universally applied. In the classical world, inequality was a natural feature of life. The emphasis on distinction and hierarchy within humanity in much of Greek philosophy meant that dignity, implying honor and esteem, was not viewed as an inalienable characteristic of all humankind, but rather as something that only a few possessed; human value was acquired rather than inherent.

Christian theological traditions have generally rooted themselves in the fundamental concept that human dignity should be viewed as universally applicable. The concept of *imago Dei*, of human beings as made in the image of God, has been a central concept for elaborating the relationship between man and God: "Then God said, 'Let us make humankind in our image, according to our likeness.'"[38] The phrase signifies that human beings are created by God purposefully, not just as his creatures but as creatures who themselves are godlike in some way. The Hebrew word denotes both the sense of likeness and image. Although the first chapter of Genesis does not speak of God as a visible image, it speaks of a God who creates and who has created humankind in his own image. However, there is no precise explanation of what this likeness implies, and Richard Middleton has argued that the few biblical references to *imago Dei*, including only two texts in the New Testament, have left the way open for a wide variety of philosophical and theological interpretations of this concept.[39]

In Islam, the Qur'ānic account of the creation of humankind is simultaneously also an account of human vocation:[40]

> [Prophet], when your Lord told the angels, "I am putting a successor[41] on earth," they said, "How can You put someone there who will cause damage and bloodshed when we celebrate Your praise and proclaim Your holiness?" but He said, "I know things you do not." He taught Adam the names of all things.[42]
>
> Your Lord said to the angels, "I will create a man from clay. When I have shaped him and breathed My Spirit into him, kneel down before him."[43]
>
> Read! In the name of your Lord who created: He created man from a clinging form. Read! Your Lord is the Most Bountiful One who taught by [means of] the pen, who taught man what he did not know.[44]
>
> We create man in the finest state.[45]
>
> He shaped you, formed you well.[46]

These verses indicate multiple perspectives on human beings, their physical nature and place in creation, and their relationship with God. First, the creation of humans was not a quiet affair; rather it was announced to the angels as a turning point in the destiny of the earth itself. Indeed, the objection that the angels raised about the need to bring human life into existence, and the consequent destruction on earth, develops into one of the first Qur'ānic conversations affirming humanity's place in creation. Second, humanity's relatively lowly but complex nature, that is, physical essence, which is clay or dust (*ṭīn*), contrasts with the lofty moral status God bestows on humans, that is, representative (*khalīfa*). God has spent time on the formation and image of humankind, and God distinguishes human beings from other beings by breathing into Adam of his own spirit; thus humanity comes into the fullness of its being only through that final breath, the element of divine origin in the human makeup. Exactly what is meant by *khalīfa* in this context is open to interpretation, as with *imago Dei*, except that *khalīfa* does imply some kind of successor or deputy who will settle on earth. Early Muslim commentary also suggested that Adam, implying the generic concept of humankind, may be God's representative in "exercising judgment with justice."[47] The Qur'ān advises Adam and the sons of Adam that the status of *khalīfa* means that they are being entrusted with looking after the earth—the earth and its riches are in human care (*amāna*):

> We established you [people] on the earth and provided you with a means of livelihood there.[48]

> [People], do you not see how God has made what is in the heavens and on the earth useful to you, and has lavished His blessings on you both outwardly and inwardly?[49]

There are verses that explicitly convey the exalted status given to humanity: "We have honored the children of Adam . . . and favored them specially above many of those We have created."[50]

The creation of humanity is simultaneous with a given status for humanity, for this is part of the gradual unfolding of the divine plan. But in the act of creation, God himself remains transcendent and untouched. In the Qur'ān at least, human beings carry an inherent dignity and honor conveyed in the very manner of their creation, but God's love (*ḥubb*) is not expressed as a reason for human creation. Moreover, the Qur'ān does not say that human beings are created in God's image, even if they are created in the best of forms. The divine breath is an essential element in the completion of humankind, but it does not explain how and if this makes humanity godlike in any way.

This is not because there is no reference to images of God in the Qur'ān but because the dominant message of the Qur'ān is that "there is nothing like him [God]."[51] While the absolute transcendence and oneness of God are major Qur'ānic themes and the fundamental core of Islamic monotheism, Muslim theology from the second/eighth century onward wrestled with how transcendence could be reconciled with immanence, and how God, who does not reveal himself in his interaction with humankind, could be known. How could human beings understand a transcendent God who exists in preeternity as well as in posteternity, whereas human life, intellect, and perception are all finite? The issue, it seems, is that transcendence does not mean distance, for God does want to be known. God is near man, "closer to him than his jugular vein";[52] he can be known by his attributes (*ṣifāt*) of which he speaks directly through the Qur'ān; he is "light upon light" and he is defined by his "most beautiful names" (*al-asmā' al-ḥusnā'*), traditionally numbering ninety-nine.[53] All this formed the basis for a systematic theology about God's essence (*dhāt*).[54] Conversely, even if God wants to be known, humankind is incapable of knowing him. Despite a variety of opinions on the knowability of God's essence and God's attributes, Abū Ḥamīd al-Ghazālī (1058–1111), perhaps the most prominent and celebrated theologian of Islam, concluded: "The end result of the knowledge of the *'ārifīn* is their inability to know Him, and their knowledge is, in truth, that they do not know Him and that it is absolutely impossible for them to know Him."[55] It is important to point out here, albeit briefly, that the tension between self-revelation and complete transcendence has exercised the minds of Christian and Muslim scholars for centuries—reconciling a God who is radically one and transcendent and a God who reveals himself for a purpose. Against the background of the concept of *imago Dei*, Christians disputed how much the image of God had been damaged by the fall of humanity, whereas Muslims focused on the necessity of human submission to God. In their thinking about the relationship between the divine and the human, Muslims focused on the revelation in the Qur'ān as inspiring a doctrine of purpose and obedience, whereas Christians saw the revelation in Jesus Christ as bringing redemption from sin.

In Islam, the dominant conceptual framework for human relations with God is that of servant to master. Whereas servility is not a condition of human creation, it is in fact implied in the question asked by God: "[Prophet], when your Lord took out the offspring from the loins of the children of Adam and made them bear witness about themselves, He said, 'Am I not your Lord?' and they replied, 'Yes, we bear witness.'"[56] Syed Nomanul Haq writes, "so powerful is this narrative that humanity in the very principle of its being has testified to the majesty of God. In other words, human nature is essentially theomorphic."[57] Humans' nature (*fiṭra*) inclines them toward God; thus the servant–master (*'abd–rabb*) relationship between a human and God is a natural state, not a servile state. The significance of this relationship is that human beings can understand neither themselves nor the universe on their own but only in the context of their relations with God.

Human creation, alienation, and destiny all depend on the unique relationship of human beings to God. Although weak, they are asked by God to be his successor (*khalīfa*) on earth; although free to choose, they must live the moral life revealed to them; and finally, although mortal, they must prepare for their final destiny with God. The necessary corollary of this relationship is free will, which allows human beings to make choices and judgments using their own intellect. Human freedom is the greatest human gift, not because animals and other life forms are not free but because human freedom is aligned with human accountability. The exercising of this freedom is intrinsic in the very obligation of stewardship. Curiously, according to the Qur'ān, God offered moral responsibility to the heavens and the earth but they refused out of fear, yet humanity accepted it in foolishness.[58] The Qur'ān reveals humankind as ready to assume its ambivalent role of stewardship in the natural world, but there is no sense that humanity really understands the onerous responsibility of a just stewardship of the natural world and a just moral order for humankind. While the Qur'ān repeats that "control of the heavens and the earth" belongs to God, there is a transition of responsibility to human beings that becomes a defining moment in human destiny.[59]

In the Qur'ānic story of Adam's creation and his eating from the tree of knowledge, Adam's first act of disobedience is also his first act of human freedom. The whole cycle of human existence—creation by God, alienation from God, and final destiny with God—is contained within the verses of the creation narrative. Having silenced the angels' objections by revealing Adam's knowledge, God's second conversation is with Iblīs, who also raises an objection, refusing to prostrate himself in front of Adam. The Qur'ānic narrative around these two conversations is hurried, for the real story is that of human beings, not of those who were created before Adam even if their devotion is total. The significance of the angels and of Iblīs is now relative to the creation of humanity. If Iblīs's pride leads to his downfall, his downfall leads in turn to humanity's first transgression. Most religions, cultures, and philosophical traditions have their own story of how humans eventually become estranged or alienated from a god, from gods, or from a bountiful nature. The Christian lament concerns human alienation from God as a result of the fall from grace and the consequent need for the messianic mission to rescue humankind. However, the concept of alienation in Islam is different. It certainly recognizes the impact of human disobedience and humanity's loss of a certain Edenic state, but it does not see this loss as radically determining our earthly existential paradigm. Even if humankind is now expelled from paradise, paradise remains the ultimate goal and paradise or salvation is still attainable. The Edenic status is no longer a gift but can be earned once again through good works and devotion. Yet, on a prior transcendental plane, humanity has already accepted the stewardship of the earth in response to an offer from God, so the descent from paradise to earth is the loss of one world but the challenge of another. Indeed, the poet and philosopher Muhammad Iqbal sees the consequence of this transgression as a key step in human development: "The Fall does not mean any moral depravity; it is man's transition from simple consciousness to the first flash of self-consciousness, a kind of waking from the dream of nature."[60]

It is in the earth as sacred territory, with the cycle and rhythm of nature that are also the signs of God, that humankind must once again turn to divine guidance to reestablish a just order; this is the struggle for success (*falāḥ*). Revelation in the form of divine guidance does not automatically release humanity from this struggle but provides the only hope of deliverance from a relative loss to a higher success. In other words, although God remains the supreme arbiter, salvation lies within human beings.

The human condition is perceived in different ways, and in much of Sufi poetry, the struggle is not real because even the world itself is not real:

> So this world
> Seems lasting, though 'tis but the sleeper's dream.[61]

In Islam, being human is forever to wonder what it is to be human. It is to realize our desires and to cope with that which lures us away from God. It is to live with both the faith and the risk God has placed in humanity while all the time reflecting on our final destiny. Believers live with the dilemma of God's nearness to humanity but humanity's persistent failure to turn to God. Human beings can be strong in the face of adversity but weak in the face of temptation set before them through the expulsion of Iblīs from God's favor. Yet, even if humanity is caught in the cycle of sin and repentance, there remains one ultimate source of deliverance, and that is divine mercy or *raḥma*. The overriding image of God in the Qur'ān is contained in that single epithet that has come down in Muslim intellectual and popular tradition as God's most widely used invocation: *al-Raḥmān*, "the Merciful." If there is one divine attribute that could be the reason for the creation of humankind, it is divine mercy. It is God's act of mercy by which creation came into being, by which humanity, conscious of its distinct role in creation, is endowed with intelligence and freedom to know God.

Indeed the Qur'ānic discourse is firmly rooted in God's intervention and signs in human history as acts of divine mercy. His signs are prophets and books, and while belief has never been forced upon humanity, belief has always been invited:

> And we have sent down to you the Book in truth, confirming the Book that existed already before it and protecting it. . . . For each one of you [several communities] We have appointed a Law and an open way. If God had so willed, he would have made you all one community, but [He has not done so] that He may test you in what He has given you; so compete in goodness. To God shall you all return and He will tell you [the Truth] about what you have been disputing.[62]

Divine intervention demands that humanity defines a relationship with God. In Islam, the authority of the Qur'ān and the wisdom of the Prophet and prophets offer guidance, but human beings have the freedom not to respond. Against this freedom to reject the signs of God is the Qur'ānic exhortation to turn to God in worship. Prayer develops a person's sense of self and a yearning for God; it is an instinctive desire to speak to someone in the silence of the universe, but worship, both individual and congregational, also reflects humanity's awareness of the ethical bond shared with others.

The one who does not worship God in this world is "deaf, dumb, and blind"; the one who refuses to accept the salvific message of monotheism is in darkness, and the one who mocks God will be mocked by God.[63] Vivid images of the torments of hell and the pleasures of paradise convey the literal or metaphorical outcomes of a virtuous or wicked life. Whether humankind has bowed to gratitude (*shukr*) or denial (*kufr*), it is without doubt that a person's own limbs will testify to the kind of life lived.[64] The ledger of deeds (*ṭā'ir*) will hang around each man's neck to be read on the Day of Judgment.[65] The essential premise of worship is not that God gains anything by human obedience but that humanity realizes its ultimate goals through recognition of the sovereignty of God, rejection of false gods, and development of god-like attributes.

Max Weber is right to say that Islam lacks the sense of the tragic that comes from the feeling of sin.[66] Yet while this is true in terms of a strict comparison with the Christian doctrine of original sin and redemption, human beings still commit sin; they wrong themselves and they wrong others. The whole context of our earthly existence is based on human transgression, forgetfulness, and divine forgiveness. So powerful is this emphasis that the Qur'ānic message contains an almost desperate sense of divine forgiveness:

> Say, "[God says], My servants who have harmed yourselves by your own excess, do not despair of God's mercy. God forgives all sins: He is truly the Most Forgiving, the Most Merciful."[67]

> My mercy encompasses all things.[68]

The same emphasis is found in perhaps the most poetic and moving Prophetic ḥadīth:

> O son of Adam, so long as you call upon Me and ask of Me, I shall forgive you for what you have done, and I shall not mind. O son of Adam, were your sins to reach the clouds of the sky and were you then to ask forgiveness of Me, I would forgive you. O son of Adam, were you to come to Me with sins nearly as great as the earth and were

> you then to face me, ascribing no partner to Me, I would bring you forgiveness nearly as great as it [i.e., the earth].[69]

God expects human beings to commit sinful acts, for the possibility of sin will always accompany human freedom. But the possibility of goodness also accompanies human choice, and goodness knows no limits; it is far reaching and can be imagined in multiple ways. The emphasis in the Qur'ān is less on human transgression than on the imperative to turn to God for forgiveness. If divine mercy is ultimately the binding force between humankind and God, it is also what directs human beings to faith and good works. In other words, both the God–human relationship and relationships between human beings must have an essential ethical character.

While Muslim schools of theology disputed the exact relationship between right belief and right practice required to attain success and avoid perdition, the overarching belief in divine mercy could never be eclipsed. It is humanity's destiny to be caught in the triangle of a covenant with God and Satan's pact with God, a triangle that is broken only in the next life. Until then, "enjoining what is right and forbidding what is wrong" is the premise for human flourishing. Only in the words of the great Sufis does one detect desperation to be with God again, a restless desire to do away with that which separates humankind from God even in this life. Perhaps nowhere has this been expressed more hauntingly than in the words of the great Sufi saint Abdul Quddus of Gangoh: "Muhammad of Arabia ascended the highest Heaven and returned. I swear by God that if I had reached that point, I should never have returned."[70] Basing his desire to be with God on the narrative of Muhammad's ascension to heaven, this Sufi saint questions the Prophet's return. The mystic longs for that vision that the prophet has already experienced. The Prophet has returned, whereas the mystic would find any other experience now meaningless. For those of us believers who are neither mystics nor prophets, the struggle to find and hold onto the sacred in the profane, the sublime in the ridiculous, and the divine in the ordinary is itself no less of a challenge.

CHAPTER TWO

Living with Difference

2.1 Affinity, Inclusion, and Mission

Christian Resources for Living with Difference

Michael Ipgrave

How do Christians live with difference? What resources and approaches do they bring to the challenge of diversity? That is the task I have been asked to address, with particular reference to issues of ethnic and cultural diversity, and of gender difference. Perhaps I can begin by pointing out something rather obvious but very important: that, for Christian faith, diversity in creation is an acknowledged and celebrated feature of the universe. "O Lord, how manifold are your works! In wisdom you have created them all; the earth is full of your creatures," the Psalmist exclaims.[71] In more systematic mode, the Bible's opening account of Creation provides a map of the range and complexity of the created order, concluding that: "God saw everything that he had made, and indeed, it was very good. . . . Thus the heavens and the earth were finished, and all their multitude."[72] The diversity of creation, rightly understood, is a visual language expressing the abundance, richness, and wisdom of the life of the Creator[73]—what Aref Nayed, in a lecture in an earlier Building Bridges seminar, described as "āyatology," a divine semiology.[74] This seems a clear enough position so long as the created order is received as the work of God, but the question before us now is that of the human order. Nayed went on to describe the incursion into āyatology of humanly created technology and the devastating effects on biodiversity that this intervention could have.

These ecological questions are taken up in other contributions to this volume, but the human order also has its own markers of diversity and difference. How are these addressed in Christian understanding and practice? Are the differences of human beings also seen as an expression of the divine fecundity, or at least located within the ambit of the divine providence?

Strands of Difference and Diversity

Although the question of difference and diversity within Christianity is central to our subject, it is not possible to answer it in general without asking what kind of human differences are being discussed. It is important at the outset to recognize what we might call the diverse diversities, the different differences, with which we are dealing. To avoid cumbersome language of this kind, I shall use the unmemorable expression "strand." In its legal sense, this is a word with—as far as I am aware—no theological resonance whatever; indeed, it has been only recently coined in the context of human rights discourse. In common with that of other members of the European Union, U.K. equalities law now recognizes six distinct grounds on which discrimination can be recognized and should be combated, and these it refers to as strands: namely, race, gender, sexual orientation, religion or belief, age, and disability. This list is not in fact exhaustive for antidiscrimination provision: in some cases, for example, different languages are also protected by law.

We can note that these strands, first enumerated in a human rights context, are seen as marking differences that could be causes of shortfall from an agreed objective of equality. Although there may be in this secular thinking an implicit space created for the celebration of diversity, the emphasis is on restricting the effects of that diversity insofar as those effects are seen to imperil the project of equalized status. I am not called on to address Christian attitudes to each of these strands today; in particular, we are not in this session focusing on Christian (or Islamic) evaluations of the significance of religious diversity. Nevertheless, it will be immediately obvious that, severally and individually, the different strands raise extensive, deep-seated, and very different challenges for contemporary Christian believing and living. However, these challenges are not without precedent in the life of the Christian community, as can be seen by looking at a rather shorter list of strands embedded in one of the key New Testament texts on "difference."

In a powerful passage arguing for the freedom of the children of God that is guaranteed for them by their incorporation into the body of Christ, Paul writes to the Galatian Christians: "As many of you as were baptized into Christ have clothed yourselves with Christ. There is no longer Jew or Greek, there is no longer slave or free, there is no longer male and female; for all of you are one in Christ Jesus."[75] Like many Pauline texts, this verse has had an impact far beyond the immediate context of its setting in the epistle's argument, and it is of particular resonance for us today because it names three strands of difference among those with which the apostolic church had to engage. That this is not an issue limited to the Galatian community is shown by another catalogue of strands appearing in the letter to the church at Colossae: "There is no longer Greek and Jew, circumcised and uncircumcised, barbarian, Scythian, slave and free; but Christ is all and in all!"[76]

Although the structure of the two lists is similar, the contents are different; I want to concentrate on the better-known Galatian verse. Here it will be seen that the first and third of the three strands Paul mentions can be broadly aligned with those identified in contemporary European legislation, namely race (Jew or Greek) and gender (male or female), while the second is one that is not mentioned (slave or free); more generally, the first refers to ethnic and cultural diversity, but not—as the baptismal setting makes clear—to differences of religion or belief.

The three Galatian strands of ethnicity or culture, of gender, and of slavery have been handled very differently within the Christian tradition, yet it is striking that Paul unquestioningly coordinates them in this text. Taking this cue from the apostle, I wish first to look briefly at the development of Christian attitudes to slavery—or, more precisely, attitudes to the difference between enslaved people and free people—before turning to questions of ethnocultural and gender difference. I take this course in the hope that the history of the former can cast some light on the theological processes shaping the latter two. I owe this method to the lead recently given by Richard Burridge in his fine study of New Testament ethics, *Imitating Jesus*.[77]

Living with the Difference between Slave and Free?

The New Testament holds together the practical issues of living in a slave-owning society with the spiritual reality of slaves and free having equal access to God in baptism. At some points the distinction between these two spheres of relationship is carefully maintained—after the exhortation "Let all who are under the yoke of slavery regard their masters as worthy of all honor" follows the warning: "Those who have believing masters must not be disrespectful to them on the ground that they are members of the church."[78] By contrast, in Paul's letter to Philemon, returning the runaway slave Onesimus, the two relationships are brought into a close, paradoxical contrast: Paul says Onesimus is to be received back "no longer as a slave but more than a slave, a beloved brother."[79] The tension of these two ways of looking at slave–free relationships held for centuries and was particularly sharp in situations where Christianity was the religion of a dominant slave-owning group, still more when the church itself institutionally possessed slaves. Burridge points out that there were many who were ready and able to defend the distinction between slave and free on the grounds of scriptural texts.[80]

Eventually, however, and after considerable struggle, slavery came to be regarded as indefensible by Christians. Although this judgment was expressed as an absolute moral repugnance, it had its origins in the impossibility of sustaining within the Christian community a tension between baptismal equality and the exigencies of slave owning. This history, of course, is quite different from those of the "ethnic-cultural" and "gender" strands of difference. While living with the slave–free distinction was eventually judged to be incompatible with the Christian commitment to spiritual equality in baptism, in the case of the two other strands Christianity has come variously to accommodate, to affirm, and to celebrate diversity and difference within the life of the church. In terms of the question I posed at the beginning, the distinction between slave and free came to be seen as a merely human difference, and indeed one opposed to the divine will, whereas culture and gender continue to be seen as aspects of diversity within God's providence. So it may be that understanding the processes leading to the eventual Christian rejection of the slave–free difference can help in discerning how to respond to the other strands of difference.

Burridge points out that the decisive change in Christian attitudes to slavery was effected by extending the community of interpretation that addressed the scriptural witness to include those who had direct experience of both sides of the slave–free polarity:

"If there was biblical study driving the abolitionists, it was a result of reading and re-reading their Bibles in the light of that listening to the experience of former slaves and slave-traders."[81] He also stresses that the process of interpretation involved not only reading off ethical teachings from the text of the scriptures but also seeking to follow the way of life of Jesus, who reached out to the poor and oppressed: "To imitate Jesus, it is not enough simply to extract his ethical teaching from the Sermon on the Mount; we must also imitate his loving acceptance of others, especially the marginalised, within an open and inclusive community."[82] Indeed, once they are welcomed, the marginalized are no longer on the margins. Central both to the widening of the interpretative circle and to the project of shared discipleship is then the sense of the community of Christ's body, which is open to all, and in which all have an equally honored place. In one sense, the very injunctions addressed to slaves in the New Testament point to the security of the place they enjoy in the community because they would not otherwise be counted as recipients of the exhortatory messages. But in another sense Christian abolitionism implies a rejection of an overaccommodating worldly view of the church through a renewed emphasis on its spiritual reality as a community of the baptised with equal access to God.

Two other points must be factored into this brief account of the development of Christian attitudes to slavery. First, the decisive movement to abolition came after a period in which slave owning had been justified by many precisely to the extent to which it did not extend to the ownership of Christian slaves. Slaves should not be baptized, some argued, because it would then be necessary to grant them freedom. This argument was applied in contexts where slave owners were of different ethnic and cultural groups from their slaves, so it was possible to draw a distinction, supported by some forms of Calvinist theology, between historically "Christian" nations and "heathens." Against this, however, as European Christians established themselves in different parts of the world as dominant groups, the religion that they took with them demonstrated in many cases that it had a surprising missionary impulse to it: not content with restricting their ministrations to expatriates and their descendants, chaplains and other clergy brought the Gospel to those who were enslaved. Conversely, for many slaves, Christian faith—although seen by many as the religion of the oppressor—was received by others as a message of liberation and hope, able to transform their lives. There is therefore a missiological transformation lying behind Burridge's "widening the community of interpretation."

Second, in the debate among Christians about the status of slaves in relation to free people, the most telling argument was a simple appeal to a sense of shared humanity—or, more strongly, of kinship. The mass-produced medallions of Josiah Wedgwood visually encapsulated this with a picture of a slave with the slogan: "Am I not a man and a brother?" It is important to note here that an even more fundamental affinity is being claimed than that of shared baptism: whether Christian or not, the slave shown in the medallion is seen as a human being with an equal entitlement to recognition as one made, like the purchaser of the medallion, in the image of God. In the order of creation as of redemption, there is to be no distinction between slave and free. Like the baptismal regeneration that guarantees access to the Father through sharing in the death and resurrection of the Son, the image of God is an intrinsically relational marker of human identity, affirming both slave and free as the sons or daughters of God.

Within the developing history of Christian attitudes to slavery, then, it is possible to identify three related and mutually reinforcing factors: the opening to true inclusion of the Eucharistic community, gathered around the imitation of Jesus and the interpretation of his words; the provision of that community with new members through the missionary imperative of communicating the Gospel; and the affirmation of the kinship of all humanity marked by bearing the image of God the Father. In the history of this strand of difference, the ultimate outcome of these factors was the denial of any validity to the distinction between slave and free. In the case of the other two strands to which I now turn—ethnicity or culture, and gender—the outcome of the Christian project of living with diversity may be quite different; indeed, these are projects whose histories are still being formed. Nevertheless, I shall argue that these same three factors provide core Christian resources for living with difference here also.

Living with Differences of Ethnicity or Culture and of Gender

There are evidently fundamental dissimilarities in the ways in which the two strands of "ethnicity or culture," on the one hand, and "gender," on the other hand, mark the ordering of humanity. Most obviously, the former is multiply diverse while the latter is only dual: the nations of the world are many while male and female are only two. For this reason, it is possible to speak of diversity in relation to ethnicity or culture but of difference with regard to gender. Moreover, in some respects at least the former seems to admit of a more obvious human contribution to its formation compared to the latter. In accordance with the terminology of this seminar, I have used the rather wide term "ethnic or cultural" for the first strand, which in reality represents a spectrum of markers of human identity; the "cultural" end point of this spectrum certainly is created by human production even if the "ethnic" end has a greater sense of givenness. Contrasted with this, "gender" may appear as much more of a naturally provided category—although even here as well modern gender studies point to the part played by socialization in learned gendering as distinct from biological sex. A further dissimilarity between the two strands is that there are very few communities in which gender difference can be ignored, and those that there are have a certain artificiality about them; gender difference is indeed the foundation of the intimacy that forms social bonding. There have been and continue to be communities, however, in which ethnic and cultural differences are absent or can be safely ignored; where they are obvious, they may well be pressed into service as lines to divide people from one another rather than to bond them together.

It is perhaps not surprising, considering these differences, that Christian tradition has generally been more theologically appreciative of gender difference than of cultural diversity; the tendency has been to see the former as more immediately God-given while the latter has often been viewed with some ambiguity, as embodying elements of human rebelliousness as well as of providential ordering. That said, the resources of scripture and their development and application in Christian thought and practice are many-layered and complex in relation to both strands, moving in contradictory or contending directions, and still open to a wide variety of interpretations. It would be wholly misleading to identify one homogeneous Christian account of living with difference in relation to either strand. However, in relation to both, as in relation to the distinction of slave and free, Christians have sought to work on two different planes simultaneously, holding in tension, on the one hand, the exigencies of practical accommodation to social contexts marked by ethnic or cultural and gender differences with, on the other hand, the spiritual reality of Jew and Greek, man and woman, being called through baptism into a community of equal access to God through Christ.

In relation to these two strands as in relation to slavery, the same three factors provide basic Christian resources for dealing with difference: namely, the recognition of affinity provided by a common marking with the image of God; the widening of the community of interpretation and discipleship through the inclusiveness of the Eucharistic gathering; and the missionary impulse to communicate with the other in order to commend ultimate truth. As it has perhaps been less intensively discussed in Christian theology, in what follows I shall in each case focus mainly on ethnic and cultural diversity with rather more glancing references to issues of gender difference.

Affinity through the Image of God

In the first place, there is the sense of affinity across difference produced by sharing the image of God. It must be recognized that the idea of "image" in the "Priestly" account of humanity within the overall account of Creation, whatever its original signification may have been as the Hebrew *ṣelem*, has been developed in Christian thinking into a richly relational, even communitarian symbol of the way in which human diversity can mirror the richness of God's life. Taking their cue from the plural form of the divine speech announcing the creation of humanity, "Then God said, 'Let *us* make humankind in our image, according to *our* likeness,'" some Christian commentators have seen here a reference to the ensemble of Father, Son, and Spirit acting together to create the *imago Dei*, from that concluding that the divine image in humanity has itself a Trinitarian reference, whether the referent be taken as the relation of humans in community or as traceable within the human individual.[83]

With more textual plausibility, others have drawn attention to the shift in the object in the verse of creation, involving both a change of number and the inclusion of a new gender: "So God created man (*hā ādām*) in his own image, in the image of God he created him (*ōthō*); male and female created he them (*ōthām*)."[84] This, it is argued, shows that the *imago Dei* implies gendered relationship as constitutive of humanity. In the following chapter of Genesis, indeed the man is created first, and the woman is subsequently formed from his rib, giving rise to an exegetical tradition, found even in the New Testament, that accords primacy to one gender over the other.[85] Yet in the Priestly text that speaks of creation in the image of God, the narrative is rather of simultaneous creation with implications of mutuality, codependence, and equality of esteem. *Imago Dei* here seems to function as a marker that affirms gender parity in the context of relationship to one another and to God, and that conversely points to the possibility of interpersonal relationships subsisting within the very life of the God whom humans image.

In relation to ethnic and cultural diversity, the theme of the *imago* is not explicitly developed, but the same line of thinking about affinity can be traced in the motif of *syngenesia*, the belief—shared with much of the Greek philosophical tradition—that the diversity of human races and cultures all derive from and can be traced back to one parental source. This is of course implicit in the ancestral narratives of Genesis, which in fact present two origin stories for cultural and ethnic diversity. The first, concerning the sons of Adam and Eve, identifies Cain and Abel as types of the two key cultural patterns of Ancient Near Eastern society, respectively agrarianism and pastoralism.[86] It is true that the story appears to privilege one culture over the other because Abel's offering is accepted by God and Cain's is declined, yet even here there is ambiguity, for God puts his protective mark on Cain.

The second account of ancestral genesis follows the narrative of the flood, when the earth is repopulated through three distinct ethnicities descended from the three sons of Noah: Shem, Ham, and Japheth.[87] Here too a partisan and discriminatory interpretation is possible, building on the account of Noah's curse of Ham.[88] The story of the curse, extended by imaginative interpretation to apply to contemporary Negro people, was indeed used by biblical defenders of the institution of slavery. However, the following chapters of Genesis, showing the work of the Priestly compiler, use the account simply to chart the peopling of the known earth.

It is this nonpartisan, universalistic account of *syngenesia* that is taken up in the New Testament in Luke's account of Paul's speech on the Areopagus: "From one ancestor he [God] made all nations to inhabit the whole earth, and he allotted the times of their existence and the boundaries of the places where they would live."[89] Note that Paul's literal words are not gender specific: the text reads, according to different variants, either "from one" (*ex henos*) or "from one blood" (*ex henos haimatos*). The emphasis is on unity of origination, not on a biological prioritization of one gender over the other. More significantly, as in other parts of the biblical witness, here the teaching of a common descent from one human ancestor leads naturally to an affirmation of a shared spiritual parenthood in the person of God the Father—Paul quotes the words of the pagan Greek poet Aratus: "For we too are his offspring."[90]

In the case of both gender and culture or ethnicity, then, there is a cluster of biblical teachings around *imago Dei*, *syngenesia*, and the universal Fatherhood of God, which together emphasize an affinity of humans grounded in their relationship to God and one another. While they are expressed in narrative forms that can lend themselves to subordinating or partisan interpretations, these affinity teachings have also provided rich resources for those wishing to affirm a basic equality between humans that crosses divisions without in any sense seeking to abolish the significance of the underlying differences. Affinity is compatible with a continuing recognition of the reality of diversity or difference within both ethnicity or culture and gender. In this respect, its effect is different in these two strands from the case of slavery, where the affirmation of a common humanity eventually resulted in the refusal to countenance a continued distinction between enslaved people and free people. Whereas the slave–free distinction could only be read as the priority of one and the subjugation of the other, cultural and gender differences could be interpreted as complementary expressions of a fundamentally equal status in relation to God, and so, in light of "image" teaching, as providential ordering, not merely human construct.

Widening the Community of Interpretation and Discipleship

While *imago* and *syngenesia* are motifs applicable to the whole human race, whatever its members' religious affiliation, the second factor I identified as changing attitudes to slavery is by definition limited to the Christian community: namely, the opening up of the Eucharistic assembly of interpretation and discipleship to all those who seek to follow Jesus. While the church has always included people of both genders, and throughout history has subsisted in different cultures and among people of different ethnicities, the present age has seen an unprecedented awareness of the importance of explicitly attending to these strands of diversity within the body of Christ.

This awareness is evident at the level of biblical and theological study, where scholars may well write avowedly from a feminist perspective, or may expressly reflect on Christian faith from the contexts of their own ethnic or cultural standpoint. It is instructive to reflect on the pace of change here. At a very practical level, for example, in the Church of England women have only been ordained priests since 1993, yet in 2006 for the first time more women than men were ordained priest; overall, more than a quarter of our clergy now are women. Given that one of the priest's most important responsibilities is to expound the scriptures at the Eucharist, it follows that the community of interpretation has significantly broadened in gender terms. In relation to cultural and ethnic diversity, in 1990 the Indian theologian R. S. Sugirtharajah introduced a volume of studies bearing the significant title *Voices from the Margin* with these words: "It highlights the struggles and exegetical concerns of those who are on the periphery of society. Generally, the dominant biblical scholarship has shied away from the needs of the weak and needy. . . . These essays embody the needs and aspirations of those who are not normally at the forefront of things."[91] As the pace of globalization has accelerated, it remains true that the weak and the needy are not normally at the forefront of things politically and economically, yet it is remarkable to see the way in which the academic community of interpretation has expanded even since that volume's publication to include a whole diversity of voices. In theological discourse, it is no longer so easy to identify who is "on the margin" and who is "at the center."

This in turn applies with increasing effect also to processes of ecclesial decision making, where global communions are all struggling in different ways to adjust both to the rebalancing of the Christian world toward the South and to continuing changes in the way that men and women understand their relationship toward one another. Despite the pain and confusion of these processes, which Anglicans know only too well, they can be seen as an inevitable corollary of what Burridge calls the opening of the community of interpretation and discipleship into a more inclusive reality.

The effects of globalization, though, are not only seen at a global level; local churches also can be transformed by the impact of migration on communities. London, where I now minister, is a truly microcosmic city, with people who can trace their ancestries or their own earlier lives to all parts of the world and who maintain a strong sense of identification with diverse cultural traditions. We are catching up with the historic diversity of a city such as Singapore. This diversity is not just an external feature providing a context for the mission of the Christian church; it is also internally constitutive of our very life as our congregations regularly include worshippers from across the world, worshippers who are together shaping new expressions of what it means to be a Christian community marked by diversity. While this may seem a new and, in general, a renewing experience for the Church of England, it can also be seen as a recovery of the formative context of the original Christian movement in the cultural and ethnic pluralism of cities such as Corinth: "The new municipalities [of the first century Roman Empire] were to be meeting-places for ethnic and religious diversity, settlers found themselves alongside people who were 'different,' and needed to develop new patterns of community life as they faced pluralistic and social challenges unknown in their countries of origin."[92]

Wayne Meeks some years ago pointed out that this complex social setting has left its ineradicable mark on the identity of the apostolic church: "Its complexity, its untidiness to the mind, may well have been felt with special acuteness by people who were marginal or transient, either physically, socially or both, as so many identifiable members of the Pauline churches seem to have been. In any case, Paul and the other founders and leaders of those groups engaged aggressively in the creation of a new social reality."[93] It follows that local Christian communities today shaping new identities for the *ecclesia* through the negotiation of difference between people of different diasporas are rereading the Bible in a context close to its original; the opening of the community of interpretation to diversity renews its authenticity. In doing that, we are finding that issues of cultural diversity are encoded into the very logic of, for example, Paul's letters. Likewise, perhaps, in relation to the other strand, of gender, the New Testament can also be interpreted as inscribing gendered memory through the witness of "Mary, who treasured all these words in her heart and pondered them."[94] It is through a widening of the community of interpretation that these textually embedded diversities become once again apparent to us today.

The Missiological Impulse to Communicate

Christians living with difference have as a resource the missiological impulse that motivates the church's life. This might at first seem a perverse element of the Christian faith to identify as a resource in contexts of difference and diversity; surely, it could be thought, it would be much easier to live with differences if everybody were just to keep their opinions and activities to themselves, and learn to accept that others had their own opinions and activities. Yet this is to misunderstand the nature both of Christian mission and of the things that make for the health of diverse societies. The mission into which the Spirit leads the church is not an exercise in interfering with others' ways of life; it is rather an entering into communication across difference, inspired by the desire to commend truth. And diversity is not best honored through drawing protective lines between different communities but through enabling open, honest exchange between people and groups who differ from one another.

The paradigm for this communicative mission impulse is the Pentecost event, at which the Spirit enables people of different languages to speak to and to hear one another as they tell of the mighty acts of God; this confession of saving truth then necessarily spills over into mission to the surrounding community. To appreciate the import of Pentecost, it is necessary to set it against the background of the Genesis story of the tower of Babel, that highly ambiguous narrative on the origin of human linguistic—and implicitly also of cultural and ethnic—diversity: "The whole earth had one language and the same words. . . . Then they said, 'Come, let us build ourselves a city, and a tower with its top in the heavens, and let us make a name for ourselves; otherwise we shall be scattered abroad upon the face of the earth.' "[95]

Rabbi Jonathan Sacks describes Babel as "the first global project" and remarks that the significance of God's decision to bring it to an end by "confusing the language" of humanity is that it is not the divine purpose to create a universal order because "Babel ends with the division of mankind into a multiplicity of languages, cultures, nations and civilisations."[96] It would be interesting to know how this sounds from an Islamic perspective; to me, it seems to resonate with the Qur'ānic verse "To each among you have we prescribed a law and a way. If God had so willed, He could have made you a single people. But his purpose is to test you in what he has given each of you."[97]

Sacks insists that this does not imply any questioning of monotheism, but it does require an acknowledgment of the diversity of ways in which the one God addresses people: for Judaism, "The God of Abraham is the God of all mankind, but the faith of Abraham is not the faith of all mankind."[98] It seems to me, though, that Christian faith cannot rest content with a pluralism like this but is impelled to say that the truth that has grasped us in Jesus must in some sense be true for all. This missionary conviction leads to the imperative to communicate across differences; the Pentecost event guarantees that such communication is a possibility capable of realization as Spirit-enabled dialogue replaces the cacophony of Babel. Christianity thus engages with diversity not only through accepting its reality but also through seeing it as a context for communication.

When mission is seen in this way, as communication in the service of divine truth, rather than as an attempt to extend institutional hegemony, or to enlist others to our side, or to replace one way of thinking by another, two points become clear. First, mission belongs to God, not to Christians; and God has appointed that it should take place within a context of diversity and difference. The missiological impulse of the Spirit is thus ineluctably linked to living with difference, whether we like it or not.

Second, mission as communication involves a two-way flow of ideas, a joint exploration of a truth that has been given in which each party will be enriched by the other. Indeed, this can be seen right at the outset of Christianity, when the first mission proclamation of the church, "He is risen," is communicated in gendered complementarity, entrusted to the women at the tomb to convey to the apostles—so that these women are hailed in Eastern tradition as *isapostoloi*, "equal to the apostles." In terms of cultural history, too, the ability of mission to lead to mutual enrichment is no mere ideal but an actual reality, as is shown by the fact that much of the earliest reliable knowledge of other societies and cultures to reach western European Christians was brought to them by missionaries or scholars linked with the missionary enterprise. The subsequent transformation of the Christian community through the incorporation of people of different cultures has given us an ecclesial resource for living with difference in the shape of the glorious and growing diversity of the Body of Christ.

A Trinitarian Contour

The sense of universal affinity through the shared divine image, the establishment of the Eucharistic community as an inclusive site of interpretation and discipleship, and the missiological impulse leading to mutual communication across difference, then, provide three key resources for Christians living with difference and diversity. These are not peripheral to the faith. On the contrary, they can be seen as reflective of an underlying Trinitarian contour that shapes the distinctive patterns of Christian believing: the fatherhood of God provides the ultimate ground in which humanity shares its kinship attested by the divine image; the lordship of Jesus around whom the diverse ecclesial community gathers is expressed through teaching and example; the energy of the Spirit renewing God's people in mission is that which enables communication across difference. This is not to impose a Trinitarian pattern too neatly on the complexity of Christian attitudes to diversity, but it is to recognize that the core features of Christian faith can be discerned as shaping those attitudes. Living with difference is a theme that leads straight to the heartland of Christian believing.

2.2 Islam and Human Diversity

Vernacular Religion Confronts the Categories of Race and Culture

Vincent Cornell

The first morning that I ever spent in Singapore was in December 2004, exactly on the day of the earthquake and tsunami that devastated the province of Aceh in Indonesia and wreaked havoc throughout the Indian Ocean region. On that day, a group of Muslims from the Abdul Aleem Siddique Mosque took me to the shrine of Habib Nuh al-Habshi, a Sufi saint whose tomb is found just behind a freeway off-ramp in Singapore's port district. My new friends told me that Habib Nuh, along with three other Muslim saints in the Singapore region (one in Malaysia and the other two on nearby islands of Indonesia), protected Singapore from earthquakes and typhoons, which had never occurred in the city's history.

Since that time, I have made it a point to pay my respects to Habib Nuh al-Habshi whenever I visit Singapore. This follows a longstanding Muslim tradition of paying respects to the "Masters of the Land" (*rijāl al-balad*) whenever one visits a new country. For me, Habib Nuh and his tomb represent the religious and cultural diversity that make of Singapore a beacon of cosmopolitanism among the great cities of Asia. Habib Nuh al-Habshi was a sayyid, a descendant of the Prophet Muhammad, who originally came from Hadramawt in South Yemen. Across the street from his shrine is a Taoist temple surrounded by yellow flags. Habib Nuh's shrine is a rectangular structure on a hill, rising many dozens of steps above the ground. The building that houses the grave looks more like a Hindu *chandi* shrine than a typically Muslim building. Overall, the impression that the shrine gives the visitor is more Mayan than Muslim, and it evokes the feeling of climbing the steps of temples in Uxmal or Chichen Itzá in Yucatán, Mexico. The anthropologist Engseng Ho describes Habib Nuh's tomb in the following way:

> The tomb is covered by the green cloth of Islam and surrounded by golden yellow drapes, the colour of Malay royalty. Pilgrims and supplicants from all ethnic groups—Malays, Hadrami Arabs, Chinese, and especially Indians—come to visit and sit quietly a while. On the walls are framed genealogies, pointing to Habib Nuh's siblings in Penang, Singapore's predecessor port city at the northern end of the Strait of Melaka, and to ascendants in Hadramawt. The line from Singapore to Penang reaches west to other port cities, which until two generations ago were Crown Colonies of Britain's empire of free trade: Colombo, Bombay, and Aden. Along this old trunk route of world trade, and along the smaller branches that feed into it, are older ports settled by Hadramis, and housing tombs like Habib Nuh's.[99]

One would be hard put to find a better example of the cosmopolitanism that characterizes the culture of Islam than this Muslim tomb in the largely Chinese city of Singapore. The theological basis of this cosmopolitanism can be found in the following two verses of the Qur'ān, which are among the most famous verses in Islamic scripture:

> Among [God's] signs are the creation of the heavens and the earth, and the differences of your languages (*alsinatikum*) and colors (*alwānikum*). Herein indeed, are portents for those with knowledge.[100]

> Oh humankind! We have created you male and female (*min dhakarin wa unthā'*), and have made you peoples and tribes (*shu'ūban wa qabā'ila*) so that you may know one another. Verily, the noblest of you, in the sight of Allah, is the most God-fearing of you (*atqākum*). Verily, Allah is the All-Knowing and the Aware.[101]

Muslims often cite these two verses of the Qur'ān in interfaith gatherings to demonstrate that Islam is tolerant in spirit and to argue that God encourages Muslims to embrace religious diversity. As a practicing Muslim and scholar, I too believe that the diversity of the world's religions is part of God's plan for humanity. However, I am also aware that when we use these Qur'ānic verses to argue for religious pluralism, we overlook the fact that although they are indeed about difference, they say nothing on the surface about *religious* difference. Instead, they speak about differences of language (Ar. *lisān*, pl. *alsina*), color (Ar. *lawn*, pl. *alwān*), gender (Ar. *dhakar wa unthā'*, literally "male and female"), peoples (Ar. *sha'b*, pl. *shu'ūb*), and tribes (Ar. *qabīla*, pl. *qabā'il*). When we argue, as we often do, that these verses advocate religious pluralism, we are in fact "pushing the envelope" of Qur'ānic exegesis. Literalistic commentators could even argue that such an interpretation has no basis in the text. Although I prefer not to agree with them, I must concede that they have a point. Here, then, I take the opportunity to concede their point and talk about what these verses actually say, instead of what many of us would like them to mean.

More than fourteen hundred years after these verses were first revealed, we can still recognize two of the categories of which they speak as primary categories of human identity. These are the categories of language and gender—or in the exact words of the verses themselves, of "tongues" and of "men and women." As for the other categories of which these verses speak, they are somewhat alien to us, just as our own ways of speaking about difference would be alien to those who lived in the time of the Prophet Muhammad. Instead of speaking about "colors," we are now likely to speak about "race." Instead of talking about "peoples," we would probably talk about "nations." Instead of referring to "tribes," we would use words such as "societies," "ethnicities," or "cultures." Each of these modern categories—race, nation, society, ethnicity, and culture—is a complex ideological concept that carries with it a particular genealogy and set of meanings. All of these terms are as heavily charged with politics as they are with the categories of social science. As ways of conceptualizing human diversity, they would be as alien to the Prophet Muhammad and his followers as Einstein's general theory of relativity. The idea of difference certainly existed in the Prophet's time and later on in Islamic history, but not in these terms. Unlike us, when premodern Muslims talked about colors, peoples, and tribes, they really meant colors, peoples, and tribes. We moderns are the ones who turn colors into "races" and turn peoples and tribes into "nations."

The truth of this assertion is borne out when one looks carefully at ḥadīth accounts and early commentaries of sacred texts. For example, a ḥadīth transmitted by Bukhārī and Muslim states, "Verily, my friends and allies are not of the tribe of so-and-so. Rather, my friends and allies are the pious, wherever they may be." This tradition provides evidence that the world in which the Holy Qur'ān was revealed was a world of tribes and peoples, but not of "cultures." This conclusion is reinforced further by the influential Qur'ān commentary (*tafsīr*) of Muḥammad ibn Jarīr al-Ṭabarī (d. 923 CE). In this commentary, Ṭabarī does not discuss the "nations and tribes" passage of *al-Ḥujurāt* 49:13 as a text speaking about cultures or even about peoples. Instead, he thinks only about false notions of genealogical (i.e., tribal) superiority and inferiority: "When the verse says 'so that you may come to know each other,' it means, 'so that you may know each other with respect to genealogy' . . . not because you have any superiority to others in that respect nor any nearness which will bring you closer to God, but because the most distinguished among you is the most pious among you."[102]

However, to conclude from Ṭabarī and other sources that early Muslims did not think in terms of race and culture is not to say that prejudice did not exist in premodern Islam or even among the Prophet's own community. In a recent article on the concept of race in Islam, the African American Muslim scholar Paul Hardy notes that the "nations and tribes" verse was revealed immediately after the Prophet Muhammad's conquest of Mecca. After granting immunity to the tribes of Mecca that had fought against him, the Prophet asked Bilāl the Ethiopian to call the people to prayer. A group of three recently converted Arabs watched Bilāl make the call to prayer. One of them remarked how happy he was that his parents were not on hand to see such a disgusting sight. Another found it remarkable that the Prophet could find no one other than a black slave to call the Muslims to prayer. The third refrained from making any negative comment at all, lest God send a revelation to the Prophet to deal with what they had said. In modern parlance, we would call the first of these people a racist, the second a snob, and the third, a hypocrite. As the hypocrite expected, God indeed sent the angel Gabriel to inform the Prophet of their discussion. The Prophet asked the three men about what they had said, and they confirmed what Gabriel told him. God then revealed the verse to proclaim that the only criterion He uses to judge between believers is piety, a virtue that Bilāl possessed to a greater degree than his critics did.[103] This verse of the Qur'ān would not have been revealed if these Arab Muslims had not discriminated between themselves and Bilāl, a black African, based on their color and origin.

Muslims, like most human beings, are not free of prejudice. Thus, one finds repeated reminders in Qur'ān and ḥadīth that God ranks people according to their inner worth, not according to their outer characteristics. The world of late antiquity, including the region where Islam was born, was full of status distinctions in which most people lived at a disadvantage compared with a more privileged minority. Common status distinctions in this period included rich versus poor, owner versus slave, man versus woman, Arab versus non-Arab, cultured (mostly in Greek) versus uncultured, conqueror versus conquered, dominant tribe versus subordinate tribe, and high lineage versus low lineage. Most of these status distinctions continued from the pre-Islamic *Jāhiliyya* period into Islam, with the exception that literacy in Arabic or Farsi replaced literacy in other languages. However, even at its worst, one is hard put to find in the Late Antique world any prejudice as comprehensive and deeply rooted as the modern concept of race. It would have been unthinkable not only for early Muslims but also for Late Antique Mediterranean people in general to define the worth of human beings solely on the basis of how one looked, as is done in modern racism.

A famous ḥadīth of the Prophet Muhammad in the *Musnad* of Aḥmad ibn Ḥanbal (d. 855 CE) states: "There is no preference for an Arab over a non-Arab, nor for a non-Arab over an Arab; nor for a red man over a black man, nor for a black man over a red man; except through piety." In another ḥadīth, the Prophet said, "I was sent to the reds and the blacks." Notice that the phrase "white people" does not appear in these traditions. In traditional Islam, color was a distinction but not a fundamental defining characteristic. To a certain extent, the existence of racism in Western societies is an accident of history and geography. The lack of pale-skinned, blonde-haired people in the Mediterranean world turned color prejudice into what Sigmund Freud called the "fetishism of small differences." Because people did not differ greatly in appearance, more was made of differences in genealogy, language, and modes of livelihood. It is easier to be a true racist where differences in color, hair, or skin and bone structure are the sharpest. The ideology of racism is an ideology based on perceived differences in outward form, such as color and body structure. This is one reason why racism tended to develop in countries that possessed colonies far from the metropolitan "homeland" or in societies that were based on plantation or slave economies where labor was imported from different continents.

Large-scale agricultural slavery was rare in the premodern Muslim world outside of modern-day Tunisia (in the region of al-Qayrawan) and Iraq (in the al-Sawad agricultural region). It is probably not a coincidence that the only major political movement in Islamic history that reflected what we today would call a strong "racial" component was the revolt of the Zanj, the black agricultural slaves of Iraq, between 869 CE and 883 CE. For the most part, however, color was of limited importance, and the whiteness or even lightness of a person's skin was not seen as phylogenetically better than the norm. In the premodern Muslim world, color difference was a matter of aesthetics, not of race. To be reminded of this fact, one need only recall the passage in T. E. Lawrence's *Seven Pillars of Wisdom*, where the famous Lawrence of Arabia frightens a Bedouin child because his blue eyes remind the boy of blue sky shining through the eye sockets of a skull. Similarly, when I lived in Morocco in the 1970s, the Senegalese wife of a wealthy executive from Fes told my Moroccan wife that Fasis chose Senegalese women because they liked the contrast of gold jewelry on black skin.

However, as the Zanj revolt in early medieval Iraq indicates, blacks were still likely to have a greater problem with prejudice under Islam than other people were. In twelfth-century North Africa, for example, the Sanhaja Berbers of Morocco prohibited marriage and even concubinage with black women. Marriages between Sanhaja men and black women were so rare that when a Sanhaja disciple of the Andalusian Sufi Abū Madyan (d. 1198 CE) married his master's former concubine, it was considered a minor miracle. After the marriage, the couple had to move from the Maghrib to Egypt to find a place that would accept such a mixed marriage. Widespread acceptance of what we today would call "interracial" marriage developed only after the Arabization of Morocco, following the migrations of the Banū Hilal Arabs from Palestine and Egypt and the Banū Ma'qil Arabs from the Yemen.

The famous Arab writer and theologian of Baghdad Abū 'Uthmān al-Jāḥiẓ (d. 869 CE), probably the greatest essayist in the history of Arabic literature, was considered ugly not only because he was short and goggle-eyed (the meaning of *al-jāḥiẓ*) but also because he had black skin. In defense of his condition of birth, he wrote an essay called *The Glory of the Blacks over the Whites* (*Fakhr al-Sūdān 'alā al-Bīḍān*). This work is interesting partly because it draws one of the first clear distinctions between "black" and "white" in Muslim literature. However, it is even more valuable for what it says—or does not say—about the concept of "race" in premodern Islam. Jāḥiẓ's work is an apologia for blackness, and he begins by mentioning famous black people in Islamic history. Included in this list is Bilāl the Ethiopian, whom the Caliph 'Umar ibn al-Khaṭṭāb (d. 644 CE) called a "lord" and "one-third of Islam."[104] The second part of the work consists of a collection of verses from black poets of the Umayyad period (661–750 CE). Most of these poems are witty and sometimes vulgar responses to Arab poets who insulted their blackness.

The third part of the work makes use of the *faḍā'il* (exploits) genre of Arabic literature. Here Jāḥiẓ glorifies black heroes from before and after the advent of Islam and recounts the virtues of what we in the United States would call "black culture." In this section, Jāḥiẓ makes ample use of stereotypes that today would be seen as racist. For example, he asserts that blacks are more generous than others are, they are excellent singers, they have great strength and vigor, they are brave and generous, and they are loquacious speakers. "One of their men will lecture (even) a king from sunrise to sunset," says Jāḥiẓ, "and will not be content to drop the subject or to be quiet until he has finished what he wanted to say." He also states, "You will never see a black with anything but the most pleasant disposition, a tongue disposed toward laughter, and the best impression of others."[105]

One of the most revealing passages in this section confirms that blacks were often ridiculed as slaves or former slaves in the generation before the Zanj revolt at the end of the ninth century CE. Jāḥiẓ states, "The Blacks have said to the Arabs, 'Out of your ignorance you considered us as belonging to you, just as you considered your women your property in the *Jāhiliyya* period. When the justice of Islam came, you understood that this was evil, yet we still have no desire to desert you. We have filled the country through intermarriage. We have prevented your destruction and protected you from your enemies.'"[106] Apparently the accusation that Arab men mistreated their women was just as stinging a rebuke in the early 'Abbāsid period as it is today.

However, the assumption among some Africans and African Americans that Muslim Arabs were just as racist as some Europeans and Americans is contradicted by Jāḥiẓ's discussion of color differences.

> The number of blacks is greater than the number of whites, because most of those who are counted as whites are comprised of people from Persia (Fars), the mountains, Khurasan, Rome, Slavia, the land of the Franks, and al-Andalus, and anything apart

> from these is insignificant. But among the blacks are counted the Zanj, the Ethiopians, the Fezzan, the Berbers, the Copts, the Nubians, the Zaghawa, the Moors, the people of Sind (modern Pakistan), the people of the Indus Valley, the Qamar, the Dabila (South Indians), the Chinese, and those who are beyond them. The islands of the sea between China and the land of the Zanj are full of blacks, just as are Sarandib (Sri Lanka), Kalah, Amal, Zabij, and the islands up to Hindustan and China (modern Indonesia).[107]

This passage is clear evidence that the concept of color was a main factor of human difference for Jāḥiẓ. However, this was not racism in any meaningful sense of the term. No modern observer would consider Chinese, South Asians, and Indonesians to be of the same "race" as sub-Saharan Africans. Actually, it would be more accurate to say that Jāḥiẓ considered the lightness or darkness of one's skin but not one's color as a marker of "color" difference. In this passage, he ignores both skin color and structural characteristics—two major determinants of the modern concept of race—in defining the parameters of human "blackness."

In Jāḥiẓ's time, the Arabic language had no word that would correspond to the semantic range covered by the English word "race." The word that is usually translated as "race" in medieval and modern Arabic texts is "*jins*." *Jins* comes from the Latin *genus* and literally means "category." It is also the Arabic term for "sex," as in gender. *Jins* is a classificatory term that was taken over from Greco-Roman philosophy and science. It was used in Islamic law, for example, to define the value of commodities. In other words, one *jins* of a commodity would have a different unit value than another *jins* of the same commodity. By contrast, the eleventh-century Central Asian jurist Abū Bakr al-Sarakhsī saw *jins* as a way of characterizing human worth based on status distinctions: "The free person and the slave are of one *jins*. As far as his origin is concerned, every human being is free. Slavery intervenes as an accident. . . . Thus slavery does not bring about a change in one's *jins*."[108] Although for Sarakhsī *jins* is a marker of worth, it is clearly not an indicator of "race."

If it is possible to say "race does not matter" about premodern Islam, it is also possible to say much the same about "culture." Historians have long observed that the shock of European colonialism in the Muslim world was exacerbated by the fact that Muslims traditionally considered Northern Europeans to be uncivilized barbarians. Premodern Muslim terms that designated ethnicities were usually based on regions or modes of livelihood. Europeans were *al-Ifranj*, a word that stood for "Franks"; a *Hindī* was a person from the Indus Valley. *Al-Sūdān*, the "Land of the Blacks," was an anomaly in that it was based on skin color. The word *'arab* for "Arabs" referred to a people, but the term was based not on the modern concept of culture but on the socioeconomic basis of the Arab lifestyle. An *'arabī* was a pastoralist or a herdsman; thus, the term could be used for any pastoralist, irrespective of whether a person was "Arab" by culture. For example, a thirteenth-century historical work from Morocco describes the so-called Arab tribe of Banū Marin entering the Rif Mountains.[109] We would not call these people Arabs today. Ethnically, they were Amazigh people or Berbers; they spoke the Tamazight language and considered themselves distinct from Arabs. The only thing that made them Arab to this medieval Moroccan historian was their pastoralist way of life.

'Ajamī, the antonym for *'arabī*, in premodern Muslim usage, was not a socioeconomic category but a linguistic category. Originally, it meant someone who did not speak Arabic, in the same way that the word "Berber" comes from the Greek *barbaros*, which meant someone who did not speak Greek. Eventually, *'ajamī* became a synonym for "Persian" because Persian-speakers were the most significant group of non-Arabic speakers on the borders of the Arabian Peninsula. However, the term did not always have to mean "Persian." The region of modern Iran that borders southern Iraq—what used to be called *'Iraq 'Ajamī*—was only partly a Persian-speaking region. Before Islam, it was ruled by Persians but most of its inhabitants spoke Aramaic, a Semitic language that was more closely related to Arabic than the Indo-European Persian language. In early Islamic times, the Aramaic speakers of Iraq were called *Nabaṭ* (pl. *Anbāṭ*, "agriculturalists" or "farmers") by the Arabs. Because they did not speak Arabic, they were also considered *'Ajamī*.

Now that we have established that our modern concepts of race and culture had no exact parallels in premodern Islam, what does this mean for our current thinking about Islam and human diversity? First, this evidence reminds us that we should not make the mistake of essentializing Muslim attitudes by assuming that the answer to the question "What does Islam say about human diversity?" is entirely scriptural. Although Muslims draw on scripture for inspiration, Muslims are not scriptural automatons who only do what scripture tells them to do. Scriptural texts are not sufficient evidence for generalization about any religious attitude. Muslims, like Christians and Jews, are informed by scripture, but are not governed by scripture.

The second lesson that we can learn from this evidence takes us back to the tomb and shrine of Habib Nuh al-Habshi in modern Singapore. Besides standing as a symbol of the cosmopolitanism of the premodern Islamic world, Habib Nuh also stands as a symbolic gesture of defiance against modernity in the guise of a freeway off-ramp. In fact, the shrine is so close to this off-ramp that one wonders what story might lie behind the freeway's location. Local Muslims claim that the government of Singapore wanted to demolish the tomb, but the bulldozers broke down every time they approached the sacred precinct. Eventually, we are told, the time-honored Chinese tradition of pragmatism reasserted itself, and the freeway was altered to accommodate the presence of the Muslim saint.

Whether or not this story is true, it provides a wonderful example of the stubbornness of tradition in the face of modernity. Even more, the shrine of Habib Nuh al-Habshi symbolizes the stubbornness of the vernacular in the face of modern religious sensibilities. As an example of vernacular Islam, there is much in this tomb and the rites associated with it to disturb Islamic modernists. Apart from the fact that it is a Sufi saint's shrine, one can cite its Hindu temple architecture, the lack of religious boundaries observed by its visitors, and the garlands of flowers on the tomb that look more appropriate on a statue of Vishnu than on an Islamic burial site. Anthropologists of religion use the term "vernacular religion" to describe culturally localized responses to scriptural teachings such as those that we have just discussed. Much like vernacular languages, "vernacular" religious discourses are juxtaposed to "standard" or official religious discourses that cut across social or geographical boundaries or locales.[110] In effect, vernacular religious discourses are socially embodied commentaries on sacred scriptures. As embodied exegetical "texts," they are just as significant in their own right as the teachings of theologians and in fact may even be more influential. One cannot claim that vernacular expressions of Islam are not "real Islam" just because they disagree with official or standard interpretations of scripture. Islamic faith is defined by Islam in practice, whether or not one agrees with the practices in question. Jāḥiẓ, the theologian and litterateur, was just as valuable an interpreter of the Islamic attitude toward human diversity as the exegete Ṭabarī was. Furthermore, by opening a window for us on what Muslims really believed—as opposed to what they are supposed to believe—we are better prepared to counter today's ideology-bound prejudices with more realistic solutions. Trying to solve real problems by spouting pious ideals is a category mistake of the first order, and it is bound to be ineffective. In many cases, we can find that having recourse to the vernacular traditions of the past can "save the text" of the Qur'ān from the imposed categories of modern ideology.

A recourse to vernacular religion also reminds us that any attempt to raise the consciousness of believers, whether of racial or ethnic diversity or of any other subject, can only be successful on the local level. In general, attitudes are reinforced but not changed by ideology. Ideologies of race and culture provide slogans; they do not provide solutions. Whenever Muslims and non-Muslims got along together, and where the problems of human difference were overcome, the solutions were most often vernacular, not ideological. Recent historical studies of Hindu–Muslim relations in South Asia have revealed that the current terms of religious conflict in India were almost entirely set by British colonialism, which imposed ideological categories on relations that were primarily non-ideological. When conflicts occurred in the past, they tended to be framed as Hindu-Turk, not Hindu-Muslim. Hindus drew distinctions between Turks, Arabs (called *Tajiks*), and Ismāʿīlī converts, and when the Delhi Sultans raided Hindu kingdoms, these kingdoms were often defended by Arabs and Ismāʿīlīs against Turks. Memorials can be found in Gujarat honoring Arab Muslims who martyred themselves fighting against Muslim Turks on behalf of Hindu kingdoms. These same kingdoms endowed mosques on behalf of Arab traders. It is at points such as these that the notions of culture and religion coincide, and they remind us that the solutions to cultural and religious conflicts alike lie in the vernacular.

As theologians, we should never forget that real tradition is always vernacular and that it expresses itself in the plural—not as "Tradition" but as traditions. The acceptance of both human and religious diversity ultimately depends on our ability to hear once again the voices of vernacular human relations. The U.S. politician Thomas "Tip" O'Neill, a former Speaker of the House of Representatives from Boston, famously said, "All politics is local." The same can be said for the politics of race, culture, and diversity in Islam.

CHAPTER THREE

Guardians of the Environment

3.1 Guardianship of the Environment

An Islamic Perspective in the Context of Religious Studies, Theology, and Sustainable Development

Azizan Baharuddin

This essay will address the topic of environmental guardianship by first stressing the need for religious studies and theology to reinvigorate their role in the context of sustainable development, and to find their way into other disciplines' ethical bases in economic and sociocultural terms. I begin from the premise that, just as the physical basis for any society is its bricks and mortar, so too in the human and social dimension of life there is a need to strengthen the belief and values basis. Guardianship as a value or belief is manifested in action in the form of sustainable development.

The Role of Philosophy

Philosophy of religion can be used in two ways: as an exercise in philosophy with religion as the subject; or as an exercise in religion where philosophy is used as an intellectual tool.[111] Philosophy is critical because it asks the questions that need to be asked if religious studies and theology (and guardianship of nature is one important aspect of theology) are to really succeed in exploring the concept of sustainable development and the most recent elaboration of sustainable development objectives, as seen, for example, in the Earth Charter (2000).[112] Philosophy can help explain the ethical foundation of principles for sustainable development, or it can help us put into religious studies the idea of sustainable development. Likewise, the idea of guardianship of nature is the foundational principle of the Earth Charter, and sustainable development can be shown to be one goal of religious instruction. Examples of questions that philosophy poses are, What do we mean? What are our reasons? What lies behind? What are the implications?

Such questions help construct a much-needed dialogue that leads to the mutual understanding and mutual borrowing that need to take place between the various disciplines currently understood as being embraced by sustainable development: economic, environmental, social, cultural.[113] Such mutual borrowing is explained in terms of transdisciplinarity, as described by Basarab Nicolescu, which can lead to a fusion of horizons between religion and science, economics, and other fields.[114]

The term "philosophy" derives from the Greek *philo-sophia*, which means the love of wisdom, *ḥikma*: knowledge of the proper place for everything. The quest for wisdom, which cannot be divorced from the truth—*ḥaqq*, one of the names of God—is at the heart of the religious impulse. Humanity has forever been looking beyond itself to find answers about itself: Where have we come from? Where are we going? How should we live? While philosophy asks the big questions, religion provides us with the grand narratives as answers, or at least clues. Philosophy also has to ask probing, critical, and analytical questions, and so the search for wisdom leads to the realm of empirical and experimental investigation and the rise of the sciences. In the Islamic perspective, philosophy (speculative) and science (empirical) are necessary for the believer to reach and to explain the religious state. In fact, the first two are subsumable under religion, which in Islam is called *dīn*, a total way of life consisting of the physical, mental, social, and spiritual. This idea is also seen in Muhammad Iqbal's description of the four phases of the religious state of belief: blind following, questioning, exploration and experience, witness and acceptance.[115]

The evolution of the religious consciousness from the first of these stages to the fourth requires the believer to have knowledge and experience of nature and life. This holistic approach to religion, and the comprehensive solutions and guidance it is supposed to offer, must make practitioners of religious studies today aware of the gap between ideal and reality in understanding, manifesting, and practicing religion.[116] For example, in explaining the relevance of religion in today's world, many Muslim believers may not really understand, or are not able to articulate, the significance either of the finality of the prophethood of their prophet or the actual "modernness" of their religion as implied by the concept of the Islamic city (*madīna*). These statements are not meant to be part of an apologetic stance but can be linked to the most recent discourses about the nature of reality currently actively pursued in the Western and "modern" or postmodern world.

It is critical to begin with this introduction for a number of reasons. To many in the West, I may be seen to represent a non-Western, non-Christian, nonmodern worldview. Therefore, it is imperative for me to share with the Western as well as the Islamic worlds the historical fact that Islamic civilization shares some elements of its origin in the Greek heritage as well as in Judeo-Christian concepts of the divine.[117] The gap between Islamic and Western worlds should not be seen as an insurmountable obstacle to fruitful dialogue, including civilizational dialogue on guardianship of the environment as a means to learn something new and to grow because of that new understanding.[118] This dialogue is critically necessary today in the context of sustainable development because the gap in relationship between man and nature lies at the heart of the religious worldview.

The Earth Charter and the Unity of Humanity and Nature

At the heart of the environmental crisis is humanity's spiritual crisis.[119] It is high time now that, despite the successes of materialistic science, we build a unity of knowledge and understanding as the basis of a more holistic (incorporating science, religion, and philosophy) worldview and actions. This is what the Earth Charter is asking us to do for the sake of our future. It clearly sends out a message to the fragmented components of our lost humanity:

> We stand at a critical moment in Earth's history, a time when humanity must choose its future. As the world becomes increasingly interdependent and fragile, the future at once holds great peril and great promise. To move forward we must recognize that in the midst of a magnificent diversity of cultures and life forms we are one human family and one Earth community with a common destiny. We must join together to bring forth a sustainable global society founded on respect of nature, universal human rights, economic justice and a culture of peace. Towards this end, it is imperative that we, the people of Earth, declare our responsibility to one another, to the greater community of life and to future generations.[120]

In Islamic teaching, the destiny of the earth and its communities is linked to the core principle of the religion: affirmation of *tawḥīd*, the unity of God. *Tawḥīd* also implies the idea of the unity of nature, man, and the Creator contained in the first *shahāda* or Islamic witness: *Lā ilāhā illā-Llāh*. This also implies the interrelatedness of all things in the natural world, and between that world and God. Muslim scientists see that nature as a whole exhibits and contributes toward such a unity since its constituent parts are related to each other in numerous ways and through numerous laws. In their practice of science they discover that the more they come to know nature, the more glaring is the truth of the unity of nature; *tawḥīd* inspires science, and science affirms *tawḥīd*.[121]

The charter also reminds us of "our responsibility to one another." In regard to the diversity of human beings, the Qur'ān tells us: "O mankind! Lo! We have created you male and female, and have made you nations and tribes that ye may know one another. Lo! The noblest of you in the sight of Allah, is the best in conduct. Lo! Allah is Knower, Aware."[122] Other faith communities also agree that morality consists in conduct that gives practical expression to ethical values, which as a product of religious studies and theology are critically required as the engine of sustainable development today.

The Challenges Ahead

The Earth Charter says of the challenge that lies ahead of us:

> The choice is ours: form a global partnership to care for Earth and one another or risk the destruction of ourselves and the diversity of life. Fundamental changes are needed in our values, institutions, and ways of living. We must realize that when basic needs have been met, human development is primarily about being more, not having more. We have the knowledge and technology to provide for all and to reduce our impacts on the environment. The emergence of a global civil society is creating new opportunities to build a democratic and humane world. Our environmental, economic, political, social, and spiritual challenges are interconnected, and together we can forge inclusive solutions.[123]

In Malaysia, the concept of civil society, or *Masyarakat Madani*, was actively debated and pursued in the 1990s. Today the trend continues with the policy of *Islām Hadhāri*, which strives to harmonize religion and development as espoused by the Qur'ān: "Seek the bounty of Allah and celebrate the praises of Allah often; that ye may prosper."[124] I offer some ideas that could be part of the inclusive solutions being sought and could share in the universal responsibility mentioned in the Earth Charter toward the emergence of a global civil society without loss of integrity and cultural independence.

We must decide to live with a sense of universal responsibility, identifying ourselves with the whole earth community as well as with our local communities. The spirit of human solidarity and kinship with all life is strengthened when we live with reverence for the mystery of being, gratitude for the gift of life, and humility regarding humanity's place in nature. We urgently need a shared vision of basic values to provide an ethical foundation for the emerging world community. In what follows I show how the ideas highlighted in the preceding quotation are indeed fundamental elements of the Islamic *Weltanschauung*. Part of this elaboration I have already described through the concept of unity, *tawḥīd*.

Gratitude for the Gift of Life

S. M. N. al-Attas explains the concept of religion (*dīn*) in Islam as connoting indebtedness, submissiveness, judicious power, and natural inclination or tendency. *Dāna*, derived from *dīn*, gives the meaning of being indebted. When we are in a state of debt, we are a *dayn* who has to follow the laws and ordinances governing such debts. A person in debt is also a *dayn* who is under obligation to a ruler or governor, a *dayyān*. *Dāna* is also connected to *madanna*, which means to build or found cities; to civilize, humanize, refine. From *maddana* in turn arise the concepts of *madīna*, the city, and *tamaddun*, civilization.[125]

In the context of environmental ethics or guardianship of nature and sustainable development, the concept of *dīn* implies that humans are indebted to the Creator for their existence to begin with, and that they already acknowledged God as their Creator the moment their souls were created. Al-Attas explains that the nature of this debt of creation and existence is so total that "at the instance he is created and given existence, man is in a state of utter dependence because 'he' (*Ādam* means 'no' 'thing') really possesses nothing himself; which means everything in him, from him and about him is what the creator (who owns everything) owns. This also means that mankind is totally dependent for his sustenance on the sustainer of Life Himself."[126] This is explained further in the Qur'ān: "When thy Lord drew forth from the children of Adam—from their loins—their descendants, and made them testify concerning themselves (saying): 'Am I not your Lord?'—They said—'Yes! We do testify.'"[127]

Because he owns nothing, man can only repay his debt with the only thing that is his, namely his consciousness. It is through this consciousness that he "returns" himself to the Creator, who owns him absolutely. This is why in Islam *dhikr*, or "remembrance," is so crucial. It is the means for "returning," and hence for attaining *ḥikma*—"wisdom."

Ḥikma underlies man's thoughts, intentions, decisions, and actions, the sum total of which is *'ibāda*, service or good works—the original reason for man's creation.

To be of service or do good works, man needs nature or the environment; the Qur'ān explains that this has been made malleable for him (*taskhīr*). The environment is the theatre for his *'ibāda*. For example, to perform the *zakāt* (tithe[128]), man needs to have worked the environment by farming, cultivation, and so on, and for this he must possess scientific and technological knowledge and skills for the "what" and "how" of his use of nature. Nature is not his but is given to him only for his sustenance, comfort, and entertainment as a trust (*amāna*). His relationship to nature is in the capacity of *khalīfa* or vicegerent.[129]

This state of being in which man gives back to God does not mean that man is in some kind of state of unhappiness as a slave because it is in submission that man actually becomes what his inherent nature truly is. In submitting, man returns to his true nature in which he finds peace and happiness (*salām*). His "returning" is in fact a gain. This is the state of being of the *khalīfa*, the "slave" who is paradoxically vicegerent of the Almighty, microcosm of the macrocosm. He who enslaves himself gains. "Who is he that will loan to Allah a beautiful loan, which Allah will double unto his credit and multiply many times?"[130]

In the Islamic context at least, one of the basic challenges for religious studies is to show the contemporary relevance of the paradoxical position of man as slave of God yet also God's vicegerent. Nature is made malleable for him (*taskhīr*), yet he must not transgress the boundaries of what is good (*ḥalāl*) and harmful (*ḥarām*), what is just (*'adl*) and unjust (*ẓulm*). These and other values are all part of *maqāṣid al-sharī'a*, the "beneficial objectives" of the Sharī'a, regulations prescribed by revelation.

The "*ḥalāl*-ness" or "*ḥarām*-ness" of a thing or act is actually explicable from the components and processes of nature or society studied through the natural and human sciences. As such, the ethics underlying sustainable development need to be explained through both science and religion, with philosophy providing tools for connecting the two and articulating the arguments and principles arising out of their harmonization. This exercise of explaining revelation by using scientific facts is also called theology of nature, a kind of dialogue between science and religion.[131]

In using resources, in treating the environment in ways that ensure balance, peace, and sustainability, humans enslaves themselves to God in order to fulfill his commands and ordinances—"debtors," as the somber religious language describes it—to fulfill their guardianship of nature. God has not created the environment, nature, and the universe for nothing but to enable humans to do good works; in submitting, humanity intrinsically becomes "environmentally ethical," being "best in conduct." Through this "enslavement," which means being ethical and respectful of nature's ways, humans operationalize their God-given power judiciously and eventually go on to build cities. Through guardianship, humanity attains to great heights of civilizational achievement:

> And He it is who created the heavens and the earth . . . and His throne was upon the water that He might try you, which of you is best in conduct.[132]

> Lo! We have placed all that is in the Earth as an ornament thereof that we may try them: which of them is best in conduct.[133]

Misconceptions Regarding the Idea of *Khilāfa*

Lynn White Jr. once wrote that it was the concept of the vicegerency or stewardship of humanity in the Christian (and, by implication, the Islamic) worldview that was responsible for the anthropocentric attitude to nature that gave rise to the environmental crisis.[134] In the Islamic tradition, as mentioned earlier, nature has indeed been made malleable for humanity (*taskhīr*):[135]

> See ye not how Allah hath made serviceable unto you whatsoever is in the skies and whatsoever is in the earth and hath loaded you with His favours both without and within? Yet of mankind is he who disputeth concerning Allah, without knowledge or guidance or a Scripture giving light.[136]

> Hast thou not seen how Allah hath made all that is in the earth subservient unto you? And the ship runneth upon the sea by His command, and He holdeth back the heaven from falling on the earth unless by His leave. Lo! Allah is, for mankind, Full of Pity, Merciful.[137]

Despite this "power," humanity is not to transgress boundaries, as explained by the science of ecology, nor to abuse nature; hence, White's claim would be contested by Muslims. To behave in an ethical manner toward the environment is in a sense what guardianship means. In the Islamic perspective, it means that humans are fulfilling the purpose of their existence, which is to serve their Creator. In so doing, they achieve happiness, as they are naturally inclined to do. This natural inclination—connected to his natural human habits, dispositions, customs, ethics, *dīn*—is also called *fiṭra*, the pattern of God's way (*sunnat Allāh*) of creating things. This "way" is indeed what is meant by the Sharī'a of God. Behaving in accordance with *fiṭra* and Sharī'a results in harmony; it is the realization of what is actually intrinsically in one's true nature. Sharī'a is cosmos (order) as opposed to chaos, justice as opposed to injustice; justice exists when something is where it belongs.[138] Could sustainable development ultimately mean, then, that humans will discover their true states and beings as well as nature's true state and being, and that humans will live in accordance with this knowledge? Hazel Henderson and Daisaku Ikeda, both champions of the Earth Charter, may agree when they express their hope for the fostering of leaders for the creative coexistence of nature and humanity through education.[139]

Fiṭra and justice intrinsically reside in nature, and humans witness to these while doing their science. The poet-philosopher Muhammad Iqbal said that in his studying of nature, the scientist is actually in a state of contemplation and worship.[140] In this regard we are reminded of the Qur'ānic verses that speak of all creatures as "glorifying God in their own ways" according to their own natures. Interpreters have taken the latter to be the creatures' spiritual acts of glorifying (*tasbīḥ*), praising (*taḥmīd*), prostrating (*sujūd*) and praying (*ṣalāt*) to Him.[141] As such, before environmental ethics can be clearly expounded, ecological knowledge needs to be grasped through scientific observation, an exercise emphasized by the Qur'ān. Observing nature to understand creation and thence the revelation of God is an exercise called the theology of nature, the understanding of revelation by using scientific knowledge. God "hath created seven heavens in harmony. Thou canst see no fault in the Beneficent One's creation; then look again: Canst thou see any rifts?"[142]

This is also part of the meaning of submission (*islām*). Submission does not mean the loss of freedom because in fact it is freedom to live according to the demands of one's true nature, to be at one with life, which has no beginning, no end, and encompasses the seen (*ẓāhir*) and the unseen (*bāṭin*). In this way, God has created all things to distinguish truth from falsehood, right from wrong, and to set out a clear ethic, the realization of which can be seen as sustainable development: "And we created not the heavens and the earth, and all that is between them in play. We created them not save with truth; but most of them know not."[143]

Sources regarding the Environment

The Qur'ān is the most important source regarding the environment. It speaks about the cosmos, humanity, and the world of nature, all together participating in the process of revelation that is ongoing. It points to the cosmos as God's revelation, taking place in the form of the phenomena of nature including the processes in leaves, the faces of mountains, the features of animals, and the sounds of winds and flowing rivers. Every natural phenomenon is one of the signs (*āyāt*) of God, even events in the soul.[144]

Other sources and teachings on the environment include the aḥādīth (sayings and acts of the Prophet) regarding treatment of the environment; the injunctions made concerning the environment pertaining to water, soil, animals, and plants; and texts on Islamic ethics that touch upon human passions that can affect the environment. Moreover, Islamic philosophy and theology of nature are expressed in art, architecture, landscaping, and urban design. Forms of Islamic literature such as poetry also played an important role, for example among the intellectual elite of the so-called Golden Age in Andalusia (ninth to eleventh centuries).[145] In this context, S. H. Nasr quotes the famous Sufi poet Sa'dī:

> I am joyous in the world of nature
> For the world of nature is joyous through Him,
> I am in love with the whole cosmos
> For the whole cosmos comes from Him.[146]

Likewise, various literatures of the Islamic people ranging from Arabic, Malay, and Persian to Bengali and Swahili contain a vast wealth of material on the Islamic view of the relationship between man and the environment. In my own Malay-Muslim community, social wisdom is embodied in proverbs and poetic rhymes articulating principles, instructions, and guidance influenced by a religious ethic (*adab*).[147] By drawing analogies with the perceived behavior of nature's flora and fauna, these proverbs express an ethic (*adab*) pertaining to different situations in life faced by the individual, and they teach lessons to be learned.

Applying Religion for Sustainable Development: A Case Study of *Ijtihād*

The example of Umer Chapra shows that a creative interpretation of religious injunctions is possible in the area of sustainable development. Chapra has been economic adviser to the government of several Muslim countries and has written extensively on Islamic economics and finance. His most important work is *Towards a Just Monetary System: A Discussion of Money, Banking, and Monetary Policy in the Light of Islamic Teachings.*[148] He is a Muslim economist who seems confident enough in what Islam has to offer to be able to explain at length how economics, development, and religion might interact. His ideas are also set out in a work titled *Islam and the Economic Challenge.* In the context of today's economic uncertainties, Chapra earnestly appeals to Muslim countries to try out what he calls the goals of the Sharī'a (*maqāṣid al-sharī'a*) as a means of avoiding disintegration—an example of which is offered by events in Indonesia several years ago, sparked by the currency and debt crisis that hit all the economies of Asia. The people—many poor and jobless—demanded removal of their leaders through mass demonstrations. Observing the huge disparities in wealth between the various sectors of Indonesian society, they understandably felt that their leaders were corrupt and thought only of themselves. The leaders were seen to have forgotten their duties as vicegerents (*khalīfa*) of God because they neglected the poor.

The goals of the Sharī'a are, first, human well-being (*falāḥ*) and the good life (*ḥayat ṭayyiba*). To Chapra, the Sharī'a is the basis of development because, in its emphasis on socioeconomic justice, it aims to satisfy both the spiritual and the material needs of human beings. Chapra derives inspiration from al-Ghazālī, whom he quotes as saying: "the very objective of the Sharī'a is to promote the welfare of the people, which lies in safeguarding their faith, their life, their intellect, their posterity and their wealth. Whatever ensures the safeguarding of these five serves public interest and is desirable."[149]

Chapra also agrees with al-Ghazālī in putting faith at the top of the list of the *maqāṣid* because it is the most crucial ingredient in human well-being. Faith places human relations on a proper foundation, enabling human beings to interact in a balanced and mutually caring manner for the well-being of all. Faith also acts as a moral filter to keep the allocation and distribution of resources in line with requirements for unity and socioeconomic justice. Without the element of faith in human economic decisions—in the household, the corporate boardroom, the market—we cannot possibly realize efficiency and equity or avoid macroeconomic imbalances, economic instability, crime, conflict, and the many symptoms of anomie.

Chapra emphasizes that if we are to achieve equilibrium between scarce resources and the various claims on those resources, we need to focus on human beings rather than on the market or the state. It is imperative, therefore, to reinstate the human being as the foundation of the economic system. Humans must be motivated to pursue self-interest within the constraints facing the world. Truly believing in the possibility of a just and sane economic system, Chapra sets out the various stages for achieving such a system.

Like others, Chapra begins with a critique of the present situation followed by a reevaluation of principles embedded in the religious metaphysics of Islam. Using the three fundamental principles of *tawḥīd* (unity), *khilāfa* (vicegerency, trusteeship), and *'adl* or *'adāla* (justice), he describes a strategy for a more enlightened economic system. In his treatment, he deals with all the details and complexities of the modern economic system and integrates religious principles and economics throughout.

Chapra speaks of *tawḥīd*, *khilāfa*, and *'adāla* as being connected with and translatable into ideas about universal fellowship, resources as a trust, humble lifestyles, human freedom, needs fulfillment, and equitable distribution of income and wealth, growth, and stability. He suggests reviving systems laid out in the Qur'ān, such as the *zakāt* (tithe) system, and other principles pertaining to wealth. He deals clearly with an entire complex of ideas, starting with the role of the *'ulamā'* (clergy), the restructuring of policies, land and labor reforms, education and training, access to finance, and the size of land holdings, and, moving then to the restructuring of the financial and investment systems, just and efficient taxation, tariffs and import substitution, and priorities in spending.

Chapra concludes his treatise by reiterating that imbuing economics with religious values would imply a serious effort to raise (along Islamic lines) the spiritual and material well-being of all people. On the spiritual side, inner happiness can be achieved only by drawing nearer to God. On the material side, Islamization requires the just and efficient allocation of resources so that the good life (*ḥayat ṭayyiba*) can be achieved. Islamization is not necessarily against liberalization; rather, it involves passing public—and private—sector economic decisions through the filter of moral values before they influence the market. Without the integration of science, religion, and development, it would be impossible for Muslim countries to achieve development that is sustainable. Chapra observes, however, that policymakers have yet to be convinced to translate Islam's economic ideals into development policies. This is an urgent and arduous task, and the signs of the times have to be read quickly.

Conclusion

It is imperative that religious studies and theology in the different faith traditions work together to help promote the ideals of sustainable development and the Earth Charter. Through dialogue they can share their earth-sustaining principles and work out how religious studies and theology can be better taught. Dialogue, as a mechanism for achieving mutual understanding and negotiating common goals among those of the same or different faiths, needs to be properly understood and made use of. For dialogue to be effective, it has to be based on sincerity, which is a basic religious trait.

3.2 Slayers or Stewards? Ecological Guardianship in the Christian Tradition

Michael Northcott

The Book of Samuel has a heroic description of the young man who was to become Israel's favored king, David as a slayer. In the famous story, David the shepherd boy comes to the battle scene where the giant Philistine Goliath has been challenging the Israelites for a fight. David kills him with a well-aimed stone to his head from a slingshot. David then proceeds to chase after the Philistine army and slay them in their thousands. The narrator records the delight of Israel in David's power and effectiveness as a slayer as he returns from battle: "As they were coming home, when David returned from slaying the Philistine, the women came out of all the cities of Israel, singing and dancing, to meet King Saul, with timbrels, with songs of joy, and with instruments of music. And the women sang to one another as they made merry, 'Saul has slain his thousands, and David his ten thousands.'"[150]

David is celebrated not only for slaying the Philistines but also for his prowess in slaying lions, bears, and other wild animals. The biblical figure who becomes for all time the ideal king of Israel—and from whom Christ himself is said to be descended as Son of David—is first celebrated as a heroic slayer.

King David slew Philistines and lions. His son Solomon slew forests to build his great temple and enslaved his own people as loggers among the cedar trees of Lebanon. The Hebrew ancestors of the people of Israel knew slavery in the land of Egypt, but in the Promised Land, Israel's kings gradually abandoned the Mosaic law under whose terms they were to live in the land, and according to which they were to treat the land and their fellow creatures as members of a covenant community. By the time of the Hebrew prophets in the sixth century BCE, small farmers and the soil had been enslaved by Israel's kings in their imperial exploits. As the prophet Isaiah put it:

> Ravaged, ravaged the earth,
> despoiled, despoiled,
> as Yahweh has said.
> The earth is mourning, withering,
> the heavens are pining away with the earth.
> The earth is defiled under its inhabitants' feet,
> for they have transgressed the law, violated the precept,
> broken the everlasting covenant.
> So a curse consumes the earth
> and its inhabitants suffer their penalty,
> that is why the inhabitants of the earth are burnt up,
> and few men are left.[151]

The likely reason for this despoiling of the soil was salinization. Subterranean salts beneath the topsoil of the region were drawn to the surface by deep plowing and irrigation as cereal farming was taken up by the large farms that emerged under the late

Hebrew monarchy. Israel had overburdened the land, neglecting its fallow periods, and denied the soil its Sabbaths. It was partly for this reason that the Persian king Cyrus had conquered the land of Israel. When the Israelites were exiled, Isaiah decreed, the land would again get its Sabbath, and the desert and the wilderness would again bring forth fruits and vines.

It was not only on the plains that the land of Israel suffered under the growing weight of the late Israelite monarchy's imperious economy and imperial wars. Deforestation was also affecting the hills. As the mountains were denuded of trees by Israel and by her neighbors, this caused flash floods and further soil erosion. As the prophet Habakkuk suggested, the violence with which the Israelites had slain the forests of Lebanon would eventually fall upon them: "The violence done to Lebanon will overwhelm you; the destruction of the beasts will terrify you, for the blood of men and violence to the earth, to cities and all who dwell therein."[152]

The Old Testament describes humans as creatures who are uniquely and tragically divided in their vocation on earth. On the one hand, humans are earth keepers, called to tend and care for the earth and its creatures. This vocation shapes their moral character because it requires them to cooperate with the created grain of the universe; it is the vocation of the agrarian farmer to attend to the condition of the soil and to plant his crops to improve the soil, thus learning patience and peaceableness in sustaining the fertility of the earth. This sense of vocation is reflected in the narrative construction of the earth and its creatures as constituting a moral order that reflects the justice and peace of God's law, of Torah. When humans attend carefully to the soil and to the creatures that live on it, their households thrive and the Lord sends abundant rain to water the harvest and sunshine in due measure to warm the earth.

On the other hand, humans are made in the image of God—"a little lower than the angels." In this vocation they are tempted to become godlike, even to mingle with the sons and daughters of the gods, as one strand of the Genesis narrative suggests. Consequently, they tend pridefully to assert their will against the Creator. When they do this, they take up a violent relation to their fellow creatures and to one another, which neglects this original order. They learn to kill one another, as Cain first killed Abel, and as the descendants of Noah learned to kill animals for meat. And they build great monuments to their power such as the Tower of Babel, Solomon's great Temple, and the great cities whose ruined monuments still mark the present-day Middle East, for the Ancient Near East was the first place in human history where agriculture was practiced, cities were constructed, and law codes were written down. When humans constructed these new worlds in which their powers were magnified, they also learned to build empires in which they enslaved their fellow humans, worshipped idols and wealth, and went to war. The Old Testament narrators suggest that when their forbears lived in this way, they not only brought down judgment on themselves. They also subverted the created order in its original goodness and perfection, and a chasm emerged between the physical cosmos and human political community.

The "ethos of the cosmos" as described in the Old Testament is one in which the world is born not through the violent assertion of divine power—as in the Babylonian origin myth—but through the generosity of divine love and peaceable wisdom.[153] God creates a multitude of creatures who—in their beauty, diversity, and relational interdependence—reflect the glory and wonder of divine being in the godhead's own internal relations. But God goes beyond creating creatures that merely reflect the Creator's glory. God creates creatures who are like companions to the Creator, and who can freely converse and walk with their Creator in the Garden of Eden. But these godlike creatures run amok in the garden that is given to them. They refuse the original relation of service and stewardship as well as the lawful limits that the Creator had set in the fabric of being. Instead they pursue their powers to the point that they disrupt, degrade, and destroy the original goodness that the Creator had set in the order of creation—they become slayers instead of stewards.

Today in Southeast Asia the same ambiguity in the human vocation is powerfully evident, and the earth is also mourning and pining. From lands of primal jungles and rice paddies, fruit trees and coral reefs, where people lived a life of abundant leisure, planting their rice and then waiting while it grew, in the meantime doing such things as painting and flying kites, spinning tops, feasting and fishing, economic development has seen people in Southeast Asia move from the bicycle to the car, from the village to the city, and from rice growing to manufacturing computers, clothes, and cars for export all over the world. With economic development have come burgeoning cities, motorways, and suburbs; a growing pace of life; and new cultural, educational, and scientific opportunities. In the last thirty years, Southeast Asian countries such as Singapore and Taiwan have enjoyed some of the fastest economic growth of any country in the modern history of development. But this fast rate of growth and development has not been without cost.

Earlier this year I was in Kuala Lumpur, where I once lived, and flew in over new palm oil plantations that stretch from the new airport as far as the eye can see. Palm oil companies are spreading their monocrops right across this region, in many cases bribing local officials and even attracting public subsidies as they rip their way through the glorious heritage of some of the oldest rainforest on earth. Millions of hectares of Borneo and Sumatra have been burned in the last ten years to make way for palms, the oil of which is in thousands of foods, detergents, and cosmetics in Western supermarkets and which is also being turned into biodiesel to displace a percentage of the fossils that fuel European car engines, thus assuaging Europe's ecological conscience. So extensive is the burning of forestation that the whole region is often shrouded in smog in July and August. The quantity of carbon dioxide released by the burning in 1997–98 was so great that it precipitated an economic collapse across the whole region from Thailand to Indonesia.

The damage being done to the forests was brought home to me personally on a journey I made as field education director of the Seminari Theologi Malaysia in Kuala Lumpur with two of my students from Sarawak who took me and my family on a trip up the great Rajang River from Sibu to the heart of what was then known as the Fifth Division. In Sibu we met a "flying doctor" who told us she was taking medicines in helicopter trips to outlying areas where she was finding that the nomadic Penans were suffering from malnutrition. All their traditional food sources had been devastated by the loggers. With the trees mostly clear-cut over vast swathes, all the wild animals had died. The fish in the rivers had died from lack of oxygen because as the rain ran off the bare, sandy tropical earth, so much silt deposited in the rivers that nothing could survive. The area is one of the most fertile on earth—you could plant a papaya seed in the ground and within a few months you would be harvesting fruits—but greed and the quest for corporate profits had reduced nature's abundant larder to a desert. This was all craftily hidden from us because on the river and in the riverside long houses we had visited, the loggers had left a fifty-meter band of trees so tourists and visitors could not see the damage being done to the interior.

Industrial monocrop agriculture was introduced into the tropics by European Christians. British and Dutch agronomists in the nineteenth century first came and slayed the tropical forests to replace it with cash crops of rubber and palm oil. Britain paid a substantial portion of its debt to the United States after World War II with rubber and palm oil grown in Malaysia as it fought off the communists who had expected independence when the war Britain backed with the United States against Japan had ended. But Britain needed Malaya in the 1950s—these tropical soils were Britain's savior in making payments to the new imperial power across the Atlantic. Since independence, both Malaysia and Indonesia have taken up these crops with alacrity and spread them over ever-larger land areas. The rate of destruction of tropical rainforest in Southeast Asia and in Amazonia is responsible for an unprecedented loss of biodiversity on the earth in the last fifty years, which biologists are calling the sixth great extinction in the history of the planet.[154]

The burning of the forests is also the cause of significant growth in carbon emissions into the atmosphere, which are warming the global climate—20 percent of global emissions are thought to have originated in the great fires of 1996–98.[155] Global warming is already causing significant changes in tropical forests, which are thought to have precipitated a decline in amphibians such as frogs, toads, and lizards. As the air temperature rises, scientists are concerned that the hydrological cycle of the rainforest will cease to function altogether and these great gardens of biodiversity will be lost forever. Rainforests are not only a crucial carbon store, a wondrous garden, and home to millions of people and other species. They also act as natural air-conditioning; when cut down and replaced with roads and buildings, a heat island effect is produced that—in Kuala Lumpur, for example—raises temperatures between six and seven degrees centigrade at midday above what they would be otherwise.[156] This temperature change drives the use of air-conditioning in buildings and vehicles, which further exacerbates the heat island effect and increases greenhouse gas consumption.

Palm oil forests are also hotter than tropical forests because the palm oil estate is a monocrop constituted of bare earth and evenly spaced, industrially grown trees and other plants are chemically extinguished. The earth and the trees have a strong chemical smell that comes from broad-spectrum herbicides such as Paraquat, a smell I know well from much cross-country running on these estates. Agrochemical companies have developed a new way of talking about pesticides: they call them crop protectors. In the British agrochemical company Zeneca, crop protection is now included in the health and safety and quality control functions under a stewardship department. Stewardship managers at Zeneca define stewardship as "the responsible and ethical management of all activities, from innovation to ultimate use of products and beyond." The first principle of stewardship for Zeneca is that its employees are good at what they do, which is to develop and sell crop-protection products and services.[157] The application of the metaphor in the field is illustrated in a paper about the stewardship of Zeneca's Paraquat product on palm oil and rubber estates in Indonesia: Paraquat is widely associated with illness among plantation workers in Southeast Asia, but, writing in the context and frame of Zeneca's account of product stewardship, Indonesian researcher Kirniawan suggests that, if the product is used properly, it represents no health hazard. Stewardship, wise use, and good product management will turn a potentially lethal product into a harmless agricultural tool.[158]

J. R. R. Tolkien wrote his powerful saga *The Lord of the Rings* in the early days of the chemical industry when many of its scientists were dedicating their skills to the development of nerve agents and other synthesized compounds that could be used in the conduct of war, although they were later to become the fundamental ingredients of the "crop protection" strategies of the modern chemical farmer. Tolkien's imagined world is one in which there is a deep and fundamental struggle between two modes of dwelling on the earth. The one is characterized by the attempt to turn nature into service of the instruments of warfare that Sauron and his evil forces marshal in their struggle for supreme power over Middle Earth. Tolkien clearly had in mind the burgeoning of industrial technology and the technologies of warfare developed in the context of the two world wars between which he wrote his great saga. The other mode of dwelling is that of the gentle people of Middle Earth, including fairies, trees, hobbits, and wizards who dwelt in the "shires." The greatest wizard of all is Gandalf, yet he eschews lordship over Middle Earth: "The rule of no realm is mine, neither of Gondor nor any other, great or small. But all worthy things that are in peril as the world now stands, those are my care. And for my part, I shall not wholly fail of my task, though Gondor should perish, if anything passes through this night that can still grow fair or bear fruit and flower again in days to come. For I also am a steward. Did you not know?"[159] For Gandalf, stewardship is not the claim of the science-informed manager to instrumentally order a domain; his quest is to care for fruit and flower, for life itself, against the rising horde that threatens extinction.

The traditional idea of guardianship is resisted by some modern theologians because they associate it, as do the managers of Dow and Zeneca, with the managerial arrangements of private property regimes, and with the modern quest to control and reengineer the earth and its ecosystems.[160] But this is to neglect the origins of the term in the common property arrangements of hunter-gatherer and premodern agrarian and nomadic societies such as those of ancient Israel. Anthropologist Tim Ingold identifies the origins of the notion of guardianship with the earliest forms of nomadic and seminomadic agriculture in which individual family units agreed to share land according to common property arrangements that gave to each family the usufruct of a particular area of land. However, this right of use did not mean that they could deny others access to the land but only that the primary benefit of its use went to them. This sheds light on customs concerning the land in ancient Israel, such as the practice of gleaning so beautifully described in the Book of Ruth, and the injunctions of the Torah that farmers were to leave areas of land that were untilled so the wild animals would also be able to survive. Possession in traditional cultures is less a matter of ownership in the Roman and Western sense, and more of "looking after the country, or of tending the creative powers that are thought to reside in its core locales. So-called 'owners' are thus, in reality, no more than the custodians of parts of a world that belongs to all, and they exercise their rights and responsibilities on behalf of the collectivity. In other words what an owner possesses, *to the exclusion of others*, is the privilege of custodianship not that which is held in custody."[161] This is why in traditional societies the privilege of ownership is associated not with garnering and guarding a "personal" resource but rather with gift exchange, distribution, and sharing with the community hunted animal, fruits, or crops.[162] Storing up surplus as a source of personal security is seen in such cultures as threatening the common good and against nature.

We find an echo of this way of thinking in the story in Exodus 16 of the manna that sustained the Hebrews in the wilderness of Sinai after their exodus from Egypt. Each family was instructed to gather only enough to sustain them for the day, and those who disobeyed this instruction suffered illness. Later in Israelite history, Torah proscribed excessive landholdings by some gained at the expense of the poor management or poor luck of others. The Jubilee law as described in Leviticus 25 was designed to prevent debt slavery and landlessness—and hence maldistribution of the gifts of the creation—among the people of Israel. Similarly Jesus tells a parable about a farmer who had amassed so much land from his indebted or unfortunate neighbors that he needed to build bigger barns to store the surplus, plans that came to nothing because he died before he could bring them to fruition.[163]

The American philosopher Garrett Hardin wrote a famous paper some thirty years ago in which he coined the phrase "tragedy of the commons." By this phrase he describes what happens when traditional common property arrangements for using and sharing the goods of the earth fall into disuse or are ruptured by colonial and postcolonial private property regimes.[164] Under such regimes, right of use and ownership are coterminous; consequently, common resources such as earth, air, and water, because they "belong" to no one, tend to be exploited unsustainably. The modern farmer, whether he works for a corporation or owns his own farm, is trained by the modern regime of private property, and by the new conventions of chemical farming, to no longer see the soil as a shared resource that he is responsible for nurturing and passing on to future generations in a better state than he finds it.

By contrast, the traditional concept of guardianship was principally concerned with the condition of the soil. The first chapter of the Book of Genesis gives the names Adam and Eve to the first inhabitants of the earth, names that are associated with the soil and with life: Adam, *adama* in the Hebrew meaning earth or topsoil, is the son of the soil because he is formed from the dust of the earth. Eve is the "mother of all living," according to Genesis 3:20, so Adam and Eve are literally "soil and life."[165] Their vocation to steward the soil and to name and care for its living inhabitants emerges from their identification with the soil and with the living things to which they have given names. Ancient Hebrew had no word for nature apart from human beings, so stewardship neither implied that humans were responsible for something we now call "nature" nor that they were separate from it by virtue of their rule over it.[166]

On this account, the word "*radah*" in Genesis 1:28, which is sometimes translated "dominion," with its associated implication of domination over nature, is better understood as referring to the role of the human as custodian of the soil, hence its translation as vice-regent by Islamic and some Jewish exegetes. Christian biologist R. J. Berry suggests that *radah* may be best understood not as indicating human dominion or even vice-regency but as vice-gerency, in which humans are given delegated authority.[167] In other words, humanity is not given to rule instead of an absentee landlord; on the contrary, God is present to all the creatures, in the *ruaḥ* that stirs the winds on the face of the earth, and in the spirit or *nephesh* that enlivens the breath of every mammal. The concept *radah* does not imply substitution of humans for the Creator but instead continued delegated authority and hence relation between the human creature and the divine Creator. Delegation also implies right relations. When humans order their distribution and use of the earth justly and righteously—to maintain justice in the use of the land by the people and to give space to other animals—only then will their tenure be rewarded with the land's fertility, which is the sign of God's blessing of the earth, of which he is the true ruler. Hence, when humans abandon right relations with God, with each other and with the other creatures, the earth will lose its fertility and the ground will cry out for justice.[168] Here we encounter the biblical roots of the modern idea of ecological justice, which suggests that there is a relationship between the oppression of the poor and the expropriation and abuse of the earth.

The slaying of ancient forests and rare species in the modern era of technological domination of the earth indicates a radically new kind of dominion than that given to Adam in the first chapter of Genesis. It is more reminiscent of the misrule that *radah* describes in its subsequent occurrences in the Hebrew Bible—the enslaving dominion of empires or the oppressive rule of corrupt kings and merchants—than of the vocation of service to creation conferred on Adam. It is only humanity before the fall into sin to whom dominion is said to have been granted in the first chapter of Genesis. The next positive use of the word "*radah*" in the Bible is in the New Testament in association with the coming of Christ in whom a new dominion is revealed on earth, the reign of the Son of David, who is no longer a slayer but a suffering servant of the divine will to redeem creation from its subjection to sin. Christ, who is described as the *logos*, the original wisdom through which God laid out the order of creation, is incarnate on earth as a creature who restores a peaceable relation between the near divine creature—humanity—and the physical cosmos. This coming of the Creator in the form of a creature creates a new possibility for creaturely being, which has fallen into subjection to the rule of sin and corruption. This is realized in the resurrected body of Christ, which is a new creature, the form of a "new creation," as Saint Paul puts it, in which the original peace of creation is restored and even enhanced.

This sense of an enhancement of the creation as originally created is indicated in the association between Christ and animals in the birth of Christ in a stable, in his being ministered to by wild animals in the wilderness, and in the proclamation of a gospel of peace. In its cosmic implications, this recalls the prophecy of Isaiah that true shalom will not only see an end to war, and the beating of swords into ploughshares but even an end to predation as the lion lies down with the lamb. The reign of the slayer—human and wild—is at an end in the coming of the Prince of Peace.

The ecological problems that humanity faces in the modern world are a consequence, then, not of the Christian doctrine of Creation as some environmentalists have claimed, such as Lynn White in a famous essay.[169] Instead it is the atheism of modern materialism, the replacement of the divinely authored limits on human power set into creation with the dominion of economic materialism and technological rule, that have seen modern industrial civilization become the most powerful force of nature—more powerful even than the sun or the ocean with the advent of anthropogenic climate change.

The disorder of human society and ecological destruction have their root in the claim of man to be his own master. As the great Protestant theologian Karl Barth put it,

> When man, alienated from God, tries to live a lordless life, in no case does this result in his becoming the lord and master of the possibilities of his own life. The "You will be like God" (Gen. 3.5), "you will be your own lords and masters," was from the very first the promise he thought he should grasp when he started on this path. In fact, however, there never has been, is, or will be any fulfilment of this promise. In the foolish and hopeless attempt to escape from the sphere of God's lordship, it is not so simple for man to become even a little God and Lord with the implied approximation to God's supremacy and controlling power in the fashioning of human existence. Even a partially free control has always been everywhere the myth, but only the myth and illusion, of the person who thinks and claims that he has come of age and is now sovereign and autonomous. In thinking this—and the more self-consciously and emphatically he does so—the more he is overtaken by the opposite. He ceases to be the free lord and master he could and should have been in the sphere of God's lordship if, instead of fleeing from God, he had oriented himself to him. Parallel to the history of his emancipation from God there runs that for the emancipation of his own possibilities of life from himself: the history of the overpowering of his desires, aspirations, and will by the power, the superpower, of his ability. His capacities when he uses them, as Goethe describes so vividly and with such frightening profundity in his poem *The Sorcerer's Apprentice*, become spirits with a life and activity of their own, lordless indwelling forces.[170]

Barth suggests that such is the modern human revolt against the righteous command of God that Christians must be in revolt and rebellion against the disorder of modern civilization.[171] At the heart of these lordless powers are those of Leviathan and Mammon; scientific technique and monetary wealth have spread industrial suasion over every ecosystem and every community on this precious earth.[172] For Barth, the dominion of Leviathan and Mammon "reveals, though it does not constitute, the plight of man, the profound unrighteousness in which we people exist—each alone and in mutual relation—because of the basic unrighteousness of our relationship to God, the unrighteousness in which each for himself and all for all others we inevitably make life more or less difficult."[173]

Many modern Christians who claim to know the Bible but are trained by the rituals of science-informed capitalism misconstrue stewardship as indicating the rights of ownership and the power of use rather than the responsibilities of shared creatureliness. When the writers of the New Testament take up the metaphor of the steward, they point out that Christians do not even own their own bodies, let alone the forests they slay or the stores of wealth they magnify. Saint Paul tells the Christians at Corinth, who have been engaging in the licentious sexual practices of their pagan neighbors, that their bodies are not their own but instead belong to God: "Do you not know that your body is a temple of the Holy Spirit, who is in you, whom you have received from God? You are not your own."[174] For Christians, the idea of absolute ownership has no place because even the body of the Christian is not his or her own to dispose with at will. As the American farmer and essayist Wendell Berry suggests, the biblical understanding of divine ownership, "the earth is the Lord's," involves a critique of the vast accumulations of land and wealth that characterize the modern corporately controlled and managed global economy, for human ownership of land "quickly becomes abusive when used to justify large accumulations of real estate."[175]

The incarnation of God in Christ involves the affirmation that "God made the world and made it to be good and for his pleasure and that he continues to love it and to find it worthy, despite its reduction and corruption by us."[176] There is no absentee landlord here who has left the property in charge of a hireling manager. The incarnate redeemer is the Creator God who gifted the original blessing and abundance of the earth to our primeval ancestors, so "we will discover that for these reasons our destruction of nature is not just bad stewardship, or stupid economics, or a betrayal of family responsibility; it is the most horrid blasphemy. It is flinging God's gifts into His face, as if they were of no worth beyond that assigned to them by our destruction of them."[177]

Just before he stood down as the UN secretary-general, Kofi Anan said that there are two inconvenient truths in the world today. One is global warming. The other is the intent of the United States and some others to launch a new arms race to create a new generation of nuclear weapons even more fearsome, deadly, and automatically controlled by computers than the previous ones.[178] Global warming is teaching us an ancient truth. The gargantuan resources that the nations and corporations of the world have devoted to the fossil-fueled machines of war represent our modern Tower of Babel. Nations that build and acquire these great machines imagine that they will guarantee their security against external threats. But global warming is teaching us again—as in the days of Noah—that these godlike aspirations to secure security apart from dependence on the Creator, in ways that neglect the kenotic ethos of the cosmos—far from bringing security—are creating the ultimate threat to human life on planet earth. No one knows how long it will take for the ice sheets of Greenland and Antarctica to melt. But at present rates of burning of forests and fossil fuels, they will melt, and when they do cities like this one all over the world will be under water.

Civilizations have collapsed many times in human history because of this quest for material security, including the late Hebrew monarchy and the Roman Empire, both of which left their mark forever on the ecosystems of the Mediterranean region.[179] Now the world faces a civilization that has taken humanity's godlike vocation to unprecedented heights and to every corner of the earth. More than ever, humanity needs to recover the vocation of the steward, the earth keeper. Like Noah, who had to study his fellow creatures so he would know how to feed and tend them on the ark, we need to listen again to the earth, and to what the creatures are telling us. Some of them are already facing extinction, and their deaths are the harbingers of the threats to present fisherfolk and farmers, and to all future generations that global warming represents. The nations of the earth have devoted many trillions of dollars to making the weapons of war and to prosecuting wars in just the last ten years. The same quantity of wealth over the next ten years would be sufficient to provide renewable electric power, clean water, and sustainable housing for every community and household on earth. Slayers or stewards? Our God-given vocation never mattered more to the fate of the earth than it does in this generation.

NOTES

1. Robert Bellah, Richard Madsen, William M. Sullivan, Ann Swidler, and Steven M. Tipton, *Habits of the Heart: Individualism and Commitment in American Life* (New York: Harper & Row, 1985), 335.

2. Marshall Berman, *All That Is Solid Melts into Air: The Experience of Modernity* (New York: Verso, 1983), 15.

3. Calvin, *Institutes of the Christian Religion*, trans. Ford Lewis Battles (Philadelphia: Westmisster Press, 1960), 37, §1.1.2.

4. Reinhold Niebuhr, *The Nature and Destiny of Man*, vol. 1, *Human Nature* (New York: Scribners, 1941), 16.

5. Berkouwer writes: "It is actually clear enough, however, that Pascal's words in any event have nothing to do with any relativising or 'reduction' of man's misery along humanistic lines. He is not concerned with a 'greatness' which is the hidden center of man, which is 'left over' from man's apparent evil, and which finally lessens the seriousness and range of the misery. He is not speaking of a 'remainder' which shows that the damage is after all not so catastrophic. For Pascal, on the contrary, man's 'greatness' and 'misery' are closely related to each other. Man's misery is 'the misery of a nobleman, the misery of a dethroned king.' The greatness of man, created by God, is reflected in the depth of his fall. It is clear enough that Pascal is not speaking of any hidden center in man. This is a different view of greatness and misery than that given by humanism, where the greatness is sought behind the misery as the hidden center, the 'real' man in his true humanity." G. C. Berkouwer, *The Image of God* (Grand Rapids, MI: Eerdmans, 1962), 16–17.

6. Psalm 8:3–4.

7. Calvin, *Institutes of the Christian Religion*, 273, §2.2.14.

8. Ibid., 273–74, §2.2.15.

9. Berkouwer emphasizes that he is talking about "general grace" not the restorative grace of God in Jesus Christ, nor the renewing of the image of the Creator, but rather a "common grace" that limits the powers of evil. This common grace may be brought into relation with the grace of Christ in this sense, that this protection of our humanness provides opportunity for us to have salvation through Christ; but it is nevertheless not as such Christologically defined or limited. See Berkouwer, *Image of God*, 155–56.

10. Ibid.

11. Robert Louis Wilken, "Biblical Humanism: The Patristic Convictions," in *Personal Identity in Theological Perspective*, ed. Richard Lints (Grand Rapids, MI: Eerdmans, 2006), 21.

12. Gordon Spykman, *Reformational Theology: A New Paradigm for Doing Dogmatics* (Grand Rapids, MI: Eerdmans, 1992), 256.

13. Isaiah 60; and Revelation 21–22.

14. See Spykman, *Reformational Theology*, 251. Spykman also gives a word of caution, given our present fallen condition: "In our obedient responses to this cultural mandate—therein lies our blessing, our delight, our deep sense of satisfaction and service. In elucidating this cultural mandate, Scripture speaks of exercising 'dominion' over the earth and 'subduing' it. Too often these words have been cited as excuses for wantonly plundering the creational resources of land and sky and sea. Wrongly so, however, for ours is a subservient authority, to be expressed in earthkeeping and caretaking. We are not to be greedy potentates, but faithful stewards of God's good earth, treating other creatures with tender concern as we seek to meet our appointed needs." Ibid., 256–57.

15. Berkouwer gives a caution concerning the spiritual state of man in his present, fallen condition: "The image is used to stress the idea that man lost his communion with God—his religious knowledge, his righteousness, his holiness, his conformity (*conformitas*) to God's will. This latter was a radical change in man's nature, which originally was wholly turned towards God, and now after the Fall is turned completely away. Man was 'good, righteous, and holy, capable in all things to will agreeably to the will of God' (*Belgic Confession*, Art. XIV); man was created by God 'good, and after His own image; that is, in true righteousness and holiness' (*Heidelberg Catechism*, Q. 6). Man was 'originally formed after the image of God. His understanding was adorned with a true and saving knowledge of his Creator, and of spiritual things; his heart and will were upright, all his affections pure, and the whole man was holy' (*Canons of Dordt*, III–IV, I). But all this wealth vanished with the Fall." Berkouwer, *Image of God*, 38–39.

16. Genesis 1:26–28; and Psalm 8:4–8.

17. Genesis 9:6.

18. Abraham Kuyper argues that if all human life is immediately laid before God, "then it follows that all men and women, rich or poor, weak or strong, dull or talented, as creatures of God, and as lost sinners, have no claim whatsoever to lord it over one another, and that we stand as equals before God, and consequently equal as man to man. Hence we cannot recognize any distinction among men, save such as has been imposed by God himself, in that He gave one authority over the other, or enriched one with more talents than the other, in order that the man of more talents should serve the man with less, and in him serve God." Kuyper, *Lectures on Calvinism* [1898] (Grand Rapids, MI: Eerdmans, 1931), 20, 28. See also Spykman, *Reformational Theology*, 248.

19. Wilken, "Biblical Humanism," 20.

20. Michael Horton, "Human Personhood and the Covenant," in *Personal Identity in Theological Perspective*, ed. Richard Lints (Grand Rapids, MI: Eerdmans, 2006), 186. See Meredith Kline, *Images of the Spirit* (Grand Rapids, MI: Baker Books, 1980), 192.

21. Deuteronomy 16:20.

22. Exodus 22:25–27; and Deuteronomy 24:14–15.

23. Exodus 22:21–24.

24. Deuteronomy 24:17.

25. Deuteronomy 10:17–18.

26. Exodus 21:21; 23:9, 12.

27. Leviticus 19:10; see Ruth 2.

28. Leviticus 19:18.

29. Romans 8:29.

30. Calvin is concerned with our knowledge of the image of God, and thus he refers to its restoration, which is treated in the New Testament. He has in mind the words of Paul about "the new nature, created after the likeness of God in true righteousness and holiness" (Eph. 4:24) and "being renewed in knowledge after the image of its creator" (Col. 3:10)—words that obviously refer to the original creation of human beings in God's image. This line of approach is encountered

in Reformed theology, which describes the image of God as knowledge, righteousness, and holiness. See Berkouwer, *Image of God*, 87–88.

31. 2 Corinthians 3:18; Colossians 1:18; 3:10. Berkouwer points out that the word *katoptrizō* (2 Cor. 3:14–18) appears only here, and that it can mean either "reflect" or "view as in a mirror." He chooses the latter meaning: "The context does not refer to a reflection of received glory, but it does refer to the possession of glory. . . . [Paul] emphasizes this glory in its concrete outpouring and manifestation. This glory manifests itself in the now uncovered and receptive life, in the freedom and liberty of the believers, who are, says Paul, epistles which can be read by and known to all men (2 Cor. 3:2)" Berkouwer, *Image of God*, 110–11.

32. Stanley Grenz, "The Social God and the Relational Self: Toward a Theology of the Imago Dei in the Postmodern Context," in *Personal Identity in Theological Perspective*, ed. Richard Lints (Grand Rapids, MI: Eerdmans, 2006), 84.

33. Horton, "Human Personhood," 201.

34. Romans 8:20–23.

35. Isaiah 60; Revelations 21:24–27.

36. Richard Mouw, *When the Kings Come Marching In: Isaiah and the New Jerusalem* (Grand Rapids, MI: Eerdmans 1984), 6–7.

37. Anthony Hoekema, *The Bible and the Future* (Grand Rapids, MI: Eerdmans, 1982), 274.

38. Genesis 1:26–27.

39. 1 Corinthians 11:7; and James 3:9. J. Richard Middleton, "The Liberating Image? Interpreting the Imago Dei in Context," *Christian Scholars Review* 24, no. 1 (1994): 2–3. Middleton argues that throughout the centuries, theologians and biblical scholars have not asked exegetical questions of this text but rather speculative ones. In asking how human beings are like God and not like other animals, metaphysical analogies have been created between the human soul and the being of God where the content of this image has ranged from "human reason through conscience, immortality, and spirituality to freedom and personhood."

40. Qur'ānic translations in this chapter are taken largely from M. A. S. Abdel Haleem, *The Qur'an: a New Translation* (Oxford: Oxford University Press, 2004), by permission of Oxford University Press.

41. Abdel Haleem comments in a footnote that the Arabic word here translated "successor" (*khalīfa*) is normally translated as "vicegerent" or "deputy" (ibid.).

42. *al-Baqara* 2: 30–31.

43. *Ṣād* 38:71–72.

44. *al-'Alaq* 96:1–5.

45. *al-Ṭīn* 95:4.

46. *Ghāfir* 40:64.

47. *Ṣād* 38:26.

48. *al-A'rāf* 7:10.

49. *Luqmān* 31:20.

50. *al-Isrā'* 17:70.

51. *al-Shūrā* 42:11.

52. *Qāf* 50:16.

53. See *al-A'rāf* 7:180; *al-Isrā'* 17:110; *Ṭā' Hā'* 20:8; and *al-Ḥashr* 59:24.

54. Gerhard Böwering, "God and His Attributes," in *Encyclopaedia of the Qur'ān*, Vol. 2, ed. Jane Dammen McAuliffe (Leiden: E. J. Brill, 2002), 319. Böwering argues that the ninety-nine names of God function as doxology in the Qur'ān.

55. Fadlou Shehadi, *Ghazali's Unique Unknowable God* (Leiden, E. J. Brill, 1964), 37. The *ārifīn* literally means "those who know" and is used by the mystics in the sense of "gnostics." For

a detailed analysis of this issue, see Binyamin Abrahamov, "Fakhr al-Din Razi on the Knowability of God's Essence and Attributes," *Arabica* T.49, Fasc.2 (April 2002): 204–30.

56. *al-A'rāf* 7:172.

57. Syed Nomanul Haq, "Islam and Ecology: Towards Retrieval and Reconstruction," in *Islam and Ecology*, ed. R. Foltz, F. Denny, and A. Baharuddin (Cambridge, MA: Harvard University Press, 2003), 129.

58. *al-Aḥzāb* 33:72.

59. *al-Baqara* 2:107.

60. Allama Muhammad Iqbal, *The Reconstruction of Religious Thought in Islam* (Lahore, Pakistan: Ashraf Press, 1960), 85.

61. Jalaluddin Rumi, "The Progress of Man," in R. A. Nicholson, *Persian Poems*, ed. A. J. Arberry (London: J. M. Dent, 1972).

62. *al-Mā'ida* 5:48.

63. *al-Baqara* 2:15–18.

64. *al-Nūr* 24:24.

65. *al-Isrā'* 17:13.

66. See also Mona Siddiqui, 'Searching for the Face of the Lord—Hope or Heresy?', in Adrian Pabst and Angus Paddison (eds.), *The Pope and Jesus of Nazareth* (London: SCM Press, 2009), 259–260.

67. *al-Zumar* 39:53.

68. *al-A'rāf* 7:156.

69. Ḥadīth 25 and 34, related by Bukhari and al-Tirmidhi, respectively, cited in Ezzeddin Ibrahim and Denys Johnson-Davies, *Forty Hadith Qudsi* (Cambridge: Islamic Texts Society, 1997), 12.

70. Iqbal, *Reconstruction of Religious Thought*, 124. Iqbal uses this famous quote to discuss the difference between prophetic and mystical types of consciousness.

71. Psalm 104:24.

72. Genesis 1:31; 2:1.

73. Psalm 19:1.

74. Aref Nayed, "Āyatology and Raḥmatology," in *Building a Better Bridge: Muslims, Christians, and the Common Good*, ed. Michael Ipgrave (Washington, DC: Georgetown University Press, 2008).

75. Galatians 3:27–28.

76. Colossians 3:11.

77. Richard Burridge, *Imitating Jesus: An Inclusive Approach to New Testament Ethics* (Grand Rapids, MI: Eerdmans, 2007); I draw also on the presentation in Dr. Burridge's recent Eric Symes Abbott Memorial Lecture, *Being Biblical? Slavery, Sexuality and the Inclusive Community*, available at www.kcl.ac.uk/about/structure/dean/sermons-section/sermons.html.

78. 1 Timothy 6:1–2. The word used to denote church membership is *adelphoi*, "brothers."

79. Philemon 16.

80. Notably, 1 Timothy 6:1; see Burridge, *Being Biblical?* 8.

81. Burridge, *Being Biblical?* 10

82. Ibid., 9.

83. Genesis 1:26.

84. Genesis 1:27, AV; NRSV inexplicably renders "him" as "them."

85. Genesis 2:22. See also, for example, 1 Corinthians 11:9.

86. Genesis 4:2.

87. Genesis 9:18.

88. Genesis 9:22–25; the text varies between assigning this to Ham or to his son Canaan.
89. Acts 17:26.
90. Acts 17:28.
91. R. S. Sugirtharajah, *Voices from the Margin: Interpreting the Bible in the Third World* (London: SPCK, 1991), 1.
92. Andrew Davey, *Urban Christianity and Global Order* (London: SPCK, 2001), 75.
93. Wayne Meeks, *The Moral World of the First Christians* (London: SPCK, 1987), 104.
94. Luke 2:19.
95. Genesis 11:1, 4.
96. Jonathan Sacks, *The Dignity of Difference: How to Avoid the Clash of Civilizations*, 1st ed. (London: Continuum 2002), 52.
97. *al-Mā'ida* 5:48; see also *Hūd* 11:118.
98. Sacks, *Dignity of Difference*, 53.
99. Engseng Ho, *The Graves of Tarim: Genealogy and Mobility across the Indian Ocean* (Berkeley, CA, and London: University of California Press, 2006), 195.
100. *al-Rūm* 30:22.
101. *al-Ḥujurāt* 49:13.
102. Ṭabarī, *Jāmi' al-Bayān 'an Ta'wīl Ay al-Qur'ān*, Cairo: 1373/1954, II, 138ff.
103. Paul Hardy, "Islam and the Race Question," accessed at www.masud.co.uk/ISLAM/misc/race.htm.
104. al-Jāḥiẓ, *The Book of the Glory of the Black Race,* Kitāb Fakhr al-Sūdān 'alā al-Bīḍān, tr. Vincent J. Cornell (Los Angeles: France Preston, 1981), 23.
105. Ibid., 38.
106. Ibid., 39–40.
107. Ibid., 55–56.
108. *Kitāb al-Mabsūṭ*, Beirut: 1398/1978, XII, 83–84; and Hardy, "Islam and the Race Question."
109. See 'Abd al-Ḥaqq ibn Ismā'īl al-Badisi (d. after 1322 CE), *al-Maqṣad al-sharīf wa al-manza' al-laṭīf fī al-ta'rīf bi-ṣulaḥā' al-Rīf*, ed. Sa'id Ahmad A'rab (Rabat: Royal Printing House, 1982).
110. On the concept of vernacular religion, see, for example, Joyce Burkhalter Flueckiger, *In Amma's Healing Room: Gender and Vernacular Islam in South India* (Bloomington: Indiana University Press, 2006), 2.
111. See, for example, Douglas Pratt, "Philosophy of Religion," Seminar on Philosophy and Civilisational Dialogue, Centre for Civilisational Dialogue, June 26–27, 2007.
112. "The Earth Charter," www.earthcharterinaction.org/content/pages/Read-the-Charter.html.
113. Thomas Davis, "What Is Sustainable Development?" Sustainable Development Institute, College of Menominee Nation, www.menominee.edu/sdi/whatis.htm.
114. Basarab Nicolescu, "Transdisciplinarity as Methodological Framework for Going beyond the Science and Religion Debate," The Global Spiral, Metanexus Institute, May 24, 2007, www.metanexus.net/magazine/tabid/68/id/10013/Default.aspx.
115. Azizan Baharuddin, *Science and Religion: Discourse on New Perception* (Kuala Lumpur: Institute Kajian Dasar, 1994), 21–82.
116. Hazizan Noor, "Islamic Studies in Malaysian Universities: Review and Prospect," in *Dialogue on Islamic Studies Curriculum: A New Agenda for the Study of Islam and Muslims* (Kuala Lumpur: Centre for Civilisational Dialogue, 2005).

117. See Carl Ernst, *Following Muhammad: Rethinking Islam in the Contemporary World* (Chapel Hill: University of North Carolina Press, 2003).

118. Leonard Swidler, *Dialogue in Malaysia and the Global Scenario* (Kuala Lumpur: Centre for Civilisational Dialogue, 2003), 1–10.

119. Osman Bakar, *Environmental Wisdom for Planet Earth: The Islamic Heritage* (Kuala Lumpur: Centre for Civilisational Dialogue, 2007).

120. "Earth Charter."

121. Bakar, *Environmental Wisdom*, 27.

122. *al-Ḥujurāt* 49:13.

123. "Earth Charter."

124. *al-Jum'a* 62:10.

125. S. M. N. al-Attas, *Islam, the Concept of Religion and the Foundations of Ethics* (Kuala Lumpur: Dewan Bahasa dan Pustaka and Ministry of Education, 1992), 1–3.

126. Ibid. al-Attas' gender-specific language is retained in these paragraphs to make clear the personal connections drawn between contemporary humans and Adam.

127. *al-A'rāf* 7:172.

128. *Zakāt* is the giving out of a certain percentage of one's wealth that has been accumulated over a certain period.

129. See I. R. al-Faruqi and L. L. al-Faruqi, *Cultural Atlas of Islam* (Kuala Lumpur: Dewan Bahasa dan Pustaka, 1992), 334–36.

130. *al-Baqara* 2:245.

131. Baharuddin, *Science and Religion*.

132. *Hūd* 11:7.

133. *al-Kahf* 18:7.

134. Lynn White, "The Historical Roots of Our Ecologic Crisis," *Science* 155 (1967): 1203–7.

135. See al-Faruqi and al-Faruqi, *Cultural Atlas of Islam*, 334–36.

136. *Luqmān* 31:20.

137. *al-Ḥajj* 22:65.

138. al-Attas, *Islam, the Concept of Religion*, 12–13.

139. Hazel Henderson and Daisaku Ikeda, *Planetary Citizenship* (Chicago: Middleway Press, 2004), 152.

140. Muhammad Iqbal, "A Plea for Deeper Studies," Islamic Culture, vol. 3, 201–9.

141. Bakar, *Environmental Wisdom*, 63.

142. *al-Mulk* 67:3.

143. *al-Dukhān* 44:38–39.

144. R. C. Foltz, F. M. Denny, A. Baharuddin, eds., *Islam and Ecology: A Bestowed Trust* (Cambridge, Mass: Harvard University Press, 2003), 85–107.

145. S. H. Nasr, *The Need for a Sacred Science* (Albany: State University of New York Press, 1993), 129.

146. Ibid.

147. Azizan Baharuddin, "Science in the Malay World," (in Malay), at Seminar Sains dan Tamadun Melayu [Science and Malay Civilisation], December 20–21, 2006. Examples include the following: *Berani-berani lalat* ("Brave like a fly"): This proverb explains the situation of someone who is not really as brave as he tries to portray himself to be. *Seperti rusa masuk kampong* ("Like the deer entering the village"): This explains the condition or behavior of someone who is a stranger in a new place. *Seperti kerbau dicucuk hidung* ("Like the buffalo being led by the nose"): This is the condition of someone who is being bullied by someone else. *Sarang tebuan jangan dijolok* ("Do not poke the bee-hive"): This warns against "disturbing" someone or something that may be volatile.

Burung terbang dipipiskan lada ("Whilst the bird still flies, the chilli is pounded"): This proverb teaches against making preparations for the enjoyment of something that is not yet properly obtained.

148. See M. U. Chapra, *Towards a Just Monetary System: A Discussion of Money, Banking, and Monetary Policy in the Light of Islamic Teachings* (Leicester: Islamic Foundation, 1985).

149. Ibid., 1.

150. 1 Samuel 18:6–7.

151. Isaiah 24:1–6.

152. Habakkuk 2:17.

153. William P. Brown, *The Ethos of the Cosmos: The Genesis of Moral Imagination in the Bible* (Grand Rapids, MI: Eerdmans, 1999), 10–17.

154. Richard E. Leakey, *The Sixth Extinction: Patterns of Life and the Future of Humankind* (New York: Doubleday, 1995). On species loss in Southeast Asia, see Navjot S. Sodhi and Barry W. Brook, *Southeast Asian Biodiversity in Crisis* (Cambridge: Cambridge University Press, 2006).

155. Prabir K. Patra, Shamil Maksyutov, and Takakiyo Nakazawa, "Analysis of Atmospheric CO_2 Growth Rates at Mauna Loa Using CO_2 Fluxes Derived from an Inverse Model," *Tellus* Series B 57, no. 5 (2005), 357–65.

156. Sani Sham, "Physical Development and Local Climate Modification in the Kajang-Bandar Baru Bangi Corridor: Some Management and Planning Considerations," in Abdul Samad Hadi and Mazlan Othman, eds., *Tropical Urban Ecosystems Studies* 6 (1989): 299–323.

157. Bernhard Johnen, Louise Foster, and Mike Thomas, "Stewardship in the Agrochemical Industry" *Pesticide Outlook* 11, no. 4 (2000), http://pubs.rsc.org/en/Content/ArticleLanding/2000/PO/B006246O.

158. A. N. Kurniawan, "Product Stewardship of Paraquat in Indonesia," *International Archive of Occupational and Environmental Health* 68, no. 6 (1998): 516–18.

159. J. R. R. Tolkien, *The Return of the King: Being the Third Part of the Lord of the Rings* (London: Harper Collins, 1999), 20.

160. Clare Palmer, "Stewardship: A Case Study in Environmental Ethics," in *The Earth Beneath*, ed. I. Ball, M. Goodall, C. Palmer, and J. Reader (London: SPCK, 1992), 67–86; Ruth Page, *God and the Web of Creation* (London: SCM Press, 1996); Richard L. Fern, *Nature, God and Humanity: Envisioning an Ethics of Nature* (Cambridge: Cambridge University Press, 2002), 212–13; and Peter Scott, *A Political Theology of Nature* (Cambridge: Cambridge University Press, 2003), 213–18.

161. Tim Ingold, *The Appropriation of Nature: Essays on Human Ecology and Social Relations* (Manchester, U.K.: Manchester University Press, 1986), 224.

162. Ibid., 227.

163. Luke 12:17–19.

164. Garrett Hardin, "The Tragedy of the Commons," *Science* 162 (1968): 1243–48.

165. Theodore Hiebert, "Rethinking Traditional Approaches to Nature in the Bible,'" in *Theology for Earth Community: A Field Guide*, ed. Dieter Hessell (Maryknoll, NY: Orbis Books, 1996), 23–30.

166. Larry Rasmussen, *Earth Community, Earth Ethics* (Maryknoll, NY: Orbis Books, 1996), 231.

167. R. J. Berry, "Introduction: Stewardship, a Default Position?' in *Environmental Stewardship: Critical Perspectives Past and Present*, ed. R. J. Berry (London: T and T Clark, 2005), 7.

168. Rasmussen, *Earth Community, Earth Ethics*, 231; and Michael S. Northcott, *The Environment and Christian Ethics* (Cambridge: Cambridge University Press, 1996), 169–72.

169. Lynn White, "The Historical Roots of our Ecologic Crisis," *Science* 155 (1967): 1203–7.

170. Karl Barth, *The Christian Life: Church Dogmatics IV. 4, Lecture Fragments*, tr. Geoffrey W. Bromiley (Grand Rapids, MI: Eerdmans, 1981), 214.

171. Ibid., 205.

172. Ibid., 229.

173. Ibid., 233.

174. 1 Corinthians 6:19.

175. Wendell Berry, *Sex, Economy, Freedom and Community* (New York: Pantheon Books, 1992), 97.

176. Ibid., 97.

177. Ibid., 98.

178. Bob Egelko, "Climate Change Is as Serious as WMD," *Agence France Presse*, November 16, 2006.

179. Jared Diamond, *Collapse: How Societies Choose to Fail or Succeed* (New York: Penguin Books, 2005).

PART TWO

Scriptural Texts on Being Human

THIS PART COMPRISES six paired sets of readings from the Bible and the Qur'ān together with introductions given by scholars to present the texts to the seminar. The first three pairs address different aspects in the understanding of what it means to be human; in turn, they speak of human dignity, of human alienation, and of human destiny. The fourth and fifth pairs of texts engage with dimensions of the differences between humans—specifically, that of gender and that associated with ethnicity or culture. The final pair provides some scriptural perspectives on the theme of humanity and the environment.

Unusually, in the case of the second and fourth pairs, the biblical texts are introduced by a Muslim and the Qur'ānic texts by a Christian.[1]

CHAPTER FOUR

Human Dignity

4.1 Genesis 1:26–31

Ellen Davis

Although it occupies pride of place in the Bible, the Priestly poem of Creation (Genesis 1) is not an especially early text; most scholars would date it to the time of the Babylonian exile (sixth century BCE). But even if the poem of Creation comes somewhere in the middle in order of textual composition, canonical placement makes it a lens through which Jews and Christians read the rest of the Bible. The early history of humankind and Israel's history in particular, as the Bible records them, may be read largely as an account of human attempts, conscious or not, to image God in the world. Most often these attempts are arrogant and doomed to failure; throughout the Hebrew Scriptures, kings offer the prime examples of that failure. This is no coincidence. For millennia in the ancient Near East, it was believed that the king (or occasionally the queen) had a unique dignity as the human "bridge to the gods."[2] Within the Bible, some of the Psalms reflect a theology of the king's unique dignity.[3] Beginning in Genesis 1, however, the general thrust of biblical narrative and prophecy is to deconstruct any concept of the king's inherent uniqueness vis-à-vis God. In Ezekiel, Pharaoh is deluded enough to think he is himself creator of the Nile, the source of Egypt's power. In Exodus, Pharaoh's complete inability to recognize the God who made heaven and earth leads to the destruction not only of Egypt's army but even of the land itself. Israel's and Judah's own kings likewise fail in almost every case to image God's benevolent dominion in the land that is entrusted to them, so their kingdoms are also undone. Israel is destroyed by the Assyrians and Judah occupied successively by Babylonians, Persians, Greeks, and Romans. Biblical accounts of both home rule and foreign occupation explain why the Apostle Paul in the First Letter to Timothy would urge that special prayers be made for those in power;[4] they need even more help than the rest of us to claim a properly humble dignity, and they have more potential for doing damage when they miss the mark.

Against the background of that grim political history, this Priestly poem of Creation offers an exilic audience some encouragement. For a people who have lost their king, it radically democratizes the concept of creation in the image of God. No less than the king, every single human being, male and female, is created in the image of God and therefore has responsibility before God. In this matter of the egalitarian nature of human dignity, Genesis 1 prevents us from misreading Genesis 2, in which the woman is taken from the sleeping Adam's rib. Without the prior story of creation in the image of God, we might conclude that woman is a divine afterthought, with a purely derivative relationship to God.

A second element of encouragement in this poem: it restores a sense of vocation to a people who have lost land and nation-state and, it might seem, their status as God's "treasure people" (*'am segullah*).[5] It is important to recall that the Israelites were the only people of the ancient Near East who did not entirely forfeit their religion when they lost their political independence. Genesis 1 is one crucial step in the reworking of Israel's religious identity in light of the greatest disaster in its national history. The God who created heaven and earth still has an intention for this people, even in the land from which they have been exiled. This message is the subtext of Genesis 1:28, but to decipher it, you must listen to the Hebrew, or a wholly transparent translation, such as this: "And God blessed them and God said to them, 'Be fruitful and multiply, and fill the earth/ land [*'eretz* means both] *vĕkibšūhā*/and *conquer* it.'" When you hear the phrase "conquer the land," you are, narratively speaking, at the edge of the Promised Land, hearing God's promise that you (Israel) and the land will prosper if you place God's will above every other consideration. So the command, "Conquer the land/earth" places exiled Israel once more in the position of receiving God's charge and conditional promise. God still has an intention for them; they are to represent God's benevolent sovereignty on the earth, just as Israel was meant to do in the land of Canaan. (This Priestly tradition, in contrast to the Deuteronomistic tradition, downplays the element of violence in the "conquest" of the land—and that may well be closer to the historical reality.)

That message is encouraging, yet it carries a sting. An audience of exiles knows that Israel's first conquest of the land was no better than a qualified failure; they were booted out for disobedience. Therefore, implicit in the command is a warning. The original scope of the warning is that even if Israel returns to its homeland of Canaan (as in fact they did, about sixty years after the exile), they might fail again. But Genesis 1 is a liturgical poem, so its meaning continues to expand from generation to generation. For a contemporary audience, that localized warning of failure should be extended to a global level: the human project on *'eretz*, earth, might fail as dismally as did Israel's project in *'eretz kena'an*, the land of Canaan. We are perhaps the first generation in the world's history that has heard that message, a genuine part of this text but held in reserve for some twenty-six hundred years until now; its time has come.

Genesis 1 likely took shape in the face of the unthinkable: the fall of Jerusalem, the destruction of the temple, and the collapse of the "eternal" throne of David—these events were literally incomprehensible in terms of Israel's theology up to that time. This poem has demonstrated its capacity to renew its meaning in light of later events that had likewise previously been unthinkable. About six centuries after its composition, the incarnation, passion, and resurrection of Jesus Christ caused some in Israel to reckon afresh with the concept of humankind created in the image of God. In a passage that might be seen as a rereading of Genesis 1, the Apostle Paul (or someone who thinks like he does) says:

> He is the image of the invisible God, the firstborn of all creation, for in him all things in heaven and on earth were created, . . . whether thrones or dominions or rulers or powers . . . and in him all things hold together. . . . He is the beginning, the firstborn from the dead, so that he might come to have first place in everything. For in him all the fullness of God was pleased to dwell, and through him God was pleased to reconcile to himself all things, whether on earth or in heaven, by making peace through the blood of the cross.[6]

This is a remarkable, Hubble-telescopic look at the whole history of heaven and earth in Christ, from creation to a new moment that is also, in effect, "the beginning" (v. 18). Accordingly, the author picks up all the crucial elements from the Priestly poem of Creation and redefines them thus:

- the human image of God, perfect and fully visible for the first time in Jesus Christ
- human dominion: Christ has "first place in everything"
- encouragement regarding the human place in the created order: if all things and all people are created through and for Christ, then all can participate in the divine image and all can be reconciled with God
- the sting, the sobering reminder of the long history of sin and its high cost: Christ's peaceful dominion "on earth and in heaven" comes only "through the blood of the cross" (v. 20).

The Pauline corpus includes at least one more look back to the image of God. In the eighth chapter of Romans, Paul envisions "the creation wait[ing] on tenterhooks (*apokaradokía*) for the revealing of the children of God; for the creation was subjected to futility, not of its own will but by the will of the one who subjected it, in hope that the creation itself will be set free from its bondage to decay and will obtain the freedom of the glory of the children of God."[7] Paul's remarkable exegetical insight into Genesis 1 is that God gave humans dominion within the created order in an attitude of hope, and that this divine hope has not yet been fulfilled.[8] This view stands in contrast to the utter confidence that Psalm 8 expresses about human dominion; that hymn of praise was composed for or adapted by the royal house of David, and it must sometimes have served to underwrite the king's own exercise of power. But Paul's view that the creation is still waiting for human beings to look like God is more credible in this sixth great age of species extinction as we awaken painfully to the recognition that human dominion over "the birds of the air and the fish of the sea" has brought glory to neither God nor ourselves.[9] On the contrary, our subjection of creation has long been deadly and is now threatening and killing a huge proportion of God's creatures.[10]

Moreover, Paul's view that God's hope for humankind is not yet fulfilled seems to reflect a subtle aspect of the Priestly poem of Creation, a structural element that has received little (if any) attention from interpreters in the modern period. The normal pattern throughout the Priestly poem is this: a statement of divine intention, "Let there be light," followed by a notice of completion, "And there was light"; "Let the waters be gathered together . . . and it was so."[11] But no such notice follows when, on the sixth day, God creates humans in the divine image "so that they might exercise mastery among" the creatures (26; cf. 28). We are never told that "it was so." Literarily then, human dominion or "mastery among the creatures" has the status of an unfulfilled divine expectation, and that seems to me a profound theological statement (or lacuna) regarding human dignity. Genesis 1 takes a "special species" perspective; there is no question that humans are uniquely powerful. The open question is whether humans will exercise a proper mastery among the creatures, a benevolent dominion that mirrors God's own exercise of power (as distinct from an ungodly domination). That question, once opened up by Genesis 1, stands open through the rest of the Bible (as Paul's reading in Romans indicates) and even to this day.

Genesis 1:26–31

[26]Then God said, "Let us make humankind in our image, according to our likeness; and let them have dominion over the fish of the sea, and over the birds of the air, and over the cattle, and over all the wild animals of the earth, and over every creeping thing that creeps upon the earth."

[27]So God created humankind in his image,
in the image of God he created them;
male and female he created them.

[28]God blessed them, and God said to them, "Be fruitful and multiply, and fill the earth and subdue it; and have dominion over the fish of the sea and over the
birds of the air and over every living thing that moves upon the earth." [29]God
said, "See, I have given you every plant yielding seed that is upon the face of all the earth, and every tree with seed in its fruit; you shall have them for food.
[30]And to every beast of the earth, and to every bird of the air, and to everything that creeps on the earth, everything that has the breath of life, I have given every
green plant for food." And it was so. [31]God saw everything that he had made,
and indeed, it was very good. And there was evening and there was morning, the sixth day.

4.2 *Al-Baqara* 2:30–35

Muhammad Abdel Haleem

The passage chosen as a primary text from the Qur'ān (*al-Baqara* 2:30–35) comes in the context of a larger thematic unit showing human beings how bounteous God has been to them and how He has honored them, so that they should recognize this and worship none but Him. This theme starts with verse 21, which calls on people to "worship God who created them" and who provided various good things for them. Then we come to verse 29, which should be included with verse 30 in the selected text, as it helps in the comparison with the Bible. It says, "It was He who created all that is on earth for you." In the original Arabic, this statement of six words is very concise but comprehensive, using pronouns of generalization that are elaborated and detailed in scores of places in the Qur'ān, to include the worlds of animals, plants, and inanimates in the earth, sea, or skies, which God has created for humans (*khalaqa lakum*) and made of benefit or subject to them (*sakhkhara lakum*). Following this verse we have our passage as an illustration of further dignity God has conferred on humans.

The theme here is presented in a dynamic dialogue between God, the angels, and Adam, with Iblīs mentioned at the end. In concise, majestic utterance, God tells the angels the plan He has for Adam, clearly not in order to solicit their opinion or to change His plans according to their opinions but to bring out into the open what they think and to correct it: "I am going to place a *khalīfa* on earth" (30). For *khalīfa*, Arberry gives the word "viceroy." This particular meaning has become popularized in the twentieth century, but I do not agree with it, certainly not in the sense of "*khalīfa* of God," a phrase that the Qur'ān itself does not use explicitly either. A viceroy acts only if the "roy" (king) is absent, and God is never absent. The word "*khalīfa*" is derived from *khalf*, which means "behind," or "after": the *khalīfa* of the Prophet Muhammad acted only when the Prophet was dead. When I left my house in London yesterday, I repeated the Prophet's prayer, "Lord be my *khalīfa* within my family." God is ever living, ever present. My choice is "successor," not in the sense that Adam was a successor to God. Some commentators say that humans succeeded the angels or the jinn on earth. It can also mean that individuals and generations succeed each other on earth, as we find in many other passages in the Qur'ān. Thus, God is saying that humans would continue to succeed one another, just as fruits contain seeds to continue their cycle. This succession, as the Qur'ān makes clear, is so they will populate and civilize (*ista'mara*) the world while they live there "to test you through what He gives you."[12]

When God makes David a *khalīfa* in the land, He says that David should accordingly "judge fairly between people, with justice and without following anyone's desires."[13] When Moses leaves Aaron behind and goes up the Mountain, he tells him, "Take my place (*ikhlufni*) among my people, do right and do not follow the way of mischief makers."

Our passage tells us that on hearing of God's intentions, the angels protested: how could God set on earth someone who would cause corruption and shed blood? This shows that they were not talking about Adam alone, who did neither, but about his descendants as well. The Qur'ān is explicit, as we see later in our passage, in stating that angels only know what God teaches them, so some commentators say that God must have given them information about humanity's propensity to violence and bloodshed through inspiration or, alternatively, that He had mentioned this in some previous discourse. God's reply to them is, "I know what you do not know." This enigmatic answer could be explained by other passages showing that even if some humans cause corruption and bloodshed, there will be others to stand up against them, so justice and order will be restored.[14] The door is also open for them either to repent and mend their ways in this world, which in the Qur'ān wipes out all previous misdeeds, or to be judged in the hereafter.[15]

In His wisdom, God sees that the overall scheme should not be discarded because of some elements of humanity that the angels see as bad. Then God proceeds to demonstrate to them the true worth of Adam by teaching him the names of things and challenging the angels to show equal knowledge, at which they glorify God, retract their earlier protest, and say, "We only know what you tell us."

From the beginning of the Qur'ān, teaching Adam is placed on a par with creating him. Chronologically, the first revelation of the Qur'ān is "God created man . . . and taught by the pen, taught man what he did not know."[16] And another often-quoted verse says, "The Merciful . . . created man and taught him to communicate."[17]

These themes of teaching and knowing are widespread throughout the Qur'ān and are used as a mark by which humans should recognize God and His revelations. It is this knowing that distinguishes humans from other creatures. It is clear from our text that God's reason for placing Adam on earth in the role intended for him is the knowledge God has taught Adam. The words "teaching" and "knowing" occur in our passage in different derivations eight times, which highlights the importance of this theme very powerfully. It is this knowledge, rather than the claim to be "viceroy of God," that truly distinguishes Adam.

Having established for the angels this aspect of the superiority of humans, God commands them to bow themselves to Adam, and they do this. Iblīs (Satan), in his arrogance, protests and refuses.

In addition to creating man "with My own hands," creating and subjecting things to him, and teaching him, God commands the angels to bow down before man. It is clear from the passage that, in spite of the protest of the pious (the angels) and of the rebel (Iblīs), God honors humans and establishes them on earth.

A further honor that God confers on man is to admit Adam and his wife to the garden, having given them the choice to enjoy the permitted fruits of the garden but warning them not to eat the forbidden fruit and thereby disobey God. They use their choice to eat the forbidden fruit. Some Muslim theologians argue that in this respect a good human is better than the angels because he has to chosen to be good, whereas the angels by their nature are made to be always obedient to God. In the Qur'ān, moral choice and the responsibility that goes with it is called "the trust" (*al-amāna*), which man in his haste has put himself forward to bear, when heaven, earth, and mountains were afraid to do so.

I beg to differ from the popularized meaning of *khalīfa* as viceroy, vicegerent, or viceregent and from the popularized meaning of "God created Adam in His image" in the ḥadīth of the Prophet Muhammad. The Qur'ān states categorically of God, "There is nothing like Him," so I take the expression in the ḥadīth to mean what the Qur'ān states on several occasions: that God created man in the image He chose for him, "in whatever form He chose."[18] The word "*ṣūra*" as used in the Qur'ān and ḥadīth means "shape" or "form." "He shaped you in your best shape" (not His best shape);[19] "it is He who shapes you all in the womb as He pleases."[20] At birth, none of us humans selects his own shape or nature; it is God who determines these in the way He chooses. It has always been my opinion that the pronoun in "his image" has a small "h," but I felt anxious that some would say this was a figment of my imagination. A few hours before traveling here, I consulted al-Nawawī's commentary on Muslim's ḥadīth and found him citing the ḥadīth quoted in our supplementary texts as proof that the pronoun "his" refers to Adam, and not to God, so the *ṣūra* is Adam's shape, sixty cubits long.

Yet in spite of my departure from the popularized meaning of *khalīfa* as "vicegerent" or "representative of God" and the creation of man in God's image, when all is said and done, the fact remains that in both scriptures it is God who created humans and honored them. The essence is still the same in both scriptures. The two lights emanate from the same niche. Our realization of this should be the bridge that we should maintain and fortify. Furthermore, in spite of any difficulties we may encounter in fortifying the bridge or in the interfaith dialogue, we should learn from the fact that, although He knew that some humans would corrupt and shed blood, God, in His wisdom, did not scrap the whole scheme of setting humans on earth and conferring such great dignity upon them. This dignity clearly was not based on humans being pious or following any one religion or another, but God embraced those who cause corruption and shed blood. Nor is there any discrimination on the grounds of race, nationality, gender, or class; dignity is conferred on all: "We have honored the Children of Adam."[21]

Qur'ān 2:30–35

30And when thy Lord said to the angels, "I am setting in the earth a viceroy." They said, "What, wilt Thou set therein one who will do corruption there, and shed blood, while We proclaim Thy praise and call Thee Holy?" He said, "Assuredly I know that you know not."

31And He taught Adam the names, all of them; then He presented them unto the angels and said, "Now tell me the names of these, if you speak truly."
32They said, "Glory be to Thee! We know not save what Thou hast taught us. Surely Thou art the All-knowing the All-wise."
33He said, "Adam, tell them their names." And when he had told them their names He said, "Did I not tell you I know the unseen things of the heavens and earth? And I know what things you reveal, and what you were hiding."

34And when We said to the angels, "Bow yourselves to Adam"; so they bowed themselves, save Iblis; he refused, and waxed proud, and so he became one of the unbelievers.

35And We said, "Adam, dwell thou, and thy wife, in the Garden, and eat thereof easefully where you desire; but draw not nigh this tree, lest you be evildoers."[22]

CHAPTER FIVE

Human Alienation

5.1 Genesis 3, Romans 7:15–25

Mona Siddiqui

The biblical passages discussed in this essay have been selected because of their significance for Christian reflection on human alienation. There is a great deal of material in these texts suggesting tensions and difficulties in the relationship of human beings to God, to each other, and to the natural environment. The following brief comments seek to give some impression of how these passages appear when read from a Muslim perspective.

The narrative in Genesis 3 concerning the disobedience of Adam and Eve to God's commandment and their consequent expulsion from Eden is paralleled at several points in the Qur'ān.[23] The biblical and Qur'ānic accounts do, however, diverge in various ways and contain some quite different emphases. In purely narrative terms, a Muslim reading the biblical account would probably first be struck by the role Eve plays in it. In the Qur'ān there is no account of Eve's conversation with the serpent; nor of Eve's attraction to the tree and its fruit, and of her eating it before Adam does; nor of God addressing Eve and her response; nor of God's further words directed specifically to Eve.[24] The Qur'ānic accounts do not distinguish as much between Adam and Eve, and when they speak, they do so together.[25] Whereas from a certain perspective there may appear to be more dramatic interest in the more developed and individual role that Eve plays in Genesis, from a different perspective—not least that of women readers—this focus on her is not altogether welcome. In particular, the fact that Eve was, according to Genesis, the first to eat the forbidden fruit has tended to lead to the view among Christians that women are more to blame than men for humanity's sinful condition. This is a view that Adam himself appears to express when, in response to God's question at Genesis 3:11, he responds evasively: "The woman whom you gave to be with me, she gave me fruit from the tree, and I ate."[26] If anything, the Qur'ān lays responsibility more on Adam than on Eve.[27]

A question raised by this narrative that has been much debated both between Christians and between Muslims is whether there is a genuine religious basis for the subordination of women to men, and more specifically of wives to their husbands. In Genesis God says to Eve, "your desire shall be for your husband, and he shall rule over you."[28]

These words recognize at least the fact of the subordination of women to men; however, it can be argued that such subordination is not presented as God's will but rather as a regrettable result of the Fall, an outworking of human alienation from God rather than an expression of divine intention. Nevertheless, the Genesis narrative clearly can be, and has been, used to justify patriarchy. In this context we might also note a New Testament passage where the argument that it was Eve, not Adam, who was deceived by the serpent, is linked to calls for submissiveness on the part of women.[29] Christians concerned to read the Bible in ways that do not support patriarchal attitudes would argue that other, more central scriptural themes point to quite different understandings of the relationship between men and women. Reference is often made to St. Paul's words: "There is no longer Jew or Greek, there is no longer slave or free, there is no longer male and female; for all of you are one in Christ Jesus."[30] Of course, debates about the interpretation of scripture with regard to the male–female relationship also occur among Muslims, with appeals being made to a range of Qur'ānic texts in support of quite different positions.[31] It is not possible to consider the Qur'ānic material here, although it is interesting to note that it does not appear that the Qur'ānic narratives concerning Adam and Eve are as significant within intra-Muslim discussion of male–female relations as the Genesis narratives are for intra-Christian discussion of this theme.

Within the Christian tradition, chapter 3 of Genesis has been especially significant in providing the narrative basis for the doctrine of original sin. Read in this way, this passage is taken as describing humankind as created in a state of primal innocence and bliss which, through rebellion against God's will, has been lost, leading to expulsion from Eden and the consequent experience of enmity within humankind, frustration in relation to nature, and ultimately death. Some commentators have claimed that the plot of this story hinges on the idea that God does not want humanity to eat from the tree of knowledge.[32] While no Hebrew equivalent of the term "fall" is used in this context, this reading of the text sees it as providing the foundational diagnosis of the human condition as fallen, for which the only remedy is the redemption from sin that God would offer in due course through Jesus Christ. Traditional Christian exegesis has seen Genesis 3:15 as foretelling the coming of Christ and the conflict with Satan in which Christ engaged to redeem humankind. The interpretation of this narrative that has become dominant, especially in the Western Christian tradition, is that associated with Augustine, building on Paul's argument in Romans 5. This theological tradition asked questions about the manner of the transmission of original sin through the generations of the human race from Adam onward, but the text does not seem concerned to address these matters.

Here we touch on an area of significant doctrinal contrast, for Islam teaches neither that human beings exist in a state of original sin nor that resolving the human predicament requires the kind of atoning action of God through Jesus proclaimed by Christianity. It is not that Islam sees nothing wrong with humanity but that its diagnosis is less pessimistic. Some observations about the Qur'ānic Adam and Eve narratives are illuminating in this context. Certainly the Qur'ānic Adam and Eve are depicted as committing a serious error; God says of Adam that he "forgot" and was found "lacking in constancy," and Adam and Eve recognize that they have wronged their own souls by their disobedience and need God's mercy.[33] But the merciful response of God in the Qur'ān is to accept their repentance and to provide guidance that, if followed, could bring human beings to eternal salvation.[34] There is no echo here of the traditional Christian teaching that the Fall makes necessary a long process of redemptive divine intervention culminating in the sending of Christ and his death and resurrection.

Having acknowledged these major contrasts, a Muslim response to Genesis 3 might well ask whether this narrative has to be interpreted in the manner familiar in the Western Christian tradition that has been so shaped by Augustine. Muslim readers would find it significant, for example, that neither Judaism nor, indeed, all Christian traditions derive the same concept of original sin from this passage. From a Muslim perspective, it is interesting that many Christian commentators today tend to distance themselves from the Augustinian perspective. For example, one recent commentary suggests that the real purpose of Genesis 2–3 is to tell the story not of the "fall" of the human race but of its "necessary maturing." The second century Irenaeus is seen as a better interpreter of these narratives than the later Augustine.[35] Muslims are likely to find more encouraging prospects for dialogue with Christians in this kind of approach to the text than in ones that stick closer to the traditional Augustinian interpretation.

The shorter passage from Paul's letter to the Romans in many ways raises similar questions for Muslims in dialogue with Christians as the passage from Genesis. Christian commentators have long argued whether Paul is describing in this passage his past experience before his conversion or his present experience as a Christian. If one adopts the latter interpretation (held by many influential theologians such as Augustine, Aquinas, and Luther), Paul is expressing a highly paradoxical account of Christian experience; he is at the same time confident of redemption through Christ but also continues to be aware of the power of sin within him.[36] It is not entirely clear how this paradox is resolved.

The language used here by Paul to convey his experience of life as a believer would probably strike most Muslim readers as strangely negative. Returning to a point already mentioned earlier, although Islamic understandings of the human condition take seriously the human tendency to sin, they also incline to a much more optimistic picture than we have here in Romans of the capacity of human beings to receive God's merciful gift of guidance and, by following this guidance, to attain God's favor. There are more than thirty words in the New Testament that convey some notion of "sin," and Paul uses at least twenty-four of them. Paul does not define sin, but he regards the sin inherent in humankind as a barrier to fellowship with God, for it is sin that brings alienation from God. For Paul, sin was not a part of human nature as God created it, for God's creation was not flawed until Adam's sin.

As a faithful Jew, Paul recognized the Law as a blessing from God, but as a Christian, he also realized that the Law taught what sin is, and that its definition of right and wrong made plain what was wrong. In verses 7–12, Paul refers to the human enslavement to sin, suggesting that even when human beings try to do moral good by observing the Law, they cannot master their passions and desires (14–23) and end up doing what they do not want to do.

These observations give some indication as to why Paul has often been regarded negatively in the history of Islamic writing on Christianity. Muslims have often argued that Paul was responsible for initiating a process that transformed the message of Jesus from one essentially identical with that of Islam to a significantly different religion. While the relationship between God's will and human disobedience is a significant Qur'ānic theme, it bears little resemblance to the tragedy implied in the Pauline understanding of the Law and sin. One modern Muslim scholar sees Paul as responsible for the twin errors at the heart of Christianity: "peccatism" (a false diagnosis of radical human sinfulness) and "saviorism" (a false solution involving incarnation and atonement).[37] It is not the purpose of these brief comments to argue for or against this generally negative Muslim view of Paul but simply to recognize that the account of human alienation that we find in some Pauline passages is one that most Muslims may find quite unfamiliar. Therefore, in view of Paul's decisive significance in the development of the Christian faith, it is all the more important that this account should be intelligently explored in the context of a Christian–Muslim dialogue on what it means to be a human being.

Genesis 3

[1]Now the serpent was more crafty than any other wild animal that the LORD God had made. He said to the woman, "Did God say, 'You shall not eat from any tree in the garden'?" [2]The woman said to the serpent, "We may eat of the fruit of the trees in the garden; [3]but God said, 'You shall not eat of the fruit of the tree that is in the middle of the garden, nor shall you touch it, or you shall die.'" [4]But the serpent said to the woman, "You will not die; [5]for God knows that when you eat of it your eyes will be opened, and you will be like God, knowing good and evil." [6]So when the woman saw that the tree was good for food, and that it was a delight to the eyes, and that the tree was to be desired to make one wise, she took of its fruit and ate; and she also gave some to her husband, who was with her, and he ate. [7]Then the eyes of both were opened, and they knew that they were naked; and they sewed fig leaves together and made loincloths for themselves.

[8]They heard the sound of the LORD God walking in the garden at the time of the evening breeze, and the man and his wife hid themselves from the presence of the LORD God among the trees of the garden. [9]But the LORD God called to the man, and said to him, "Where are you?" [10]He said, "I heard the sound of you in the garden, and I was afraid, because I was naked; and I hid myself." [11]He said, "Who told you that you were naked? Have you eaten from the tree of which I commanded you not to eat?" [12]The man said, "The woman whom you gave to be with me, she gave me fruit from the tree, and I ate." [13]Then the Lord God said to the woman, "What is this that you have done?" The woman said, "The serpent tricked me, and I ate."

[14]The LORD God said to the serpent,
"Because you have done this,
cursed are you among all animals

and among all wild creatures;
upon your belly you shall go,
and dust you shall eat all the days of your life.
[15]I will put enmity between you and the woman,
and between your offspring and hers;
he will strike your head,
and you will strike his heel."
[16]To the woman he said,
"I will greatly increase your pangs in childbearing;
in pain you shall bring forth children,
yet your desire shall be for your husband,
and he shall rule over you."
[17]And to the man he said,
"Because you have listened to the voice of your wife,
and have eaten of the tree
about which I commanded you,
'You shall not eat of it,'
cursed is the ground because of you;
in toil you shall eat of it all the days of your life;
[18]thorns and thistles it shall bring forth for you;
and you shall eat the plants of the field.
[19]By the sweat of your face you shall eat bread
until you return to the ground,
for out of it you were taken;
you are dust, and to dust you shall return."

[20]The man named his wife Eve, because she was the mother of all who live.
[21]And the LORD God made garments of skins for the man and for his wife, and
clothed them.
[22]Then the LORD God said, "See, the man has become like one of us, knowing
good and evil; and now, he might reach out his hand and take also from the
tree of life, and eat, and live for ever"—[23]therefore the LORD God sent him forth
from the garden of Eden, to till the ground from which he was taken. [24]He
drove out the man; and at the east of the garden of Eden he placed the cheru-
bim, and a sword flaming and turning to guard the way to the tree of life.

Romans 7:15–25

[15]I do not understand my own actions. For I do not do what I want, but I do
the very thing I hate. [16]Now if I do what I do not want, I agree that the law is
good. [17]But in fact it is no longer I that do it, but sin that dwells within me.
[18]For I know that nothing good dwells within me, that is, in my flesh. I can will
what is right, but I cannot do it. [19]For I do not do the good I want, but the evil
I do not want is what I do. [20]Now if I do what I do not want, it is no longer I
that do it, but sin that dwells within me. [21] So I find it to be a law that when I
want to do what is good, evil lies close at hand. [22]For I delight in the law of
God in my inmost self, [23]but I see in my members another law at war with the

law of my mind, making me captive to the law of sin that dwells in my members.
24 Wretched man that I am! Who will rescue me from this body of death?
25 Thanks be to God through Jesus Christ our Lord!
So then, with my mind I am a slave to the law of God, but with my flesh I am a slave to the law of sin.

5.2 *al-Baqara* 2:36–39; *Ṭā' Hā'* 20:115–24

Daniel Madigan

The beginnings of this story of alienation are in the Qur'ānic text already discussed in chapter 4, "Human Dignity,"—Iblīs's refusal to obey God and bow to Adam. It is worth noting at the level of text the intertwining, interleaving almost, of human dignity and alienation. The two cannot be separated easily.

We are actually dealing here with two alienations, each quite distinct in its own way, yet also intimately bound up with the other. The human alienation that is our focus in this essay is, if anything, less mysterious than Iblīs's alienation from the God whom, according to Islamic tradition, he had served with distinction and worshipped with extraordinary devotion.

The story of Iblīs's refusal to obey is told seven times in the Qur'ān, two examples of which we have in these texts. The Qur'ān is characteristically spare in its recounting of detail, here as elsewhere addressing its hearers on the presumption that they are already familiar with the characters and the narrative. Indeed, the story of God's command to the angels to bow to the human being newly created in God's image and likeness as well the devil's refusal to bow was already found in noncanonical Jewish and Christian texts prior to the emergence of Islam.[38] For those later readers who were not familiar with the story, a wealth of detail, reflection, and explanation are to be had in the ḥadīth and in the *tafsīr* tradition, to say nothing of the extensive treatment given to the subject by poets and mystics.

Iblīs is a tantalizingly paradoxical character in the Islamic tradition. Not all commentators agree that he was an angel (as the Qur'ān texts would seem to suggest). Nonetheless, even for those who deny that he is an angel because angels are incapable of disobeying God, Iblīs's presence in Paradise and among the angels bears witness to his high status. He is presented as being heroically ascetic, a devoted worshipper, master of the seven heavens, guardian of Paradise, defender of God's throne, and yet also arrogant, prideful, and impetuous.[39]

We notice in both the texts presented here that Iblīs comes to be called Satan. According to commentators, he was previously 'Azāzīl or, less often, Hārith. The change of name in these Qur'ān texts marks a transition from Iblīs's refusal of obedience to that of Adam and Eve. While Iblīs's refusal is seen as originating within himself, rather than in the malevolence of a tempter, that of Adam and Eve is attributed to the deceit and hostility of Satan. Iblīs becomes "the accursed Satan" or literally "the stoned Satan" *al-shayṭān al-rajīm*, sworn enemy of the human person and our constant companion. Thus, there are two major strands in the discourse about the devil—the Iblīs strand (the paradoxical, tragic figure whose sin is self-motivated) and the Shayṭān strand (the constant presence of an external tempter who deceives and leads astray).[40]

In some respects, the Qur'ān texts appear to distance the human person from his or her sin, and the apparent simplicity of Adam's repentance and God's acceptance of that repentance have suggested to many readers that the sin of Adam should not be taken as seriously as Christians are accustomed to do. Yet a closer look at our texts and at some ḥadīth may perhaps show that, although there is a difference, there is less distance between us on this point than is often assumed.

The first point to be considered is that, in much spiritual writing, Iblīs's sin can be ours. Even those who have reached the heights of devotion can fall into the sin of pride. The word in Arabic is "*istikbār*," literally "to consider oneself greater." Iblīs explains to God his refusal to bow to Adam by asserting, "I am better (*khayrun*) than him!"[41] The word "*istikbār*" reminds us of the essential affirmation about God: *Allāhu akbar*, "God is greater." And so we see why *istikbār* is sinful—it is a way of associating oneself with God; it is a form of *shirk*. Iblīs is also represented in the tradition as the first to have used analogical reasoning. He explains the reason for his belief that he is better than Adam: God has made him from fire, whereas Adam was created only from clay.[42] His misguided trust in his own intellect rather than in obedience to the inscrutable command of God has brought him to a miserable end.

Second, a number of elements in the tradition can be read as a recognition that the tendency to sin is not simply external to being human but is an intimate and integral part of it. For example, according to a widely quoted ḥadīth, Satan "courses through a human being's veins (*yajrī min ibn ādam majra al-dam*)." A number of pious practices based on ḥadīth take it for granted that Satan is seeking ways to enter into people physically. Then there is the notion of the *nafs*—the (lower) soul—which provokes one to sin. It is sometimes identified with Satan and at other times is seen as his instrument.

What are we to make of Adam and Eve's readiness to believe what the deceiver tells them? According to the commentators, he convinces them that it is God's intention to send them from the Garden and that only if they eat the fruit of the tree of immortality will they be able to remain. This predisposition to suspect that God is trying to cheat them out of something they can easily have, or to which they believe they have a right, is very significant. Such a skewed, contentious, competitive relationship to God is a key element in the understanding of what Christians call original sin. The origin of this jaundiced attitude to God that leaves humans open to the insinuations of the tempter is not explained in either the Qur'ān or the Bible. It could be said that this is what Iblīs's sin and that of Adam and Eve have in common. Why then the difference in outcome? On the one hand, Iblīs is punished with the loss of everything and excluded from repentance. Adam, on the other hand, can ask for forgiveness and immediately receive it, as though his sin had scarcely touched him.

A couple of further notes on the text: The expulsion from the garden and a life on earth are not to be understood as punishments—at least for Adam. Although apparently created in heaven, human beings were created from earth and for the earth. For Iblīs, however, the expulsion and the condemnation to earthly wandering are central aspects of the punishment.

What were the "words" that, according to the Qur'ān, Adam received from his Lord?[43] These could be the verse: "Our Lord, we have wronged our souls: if you do not forgive us and have mercy we are lost."[44] There are other proposals in the commentary literature, including the following: "'O Lord, the sin which I have committed, is it something which you decreed for me before you created me, or is it something which I have invented of my own accord?' God answered, 'Rather it is something which I decreed for you before I created you.' Adam said, 'Then as you have decreed it for me, so do now forgive my sin.'"[45] This supposed dialogue between God and Adam reflects the tradition's interest in the question (never entirely resolved) of free will and predestination. A popular story describes a meeting between Adam and Moses, who questions his forebear as to why, with all the advantages he had, he would disobey God. Adam points out that such disobedience had already been decreed long before he was ever created.

al-Baqara 2:36–39

36Then Satan caused them to slip therefrom and brought them out of that they were in; and We said, "Get you all down, each of you an enemy of each; and in the earth a sojourn shall be yours, and enjoyment for a time."
37Thereafter Adam received certain words from his Lord, and He turned towards him; truly He turns, and is All-compassionate.
38We said, "Get you down out of it, all together; yet there shall come to you guidance from Me, and whosoever follows My guidance, no fear shall be on them, neither shall they sorrow.
39As for the unbelievers who cry lies to Our signs, those shall be the inhabitants of the Fire, therein dwelling forever."

Ṭā' Hā' 20:115–24

115And We made covenant with Adam before, but he forgot, and We found in him no constancy.
116And when We said to the angels, "Bow yourselves to Adam"; so they bowed themselves, save Iblīs; he refused.
117Then We said, "Adam, surely this is an enemy to thee and thy wife. So let him not expel you both from the Garden, so that thou art unprosperous.
118It is assuredly given to thee neither to hunger therein, nor to go naked,
119neither to thirst therein, nor to suffer the sun."
120Then Satan whispered to him saying, "Adam, shall I point thee to the Tree of Eternity, and a Kingdom that decays not?"
121So the two of them ate of it, and their shameful parts revealed to them, and they took to stitching upon themselves leaves of the Garden. And Adam disobeyed his Lord, and so he erred.
122Thereafter his Lord chose him, and turned again unto him, and He guided him.
123Said He, "Get you down, both of you together, out of it, each of you an enemy to each; but if there comes to you from Me guidance, then whosoever follows My guidance shall not go astray, neither shall he be unprosperous;
124but whosoever turns away from My remembrance, his shall be a life of narrowness, and on the Resurrection Day We shall raise him blind."

CHAPTER SIX

Human Destiny

6.1 Isaiah 65:17–25; Revelation 21:1–8, 21:22–22:5

Roland Chia

In the closing chapters of Isaiah we find the promise that God would "create new heavens and a new earth" that will last for all eternity.[46] This promise finds its fulfillment in John's vision of the holy city—the New Jerusalem—descending from heaven and taking its place in a creation totally transfigured by divine grace.[47] These two passages from the Old and New Testaments vividly and powerfully portray the eschatological life of the people of God mediated by the renewed creation. Accordingly, because of its future-oriented message, Isaiah 65:17–25 is read during Kingdomtide leading up to the beginning of Advent, while the passages from the final chapters of Revelation are read during Eastertide in celebration of Christ's resurrection.[48]

Isaiah 65–66 presents a vivid description of God's plan for his elect in a completely nonviolent world.[49] In one sense, these chapters recall the idyllic existence in the Garden of Eden before the rebellion of the first humans. But in envisioning the future of the created order as "the new heavens and the new earth," these chapters speak not so much about the return to the primordial Garden but the *telos* of the creation.[50] Isaiah 65–66, therefore, announces the transformation of the present creation, a future that is radically different from the past.[51]

Our passage, Isaiah 65:17–25, consists of two pronouncements, each beginning with "Behold I will create."[52] In the first pronouncement, God promises to create "new heavens and a new earth" while in the second he promises to create the New Jerusalem.[53] The emphasis on the creating activity of God here is important. Only God can create, and in Isaiah God as Creator is a dominant theme.[54] Creating refers not just to the initial work of bringing the cosmos into being but also to God's continuing work of maintenance and preservation.[55] In this passage, the verb refers to the bringing into being of new things that will supersede and replace the former things.[56]

The new creation of God is referred to as the "new heavens and the new earth," a comprehensive phrase that encompasses every aspect of the creation, including the spiritual realm. In this new creation, the people of God will forget the "former things." This expression refers not only to the "former troubles" alluded to in 16b but, indeed, to everything connected to the old existence. Not only will all the vestiges of the old order be removed when the vision is realized, the old order of existence will not even be remembered. Nothing in the new creation will prompt a recollection of the past. A general amnesia among the redeemed people of God will match the divine forgetfulness described in 65:16f. This first poetic cameo therefore speaks of the transformation of the entire cosmos resulting in the emergence of an entirely new world that will last for all eternity.

While the first pronouncement has to do with the transformation of the cosmos, the second focuses on the New Jerusalem, the holy city.[57] In the New Jerusalem there will be much rejoicing.[58] This is brought out by the use of apposition, where the nouns "Jerusalem" and "delight," and "people" and "joy" are so identifiable with one another that they are said to be the same.[59] The mood in this passage is in stark contrast to the sadness that prevails in chapters 1–39. The exhortation to "be glad and rejoice forever" indicates the eschatological character of these verses: the uncertainty and transience of the joys of this present world will be transcended by a joy that knows no end.[60] This corresponds with the announcement that the "sound of weeping and of crying will be heard in it no more."[61] In addition, the joy of the New Jerusalem is not just found among its inhabitants. It is reciprocal: God also takes joy in his new creation.[62]

By using different aspects of this present life to create impressions of the life to come, the author asserts that God's people will be completely happy, completely secure, and completely at peace in the New Jerusalem.[63] No infant will die prematurely, an elderly person will live to the fullest, and a person who dies at a hundred years of age would be but a youth.[64] This latter expression, of course, does not imply that death will still be a reality in the new heavens and earth.[65] Rather, what the writer wishes to convey is that in the new era the whole of life will be free from the power of death. In similar vein, although there will be no sinners in the New Jerusalem, the metaphor is used in 20d.[66] Not only will God's elect enjoy longevity, they will also remain in possession of their houses and enjoy the fruits of their labor.[67] When they call upon God, he will answer.[68] "With this access to God via word and answer," writes Westermann, "there is free access to the wellspring of life."[69]

The presence of verses 17a and 25 suggests that verses 19b–24 should not simply be read as merely describing the conditions of life in the present order. If these verses are taken as an integral part of this passage and not as arbitrary editorial additions, they serve as the hermeneutical key that unlocks the meaning of the entire passage. Verse 25 refers to the peace in the animal kingdom. The wolf and the lamb, which are proverbial opposites—the one aggressive and ferocious and the other weak and helpless—will feed together. The carnivorous lion will eat straw while the snake will no longer be at enmity with humankind.[70] The negative statement in 25d, "They will neither harm nor destroy on all my holy mountain," further enhances the picture of harmony portrayed in these vivid images.[71] Verse 25 therefore serves as a compendium of the messianic oracles in 11:6–9 by incorporating two virtually identical lines from it: "the lion will eat straw like the ox" (65.25b) and "they will neither harm nor destroy on all my holy mountain" (65:25d).[72] Thus, chapter 65 is of a piece with the messianic hope described in the entire book of Isaiah.[73]

The themes found in Isaiah 65 are taken up and expanded by John in his grand vision of the renewal of the cosmos in Revelation. The final section of Revelation (chapters 21–22) opens with the vision of a new heaven and a new earth, which serves as the setting for the New Jerusalem that will descend from heaven. The old order of creation, with its fragmentation and chaos, has passed away, and a harmonious new world full of life has replaced it. The righteous people of God will dwell in this world in communion with their Creator and Redeemer, and will reign with him forever. In the elegant words of Austin Farrer, here we have "the last of the Last Things and the end of the visionary drama."[74]

Structurally, Revelation 21:1–2 is modeled on Isaiah 65:17–19 and follows the same sequence of events: the appearance of the new creation, the disappearance of the old order, and the manifestation of the New Jerusalem. The passage begins with the vision of "a new heaven and a new earth," which will emerge when "the first heaven and the first earth had passed away." As in Isaiah 65:17, this phrase does not refer to the annihilation of the old created order but its transfiguration or transformation.[75] The new transfigured creation is characterized by the disappearance of the sea, the primeval ocean, which is a symbol of chaos.[76] Its disappearance signals the ultimate and total victory of God over evil: no accursed thing will be found in his new creation.

Revelation 21:2 announces the descent of the New Jerusalem from heaven. The phrase "coming down from heaven from God" emphasizes that the holy city is not simply an earthly metropolis rebuilt by human hands and will but is rather of heavenly origin.[77] The New Jerusalem is therefore a "creation of God which is to fulfil for the glorified humanity the role which the prophets saw of the earthly Jerusalem in relation to Israel (and in a less degree the Gentile nations)."[78] The double imagery of "city" and "bride" goes back a long way and is found in both the Testaments. The imagery of the "city" comes from the apocalyptic strand and can be traced to Ezekiel 40 while the metaphor of "bride" is found in both the Old and New Testaments.[79] Here as elsewhere in Revelation, "bride" is used to refer to the church.[80] The New Jerusalem can therefore be seen both as synonymous with the church or God's elect people or to the place where the saints dwell.[81]

Not only is the holy city the place where the saints will dwell, it is also the dwelling place of God.[82] The phrase "God will be with his people" is a metaphor that refers to the presence of God in victory as well as the abundance of his providential grace.[83] It is pertinent to note that John substituted "peoples" for "people," indicating that in the New Jerusalem, the many peoples of redeemed humanity will be one single elect people of God. In this holy city, God himself will wipe away every tear, and all that has damaged and disfigured the creation and human society, all the sorrow and suffering and pain, even death itself will no longer cast a shadow here.[84] The old has indeed passed away; the new has come.

The New Jerusalem is portrayed as a garden city, with lush greenery and "the river of the water of life as clear as crystal flowing from the throne of God and of the Lamb down to the middle of the great street of the city."[85] This imagery, which puts together the river of life and the tree of life, recalls the enchanted Garden in Genesis.[86] Its employment here does not indicate a return to the beginning, however, but rather that the *telos* of the creation will be in line with God's original purpose and intention. That this river flows from "God and from the Lamb" signifies that God alone is the source of life. In Revelation 21:6, God is described as the fountain, the spring of the water of life, water being the symbol of life and therefore a feature of the messianic age.[87] The river with its water of life therefore symbolizes the inexhaustible grace of God in the new heaven and the new earth.

There will be no temple in the New Jerusalem "because the Lord God Almighty and the Lamb are its temple."[88] The Old Testament prophets have already envisaged the New Jerusalem as the temple of God, but John takes a step further and eliminates the temple altogether.[89] The immediate presence of God, his *Shekinah* glory, is so pervasive that it fills the entire city and sanctifies everything in it. God is all in all, omnipresent, and he is constantly accessible to his priestly race.[90] In the New Jerusalem, there will also be no need for sun or moon "for the glory of God gives it light, and the Lamb is its lamp."[91] The uncreated light of God's glory will illumine the city. But the immediacy of God's presence is expressed supremely by the phrase, "They will see his face."[92] The inhabitants of the holy city will see what no one is able in this mortal life to see and survive.[93] To see the face of God is the deepest of religious aspirations, and its realization in the New Jerusalem "will be the heart of humanity's eternal joy in their worship of God."[94]

The throne of God, which features so prominently in Revelation, refers to the reign or kingdom of God.[95] In Revelation 21–22, "the kingdom of the world has become the kingdom of our Lord and of his Christ."[96] "Revelation's theme is the transfer of the sovereignty of the whole world from the dragon and the beast, who presently dominate it, to God, whose universal kingdom is to come to earth."[97] Revelation is indeed full of universalistic language, but it is important that we understand its universalism. John's vision that the "nations will walk in its light and the kings will bring their splendor into it" resonates with that of Isaiah and points to the ingathering of the worldwide harvest.[98] But, as Revelation 21:8 and 27 make perfectly clear, the wicked will be excluded from the New Jerusalem, emphasizing that there will be a dual outcome for humankind.[99] These verses give a clear warning to God's people that if they fail to be faithful witnesses and instead participate in the sins of Babylon, they will not inherit the holy city. In Revelation 21:8, the imagery used to describe the fate of sinners is that of divine judgment, whereas in 21:27 the imagery suggests the exclusion of the unholy from the holy city.[100] But to those who overcome, Revelation presents a wonderful promise of salvation: They will inhabit a world free from pain, sorrow and evil. God will be their God and they will be his people. And they will reign with him forever and ever.

Isaiah 65:17–25
17For I am about to create new heavens and a new earth;
the former things shall not be remembered
or come to mind.
18But be glad and rejoice for ever
in what I am creating;

for I am about to create Jerusalem as a joy,
and its people as a delight.
19I will rejoice in Jerusalem,
and delight in my people;
no more shall the sound of weeping be heard in it,
or the cry of distress.
20No more shall there be in it
an infant that lives but a few days,
or an old person who does not live out a lifetime;
for one who dies at a hundred years will be considered a youth,
and one who falls short of a hundred will be considered accursed.
21They shall build houses and inhabit them;
they shall plant vineyards and eat their fruit.
22They shall not build and another inhabit;
they shall not plant and another eat;
for like the days of a tree shall the days of my people be,
and my chosen shall long enjoy the work of their hands.
23They shall not labor in vain,
or bear children for calamity;
for they shall be offspring blessed by the Lord—
and their descendants as well.
24Before they call I will answer,
while they are yet speaking I will hear.
25The wolf and the lamb shall feed together,
the lion shall eat straw like the ox;
but the serpent—its food shall be dust!
They shall not hurt or destroy
on all my holy mountain, says the Lord.

Revelation 21:1–8; 21:22–22:5
21 1Then I saw a new heaven and a new earth; for the first heaven and the first
earth had passed away, and the sea was no more. 2And I saw the holy city, the
new Jerusalem, coming down out of heaven from God, prepared as a bride
adorned for her husband. 3And I heard a loud voice from the throne saying,
"See, the home of God is among mortals. He will dwell with them as their God;
they will be his peoples, and God himself will be with them; 4he will wipe every
tear from their eyes. Death will be no more; mourning and crying and pain will
be no more, for the first things have passed away." 5And the one who was seated
on the throne said, "See, I am making all things new." Also he said, "Write
this, for these words are trustworthy and true." 6Then he said to me, "It is done!
I am the Alpha and the Omega, the beginning and the end. To the thirsty I will
give water as a gift from the spring of the water of life. 7Those who conquer will
inherit these things, and I will be their God and they will be my children. 8But
as for the cowardly, the faithless, the polluted, the murderers, the fornicators,
the sorcerers, the idolaters, and all liars, their place will be in the lake that burns
with fire and sulphur, which is the second death."

21 [22] I saw no temple in the city, for its temple is the Lord God the Almighty
and the Lamb. [23]And the city has no need of sun or moon to shine on it, for the
glory of God is its light, and its lamp is the Lamb. [24]The nations will walk by
its light, and the kings of the earth will bring their glory into it. [25]Its gates will
never be shut by day—and there will be no night there. [26]People will bring into
it the glory and the honor of the nations. [27]But nothing unclean will enter it,
nor anyone who practices abomination or falsehood, but only those who are
written in the Lamb's book of life.
22 [1]Then the angel showed me the river of the water of life, bright as crystal,
flowing from the throne of God and of the Lamb [2]through the middle of the
street of the city. On either side of the river is the tree of life with its twelve
kinds of fruit, producing its fruit each month; and the leaves of the tree are for
the healing of the nations. [3]Nothing accursed will be found there anymore. But
the throne of God and of the Lamb will be in it, and his servants will worship
him; [4]they will see his face, and his name will be on their foreheads. [5]And there
will be no more night; they need no light of lamp or sun, for the Lord God will
be their light, and they will reign forever and ever.

6.2 *al-Raḥmān* 55:26–78; *al-Qiyāma* 75:20–25

Seyed Amir Akrami

Both of the following Qur'ānic passages refer to "that day," the last day or day of judgment on which the destiny of human beings is determined.[101] These are just two of many other eschatological passages in the Qur'ān in which the last day is described with a great variety of terms such as "the day of resurrection" (*yawm al-qiyāma*), "the day of judgment" (*yawm al-dīn*), "the hour" (*al-sāʿa*), "the day of reckoning" (*yawm al-ḥisāb*) and "the day of gathering" (*yawm al-jamʿ*). The Qur'ān also describes various events associated with the last day, such as the rolling up of the heavens, the blowing of a trumpet, and the opening of books. Muslim thinkers have reflected at great length on some of the eschatological references in the Qur'ān, for example, "*barzakh*," which is widely understood to refer to the state in which human beings will exist between death and the final resurrection.[102]

In terms of our concern here with the question of human destiny in the Islamic perspective, the eschatological passages of the Qur'ān are significant in that they establish with great emphasis the reality of a fixed point beyond this life at which God will pass judgment on every human being and will decree for each a future of either eternal reward or eternal punishment. The last day is thus a point at which, for each person, the past is reviewed and the future is decided. This review of the past will involve a total unveiling, a searching clarity before which all must stand alone. God will attend in detail to human affairs, and nothing will be left unevaluated by him. All people will be confronted with the truth of how they lived. Even a person's own limbs will bear witness to their actions.[103] Then everybody will be repaid justly, in accordance with their past life, with some being rewarded in "the garden" (*al-janna*) and others being punished in "the fire" (*al-nār*). The destiny of all human beings is thus ultimately determined by God, but this divine judgment is carried out on the basis of their behavior in this life, as expressed especially in their believing or unbelieving response to the divine message and their obedience or disobedience to it. In the Qur'ānic account of human destiny there is thus a strong link between this world (*al-dunya*) and the next (*al-akhira*). Freely chosen acts in the former will determine one's place in the latter.

Turning from these general points to the specific texts under consideration here, we note some salient features of the passage from *sūrat al-Rahmān* 55:26–78. One striking characteristic is the emphatic repetition of the rhetorical question: "O which of your Lord's bounties will you and you deny?" This is designed to provoke gratitude (very closely bound up with faith in the Qur'ān); believers are each time being invited to respond: "I do not deny."

Verses 26–27 give memorable expression to the Qur'ānic sense of the contrast between the fleeting quality of this world and the eternity of God: "All that dwells upon the earth is perishing, yet still abides the Face of thy Lord, majestic, splendid." It is a mark of genuine faith to maintain this perspective in a world where many demonstrate their failure to grasp true human destiny by living only for transient pleasures (see also 75:20–21, following).

As in many other eschatological passages, two pictures of human destiny are starkly juxtaposed: the positive picture of the destiny of those rewarded in heavenly gardens and the dark picture of the destiny of those being punished with the torments of hell (*Jahannam*). We also find the same juxtaposition, more concisely conveyed, at 75:22–25. (It should be noted, however, that although a division into these two categories is the Qur'ānic norm, one passage speaks of a third category, the "foremost" in faith (*al-sābiqūn*), who will be nearest to God.[104]) While both types of human destiny are vividly conveyed, it is notable that in the passage from *sūrat al-Rahmān*, the account of the bliss of the righteous is considerably longer than that of the punishment of the sinners. This can be taken as an indication of the primacy, in the Qur'ān, of God's mercy, which is greater than God's wrath.

A feature of the Qur'ānic portrayals of paradisiacal bliss that has attracted much comment is the presence of good and beautiful women seen as rewards for devout believers. They are mentioned in *sūrat al-Rahmān* at verses 56–58 and 70–74 and also in several other contexts.[105] The term *ḥūr*, used on four occasions to describe these women, is the source of the anglicized "houris."[106] Less often noted are references to young male servants.[107] Such passages have been variously interpreted by Muslims; alongside a widespread assumption that they are to be taken literally, different approaches have been adopted by more mystical and rationalist exegetes. More generally, while the physical pleasures and torments in the afterlife described by the Qur'ān have usually been taken by Muslims to imply the reality of bodily existence in the hereafter, there has been debate between Islamic philosophers and theologians on the nature of the resurrection and the related question of whether to interpret the Qur'ān's eschatological passages in literal or symbolic senses.

The shorter passage from *sūrat al-Qiyāma* is most notable for its reference to the vision of God (*ru'yat Allāh*) enjoyed in the hereafter by believers: "Upon that day faces shall be radiant, gazing upon their Lord."[108] Again, the history of exegesis of this passage contains divergent impulses, typified in the classical period by the literalism of the Ash'arites and the symbolic interpretation favored by the Mu'tazilites. Within the Shi'ite tradition there has been particular emphasis on the vision of God as the fulfillment of human destiny.

These texts, together with the many other Qur'ānic passages belonging to the same eschatological genre, raise many questions that have been and, indeed, continue to be debated and discussed among Muslims. Some of the most widely discussed of such questions include the following.

- How far should such eschatological texts be interpreted literally, for example in relation to what they describe of punishment and reward?
- Why does the Qur'ān place so much emphasis on physical pleasure in the afterlife when it also encourages detachment from pleasure in this world?
- Does God's mercy ultimately overrule his judgment?

Al-Raḥmān 55:26–78
26All that dwells upon the earth is perishing, 27yet still abides the Face of thy Lord, majestic, splendid.
28O which of your Lord's bounties will you and you deny? 29Whatsoever is in the heavens and the earth implore Him; every day He is upon some labour.
30O which of your Lord's bounties will you and you deny? 31We shall surely attend to you at leisure, you weight and you weight!
32O which of your Lord's bounties will you and you deny? 33O tribe of jinn and of men, if you are able to pass through the confines of heaven and earth, pass through them! You shall not pass through except with an authority.
34O which of your Lord's bounties will you and you deny? 35Against you shall be loosed a flame of fire, and molten brass; and you shall not be helped.
36O which of your Lord's bounties will you and you deny? 37And when heaven is split asunder, and turns crimson like red leather—
38O which of our Lord's bounties will you and you deny? 39on that day none shall be questioned about his sin, neither man nor jinn.
40O which of your Lord's bounties will you and you deny? 41The sinners shall be known by their mark, and they shall be seized by their forelocks and their feet.
42O which of your Lord's bounties will you and you deny? 43This is Gehenna, that sinners cried lies to; 44they shall go round between it and between hot, boiling water.
45O which of your Lord's bounties will you and you deny? 46But such as fears the Station of his Lord, for them shall be two gardens—
47O which of your Lord's bounties will you and you deny? 48abounding in branches—
49O which of your Lord's bounties will you and you deny? 50therein two fountains of running water—
51O which of your Lord's bounties will you and you deny? 52therein of every fruit two kinds—
53O which of your Lord's bounties will you and you deny? 54reclining upon couches lined with brocade, the fruits of the gardens nigh to gather—
55O which of your Lord's bounties will you and you deny? 56therein maidens restraining their glances, untouched before them by any man or jinn—
57O which of your Lord's bounties will you and you deny? 58lovely as rubies, beautiful as coral—
59O which of your Lord's bounties will you and you deny? 60Shall the recompense of goodness be other than goodness?
61O which of your Lord's bounties will you and you deny? 62And besides these shall be two gardens—
63O which of your Lord's bounties will you and you deny? 64green, green pastures—
65O which of your Lord's bounties will you and you deny? 66therein two fountains of gushing water—
67O which of your Lord's bounties will you and you deny? 68therein fruits, and palm-trees, and pomegranates—

69 O which of your Lord's bounties will you and you deny? 70 therein maidens
good and comely—
71 O which of your Lord's bounties will you and you deny? 72 houris, cloistered in
cool pavilions—
73 O which of your Lord's bounties will you and you deny? 74 untouched before
them by any man or jinn—
75 O which of your Lord's bounties will you and you deny? 76 reclining upon green
cushions and lovely druggets—77 O which of your Lord's bounties will you and
you deny? 78 Blessed be the Name of thy Lord, majestic, splendid.

Al-Qiyāma 75:20–25
20 No indeed; but you love the hasty world,
21 and leave be the Hereafter.
22 Upon that day faces shall be radiant,
23 gazing upon their Lord;
24 and upon that day faces shall be scowling,
25 thou mightest think the Calamity has been wreaked on them.

CHAPTER SEVEN

Humanity and Gender

7.1 Genesis 2:18–25; Ephesians 5:21–33

Tim Winter

Confronted with such complex texts, and with the sensitivity of the subject, I can do no more than offer a few personal reflections and reactions. Any Muslim contemplating a biblical text should recall the injunction not to rush in where angels fear to tread. It is not only that there is a formidable scholarship to assimilate. There is also the question of God's presence. The Bible's usual readers are, for us, *ahl al-kitāb*, people of the Book, and this is an honorific; indeed, the Sharīʿa typically requires us, when disposing of a text in Hebrew characters, to dispose of it respectfully, just as we do the Qur'ān. Perhaps that is why the world's richest collection of medieval Jewish manuscripts, the Cairo Geniza, was in Cairo: a Muslim context makes the survival of a Geniza relatively easy. For us there is, charges of textual interpolation notwithstanding, a kind of real presence in the text.

For the Genesis verses, I propose to invoke, not source-criticism, or Christian or even Muslim conventions of reading, but a Jewish voice: Rabbi Joseph Soloveitchik. In his book *The Lonely Man of Faith*, Soloveitchik is concerned with overcoming, to the extent that this can be possible, the alienation of modern man. In the opening primeval Genesis accounts, he finds not one but two Adams, whose interaction within us will determine our happiness.[109]

Adam I is the man of glory and mastery. He is crown of creation and, by naming the things of creation, becomes their master under God. Today this is the man of science, technology, and political acumen. Adam II, by contrast, is the "covenantal man." He is lonely: for Soloveitchik this is the key disclosure of these verses. Even before sin, he suffers from an "original solitude." He longs for a personal relationship with a personal God. In this text we are shown that this is granted paradigmatically through Eve. Here Soloveitchik is not far from many modern Christian commentators who understand the sense of "helpmeet" not as "servant" in any sense that would imply her inferiority but as someone who helps him overcome the alienation that lies in being only the man of glory.

Of course, the rabbi will not take this further, as some Christians do, to draw lessons about the internal life of God. A God with an internal relationality is not Judaically possible; indeed, the sociality created through the first human couple, and the richness of the possible human response to God that ensues, suggests that a fully rich and engaged humanity is entirely feasible without a model of a God who exists in internal relationship. The Psalms, for Soloveitchik, will certainly sufficiently prove that. Who could improve on the prayers and hymns that they contain?

I personally find this helpful; and I think it is not un-Qur'ānic. Adam is helped and healed by Eve; not many men will seriously deny this. But perhaps Muslims, unlike Jews, will be able to take this on, to the end of the Bible. If the human being who is the image of God and hence—for a creature—perfect combines what Muslims would call *jalāl* and *jamāl*: rigor and beauty, then perhaps a Muslim who ventures to read the Bible as *kitāb*, as scripture, will be less puzzled by the book of Revelation. The Jesus of gentleness, the covenantal Jesus, if you will, who is—not Adam II, but in the church's language—the Second Adam, shows his fully theomorphic nature in the book of Revelation, where he appears as a just avenger, a messiah of glory rather than of gentleness. Such a reading could restore to the Bible a symmetry that Muslims have not always found in it.[110]

What of the passage in Ephesians? For Muslims, the holy *kitāb* is primarily *Tawrat* (presumably the Pentateuch), *Zabūr* (presumably the Psalms), and *Injīl*: the Gospels. We will probably be more comfortable if we read Paul as a commentator rather than as a scripture writer. Perhaps he himself would not have argued with this.

In any case, the Ephesians passage seems to be the most sustained statement on gender in the whole Bible. Of course, reading Paul is always an exercise in careful cross-referencing, but the other texts attributed to him do not seem to change the intentions of this passage very much. There is Colossians 3:18 ("Wives, be subject to your husbands, as is fitting in the Lord"). And there is 1 Corinthians 11, which criticizes in very stern language women who pray or prophesy with their heads bare, not only because it is immodest in itself but also because the head-covering is a symbol of her husband's authority over her. For those who accept its attribution, 1 Timothy 2:8–15 takes this further still.

The better-known Pauline passage, Galatians 3:28, says: "There is neither Jew nor Greek, there is neither slave nor free, there is no male and female, for you are all one in Christ Jesus." In Muslim jargon this might be taken as abrogating the other verses, but it probably does no such thing. Paul is not suggesting that the man–wife relation is not hierarchical; he is saying that their union in Christ, without abolishing that hierarchy, utterly transcends it. Living in Christ is a true anticipation of the life of the blessed in heaven, where such interhuman power relationships cannot be expected to have meaning. But just as the moral law is not suspended for those who are in communion with the church, so too the natural hierarchy of the genders is affirmed.

Ephesians, in any case, represents the Pauline view that Christians, who believe that the Holy Spirit was operative in the exegesis of the early church, have traditionally taken as decisive. It is no more difficult to substantiate this hierarchical reading in Christian literature than in the writings of Islam on the same issue.

Here, for instance, is St. John Chrysostom, summarizing this passage: "Paul has already laid the foundations of marital love, and has assigned to husband and wife each his proper place: to the husband one of leader and provider, and to the wife one of submission. Therefore as the church is subject to Christ, so let wives also be subject in everything to their husbands, as to God."[111] No less normative is his idea that a Christian family resembles a monastery: like everything else in it, the power of the abbot exists only for the salvation of souls. There are many cases where a monk saves his soul by being in obedience to a bad, incompetent, or foolish abbot, on condition that the obedience was not in sinful things.

For the modern American Orthodox writer Alexei Young,

> Christ has taught us that happiness comes only through self-sacrifice (the husband) and obedience (the wife). . . . We are only pilgrims, preparing for the next world; therefore, how can we fail to rule wisely, lovingly, and givingly, if we are husbands? And, if we are wives, how can we fail to be meek and humbly obedient supports to our husbands? In both of these consists true happiness, for in both is to be found the essence of man and woman, the undoing of the sin of Adam and Eve, and the path—through this world—to the Kingdom of Heaven.[112]

In Western Christianity, the churches fought valiantly to uphold this particular teaching long after other battles had been lost. In his encyclical *Casti connubii* of 1930, Pope Pius XI warned about the "false teachers" who, in the name of "human dignity," would try to persuade wives to abandon the obedience owed to their husbands. "This is not emancipation but a crime," he insists.[113]

This has now, of course, substantially changed. Last year only a few traditionalists protested when Raniero Cantalamessa, the Pope's preacher, expressed his understanding of Ephesians 5:21–32. "The snag" he says, is that Paul "also recommends to women that they be submissive to their husbands, and this—in a society strongly and justly conscious of the equality of the sexes—seems unacceptable." The explanation: "St. Paul is conditioned in part by the mentality of his age."[114]

Even the Pope's preacher is now deconstructing the text. And this, for Muslims yearning for dialogue, indicates an obstacle. When St. John of Damascus argued with Umayyad clerks, or when Gregory Palamas debated with Sufis, issues were focused on the heart of religion: the teaching about God. Today, because many Christians and even more Muslims appear impatient with theology in their desire to change the world, we focus on civic issues. Yet where once there would have been substantial agreement rooted in the assumption that solemn and clear papal teaching was irrevocable, now there is serious discord and a new polemic. On occasion, Muslim–Christian encounters resemble not a meeting of minds fully representative of their conservative majorities or their historic norms but a version of the clash between the Enlightenment and traditional religion. Issues such as capital punishment, freedom of religion, homosexuality, and gender are often discussed by Christians who have consciously or unconsciously internalized an Enlightenment definition of human flowering that emerged, initially, as a reaction against classical Christianity itself and was passionately condemned by the highest church authorities of the day, authorities convinced that they were receiving the guidance of the Holy Spirit. Muslims, by contrast, tend to favor more conservative positions: even though we have no doctrine of papal inerrancy, we are mostly unimpressed by the moral consequences of modernity and of the spiritual and social atomism which it promotes. Hence the periodic sense in our gatherings that we are speaking from different universes, that modernity has made our conversation harder, not easier. The real dialogue partner is the Enlightenment.

There is no short-term answer here. It is probable, but not certain, that Islam will probably cope with the Enlightenment challenge more expeditiously than did Christianity. There are aspects to the Enlightenment to which classical Islam is not necessarily allergic.[115] But I hope, also, that Islamic ethics will remain prophetically critical of an individualism that is at the Enlightenment's heart, and that is socially corrosive. For the present, in our emergency situation, I predict two things. Firstly, that Muslims will tend to be more respectful of traditional Christian social teachings than are many modern Christians. Our dialogue may take itself to include a call to respect the past. And second, that instead of, as Vincent Cornell puts it (see his essay in chapter 2 of this volume), "pushing the envelope of exegesis" to make the scriptures say what we like, we will try to acknowledge the moral and spiritual power of traditional social orders while acknowledging that, as moral and spiritual midgets, we latecomers in religious history simply cannot carry the tougher demands of tradition. If we are honest, we will concede that a serious feminist exegesis of the Bible and the Qur'ān will always find much to criticize. But today we must make do with what we and our parishes can support: a fugitive exegesis, feeble when compared to the glory of traditional social wisdom but the most that our age can bear.

Genesis 2:18–25

18Then the LORD God said, "It is not good that the man should be alone; I will
make him a helper as his partner." 19So out of the ground the LORD God formed
every animal of the field and every bird of the air, and brought them to the man
to see what he would call them; and whatever the man called each living creature, that was its name. 20The man gave names to all cattle, and to the birds of
the air, and to every animal of the field; but for the man there was not found a
helper as his partner. 21So the LORD God caused a deep sleep to fall upon the
man, and he slept; then he took one of his ribs and closed up its place with
flesh. 22And the rib that the LORD God had taken from the man he made into
a woman and brought her to the man. 23Then the man said,
"This at last is bone of my bones
and flesh of my flesh;
this one shall be called Woman,
for out of Man this one was taken."
24Therefore a man leaves his father and his mother and clings to his wife, and
they become one flesh. 25And the man and his wife were both naked, and were
not ashamed.

Ephesians 5:21–33

21Be subject to one another out of reverence for Christ.
22Wives, be subject to your husbands as you are to the Lord. 23For the husband
is the head of the wife just as Christ is the head of the church, the body of

which he is the Savior. [24]Just as the church is subject to Christ, so also wives
ought to be, in everything, to their husbands.
[25]Husbands, love your wives, just as Christ loved the church and gave himself
up for her, [26]in order to make her holy by cleansing her with the washing of
water by the word, [27]so as to present the church to himself in splendour, without
a spot or wrinkle or anything of the kind—yes, so that she may be holy and
without blemish. [28]In the same way, husbands should love their wives as they
do their own bodies. He who loves his wife loves himself. [29]For no one ever
hates his own body, but he nourishes and tenderly cares for it, just as Christ
does for the church, [30]because we are members of his body. [31]"For this reason a
man will leave his father and mother and be joined to his wife, and the two will
become one flesh." [32]This is a great mystery, and I am applying it to Christ and
the church. [33]Each of you, however, should love his wife as himself, and a wife
should respect her husband.

7.2 *al-Aḥzāb* 33:35; *al-Rūm* 30:21; *al-Nisā'* 4:34; *al-Baqara* 2:228

Jane Dammen McAuliffe

Few verses in the Qur'ān have received more contemporary attention than those that address questions of gender difference. Literary representations of gender, whether in secular or religious texts, have become a prominent object of scholarly attention in the last several decades. Questions of gender justice occupy a central place in both domestic and international politics and they are key issues on the agendas of inter faith organizations and their activities. It is also fair to say that few issues are more controversial than those that address gender identity, gender equity, and the intimate relations between men and women.[116]

These four Qur'ānic verses are a mixture of general, ethos-setting statements and particular, prescriptive pronouncements. The more comprehensive verses are presented here first.

al-Aḥzāb 33:35

This verse appears at the mid-point of *Sūrat al-Aḥzāb* ("The Confederates"), a sūra that is dated to the Medinan period and that addresses multiple matters including relations of the Prophet Muḥammad with his family. Mentions of the "occasion of revelation" (*sabab al-nuzūl*) for this verse provide a poignant entrée to its discussion.[117] Each narrative offers an episode in which one or more of Muḥammad's wives asks a question such as "Does the Qur'ān ever mention us women?" or "Why does it speak only of the male believers *(mu'minīn)* and never of the female (*mu'mināt*)?" It is said this verse and *al-Imrān* 3:195 were revealed in response to those questions. The latter passage is also gender explicit when it says, "I do not allow the work of any worker among you, male or female (*min dhakarin aw unthā*), to be lost." A more positive recasting of this sentiment is *al-Tawba* 9:71: "And the believers, men and women, are protecting friends of one another; they enjoin the right and forbid the wrong, and they establish worship and they pay the poor-due, and they obey God and His messenger. As for these, God will have mercy on them. God is mighty, wise."

al-Rūm 30:21

The context for this verse in *Sūrat al-Rūm* is a large group of "sign" passages. Within a longer doxology (verses 17–28), verses 20–25 all begin with the phrase "and of His signs" as they speak to the wonders and the bounties of God's creation. Other than basic glossing, this passage did not attract extended exegetical treatment. Given the creation focus of the larger context, some commentators asked whether "spouses" should signify only Adam and Eve or all human spouses. The first interpretation draws the connection between this verse and *al-A'rāf* 7:189: "It is He who created you from a single person (*min nafsin wāḥidatin*), and He has created from him his wife, so that he might incline toward her."

al-Nisā' 4:34

This verse occurs in the *sūra* titled "The Women" because of the amount of material in this *sūra* that relates to the rights of women and to matters of family life, such as laws of inheritance and limits of marital consanguinity. The occasion of revelation offered for this passage concerns the situation of a woman who appealed to the Prophet after her husband had struck her. Several phrases are of particular interest to the commentators.

- "Men are the managers of the affairs of women" (*al-rijāl qawwāmūna 'alā l-nisā'*).[118] According to Ibn 'Abbās, *qawwāmūn* means those who have the rightful power over the discipline of women.[119]
- "For that God has preferred in bounty one of them over another" (*bi-mā faḍḍala Allāhu ba'ḍahum 'alā ba'ḍi*). Commentators point to the ways in which men surpass women, e.g. by requiring more blood money (*'aql*), by receiving a larger portion of inheritance and booty, by eligibility for the offices of caliph and amir, by being able to initiate divorce, and so on.
- Women are referred to as righteous (*al-ṣāliḥāt*) and obedient (*al-qāniṭāt*). For the commentators, the former refers either to those who act well toward their husbands (*muḥsināt*) or to those who do good works. For the latter, the explanations offered are that they care for their husbands' goods when their husbands are absent or that they safeguard themselves for their husbands alone.[120]
- The female conduct that is termed "rebellious" (*nushūz*) is glossed exegetically as "the wife's being hateful to her husband."[121]
- The most contested section of this verse is the three-part escalation that follows the accusation of "rebellious." "Admonishing" (*fa-'iẓūhunna*) is normally glossed as verbal exhortation. "Banish them to their couches" (*wa-hjurūhunna fi-l-maḍāji'i*) captures more comment but most of it revolves around whether this means husbands not speaking to their wives or refusing to have sex with them. For the final phrase—and phase—of marital discipline, Ibn al-Jawzī advises: "God has permitted you to beat her with a beating that is not intense (*ḍarban ghayr mubarriḥ*)."[122] He also insists that this is, indeed, a mandated sequence, that is, that corporal punishment is a final, not a first, step.[123]

Even given these exegetical restrictions, contemporary Muslim interpreters struggle with this verse. In our era, domestic violence is an important social concern. For my home city of Washington, D.C., alone, police report eleven thousand calls per year about such abuse, and five thousand women request restraining orders against their husbands or partners. A recent survey of contemporary approaches to *al-Nisā'* 4:34 groups various approaches, some of which hold the Qur'ānic text itself harmless while blaming its exegetical amplification, while others are willing to ask whether the text itself is patriarchal, androcentric, and unjust.[124] Scholars as various as Fazlur Rahman, Amina Wadud, and Asma Barlas point to the foundational ethos of the Qur'ān as one of justice and egalitarianism and cite verses such as those just discussed to support this assertion.[125] They then tend to stress the "symbolic" nature of the imperative "beat them" (*waḍribuhunna*) or characterize it as descriptive of seventh-century practice rather than prescriptive for twenty-first-century life.

al-Baqara 2:228

This verse occurs in a longer section of the second *sūra* (verses 226–43) that deals with divorce and the treatment of divorced women and widows. According to the classical exegetes, the occasion for the revelation of this verse was the practice in pre-Islamic society of women claiming to be pregnant to forestall a divorce or of hiding a pregnancy to forestall a reconciliation. Consequently, exegetical attention focuses on several key phrases in this verse.

- *Al-qurū'* (menstrual periods) is discussed via synonyms and etymological explanations. Associated ḥadīth address the problems presented by abnormal menstrual patterns.
- "It is not lawful for them to hide what God has created in their wombs" (*wa-lā yaḥillu lahunna an yaktumna mā khalaqa Allāhu fī arḥāmihinna*) is understood to mean that women are not permitted to conceal either pregnancy or the fact that they are menstruating. It also indicates, however, that women are the authority in such matters. This is, in fact, a key point about this verse.
- "Women have such honorable rights as obligations" *(wa-lahunna mithlu alladhī 'alayhinna bi-l-ma'rūfi*). The term translated as "rights" (*ma'rūf*) is understood as both the necessities of life and the ordinary associations and intimacies of marital life. A ḥadīth from the Prophet that is used as part of the commentary on this verse insists that a husband should feed his wife "when he eats, clothe her when he clothes himself" and it cautions that "he should not strike her on the face or curse her."[126]
- But their men have a degree above them *(wa-lil-rijāl 'alayhinna darajatun)*.[127] Classical commentary on this part of the verse stresses male financial responsibility as the basis of this higher "degree." Al-Zajjāj is cited for the view that both husband and wife take pleasure from each other but that a husband's precedence is a function of the money that he spends on his wife.[128]

Some contemporary interpretations of the phrase "women have such honorable rights as obligations" have read this as a statement of gender equity, that is, as an assertion that women have rights and obligations equivalent to those of men, even as they note functional differences or distinct spheres of activity.[129] The more controversial aspect of this verse, however, is the notion of "degree above." The prevailing exegetical tendency in contemporary treatments has been to limit the scope of this precedence to the situation of divorce itself, to note, for example, that men need not wait three months to remarry and that they have the authority to rescind a divorce. What such contemporary interpretations resist is any reading of "degree above" that offers men unilaterally superior rights over women or predominant ontological status.[130]

al-Aḥzāb 33:35
35Men and women who have surrendered, believing men and believing women, obedient men and obedient women, truthful men and truthful women, enduring men and enduring women, humble men and humble women, men and women who give in charity, men who fast and women who fast, men and women who guard their private parts, men and women who remember God oft—for them God has prepared forgiveness and a mighty wage.

al-Rūm 30:21
21And of His signs is that He created for you, of yourselves, spouses, that you might repose in them, and He has set between you love and mercy. Surely in that are signs for a people who consider.

al-Nisā' 4:34
34Men are the managers of the affairs of women for that God has preferred in bounty one of them over another, and for that they have expended of their property. Righteous women are therefore obedient, guarding the secret for God's guarding. And those you fear may be rebellious admonish; banish them to their couches, and beat them. If they then obey you, look not for any way against them; God is All-high, All-great.

al-Baqara 2:228
228Divorced women shall wait by themselves for three periods; and it is not lawful for them to hide what God has created in their wombs; if they believe in God and the Last Day. In such time their mates have better right to restore them, if they desire to set things right. Women have such honourable rights as obligations, but their men have a degree above them; God is All-mighty, All-wise.

CHAPTER EIGHT

Humanity and Diversity

8.1 Isaiah 2:1–5; Galatians 3:28–29; Revelation 7:9–10

John Prior

These texts on the theme "humanity and ethnic or cultural diversity" speak of fostering international peace in a time of ongoing warfare, intercultural community building without cultural imperialism, and witnessing to hope in the face of apparently impossible odds.

Some 2,700 years ago, in an age of political turmoil, shifting military alliances, and crass exploitation of the poor, the prophet Isaiah of Jerusalem inserted a vision of international justice and peace among his harsh judgment on the ruling elite. Peace among nations, but on whose terms? Seven hundred years later in what is today Turkey, small, scattered congregations of a variety of cultural and religious backgrounds struggled to form communities of faith. Ethnically and culturally diverse, on what basis could they sustain authenticity and preserve their distinct personalities? In the same area almost a half century later, these communities were being harshly harassed by the Roman colonial power. How could they remain faithful and hopeful without locking themselves into an irrelevant ghetto?

Isaiah 2:1–5

The book of Isaiah is the first of the four volumes of major prophetic literature in the Hebrew Bible. The first thirty-nine chapters form a collection of sayings delivered during the last four decades of the eighth century before the Common Era (c. 742–701 BCE). Prophet Isaiah was active in Jerusalem, the capital of Judah, during the reigns of King Ahaz (c. 734–715) and his successor, Hezekiah (c. 715–687). He lived to see the fall of the Northern Kingdom to Assyria in 722 and the supine vassalage of the Southern Kingdom to the same world power, by choice in 732 BCE and, thirty years later (701 BCE), against its will.

The times were turbulent, an age of war and rumors of war, of political expediency and duplicity. The constant warfare resulted from the imperial ambitions of ruling elites whose extravagant living depended upon the toil of the exploited majority. Assyria invaded from the north, and then Egypt from the south. One war led to the next, violence breeding violence. The ruling elite of both the Northern Kingdom of Israel and the Southern Kingdom of Judah sided with one or other of these belligerent forces.

Isaiah interprets the political chaos and coming defeat theologically: God is coming to judge, and Judah and Jerusalem will be thrown into chaos.[131] He accuses the Judean authorities of trusting in temple worship rather than seeking justice and caring for the oppressed. He condemns the rulers' rampant violation of the rights of the common people and their grabbing wealth and political power at any cost.[132]

For a while the prophet had access to both Ahaz and Hezekiah, both of whom he advised to keep out of any political or military alliance. For Isaiah, foreign alliances would be not only politically disastrous, they were also morally dubious and religiously wrong. In the face of imperial ambitions to the south and the north, insignificant Judah should place its complete trust in God alone. Judah should neither fear nor trust armed force, neither their own nor that of others. Promoting a military buildup is contrary to trusting in God alone as savior. With this background in mind, I shall now comment on the text in more detail.

> 2: 1—"The word that Isaiah son of Amoz saw . . ."

This inscription marks a new beginning, the opening, perhaps, of an older collection of prophecies now incorporated into the larger book of Isaiah.

> 2:2—"In days to come . . ."

Not at the end of time, not in another world, but in this world although in the distant future.

> 2:2—"the mountain of the Lord's house shall be established as the highest of the mountains and shall be raised above the hills."

Not so much the physical Mount Zion, which is not even the highest hill in the region, but rather a "theological" mount established and raised by God; a symbol of the meeting place between God's Word and the nations of the world.

The prophet uses mythological and cosmological language and imagery inherited from Canaanite traditions of pre-Davidic Jerusalem. Mountaintops were the homes of war-like gods; Canaanite deities lived on Mount Zaphon while the Lord of Hosts resided on Mount Zion. Mount Zion, the cosmic mountain, is invulnerable, the source of fertility and prosperity, destined to unite the nations of the world. Jerusalem on Mount Zion is hailed as a model and source of prosperity and peace for all the nations of the earth. "The mountain of the Lord's house" is being turned into a place for a school in peacemaking. Given its checkered history and ultimate defeat, Jerusalem and its inviolability has to be understood spiritually and eschatologically rather than geographically or militarily.

> 2:3—"All the nations shall stream to it, many peoples shall come . . ."

All nations of the earth become pilgrims and seek instruction and revelation; the temple represents "instruction" and Jerusalem is where the word of God resides. Thus, this universal vision remains centralized, for the Word of God radiates from Mount Zion. There are two actors, God who instructs, judges, and arbitrates and the nations who come to learn and make peace.

In this passage God no longer instructs through the temple priests but instead instructs directly, and God judges openly rather than via the fallible authorities of Jerusalem. There is no question of the nations bringing taxes or tribute to Jerusalem. The nations join Jerusalem as coequals in God's service; indeed, Isaiah may be including Judah ("the house of Jacob") as one of them.[133] Later passages in the book of Isaiah declare that other nations have to submit to Judah, but not here. Here the gathering of the nations does not imply the victory of one people over the others but universal peace, the victory of all.

> 2:4—"Nations shall beat their swords into ploughshares, and their spears into pruning-hooks."

This is surely one of the most quoted passages of the Hebrew Bible, poetic prophecy at its best, a vision of the nations of the world at peace. Not God but the nations themselves destroy their weapons of mass destruction. Although each village had its blacksmith who could beat weapons into farming implements, swords and spears were expensive; beating swords into ploughshares would entail a significant realignment of national resources. The goal is clear: investment in weapon security must be diverted to providing food security.

The new international empire that the Lord is planning with Jerusalem as its capital will be superior to Assyria. Unlike other passages in the Bible, here the Lord's victories will be achieved not through warfare but as God's initial creation was achieved, by God's Word alone. The coming world empire is a new creation. The "theological" Mount Zion will be the world center of "knowledge" of the Lord. For Isaiah, human history and the future are in God's hands, and God is the arbiter of peace.

It may well be that many of us focus our lives around one or two commanding texts that shape our horizon and guide our commitment. For many Christians one such remarkable text is this poetic vision of Isaiah 2:4: "swords into ploughshares, spears into pruning-hooks." As Daniel Berrigan puts it, "the necessary has been fused with the impossible"—necessary political pragmatism merges with "impossible" humanitarian idealism.[134]

> 2:5—"O house of Jacob, come, let us walk in the light of the Lord!"

The text concludes with a liturgical refrain, perhaps sung by pilgrims entering Jerusalem. The text on international peace under the Word of God both encourages and challenges the pilgrims. Those who already live in the presence of God ("house of Jacob") are invited to take the first steps that all nations will take one day ("in days to come"). The pilgrim people should live and witness as all nations should live and witness, a sign of universal justice and peace. A world without war emerges only when all nations turn to God and walk in God's ways.

The Isaiah text brings together the religious (instruction in God's Word) and the political (universal peace), and seeks a response from both the individual reader (longing for justice and peace) and from political leaders (international policy). The text holds out hope of what is possible to those who struggle for a more just and peaceful order. "Without visions the people perish."[135]

Isaiah dreams of a radical transformation of existing conditions between nations, a putting aside of conflict, a focus on food security. Economic security ("they shall all sit under their own vines and under their own fig trees, and no one shall make them afraid") takes away a basic threat to life, the fundamental cause of fear and suspicion.[136]

However, this text cannot be separated from the rest of the Hebrew Bible; it is but one among a number of alternative visions. The book of Joshua celebrates war and knows God as a conquering warrior, and the prophet Joel goes so far as to reverse Isaiah 2:4, "Beat your ploughshares into swords and your pruning-hooks into spears, let the weakling say, 'I am a warrior.'"[137] This Joel reversal, however, may well be ironic, purporting to record God taunting those intent on fighting, those trapped in ever more brutal cycles of violence.

Over the centuries many have interpreted this vision of international peace as an ideal beyond human history, as God's eschatological future, whereas Isaiah's counsel to kings Ahaz and Hezekiah was construed as purely pragmatic advice because Assyria and Egypt were too powerful to oppose at the time. In this reading, warfare is permissible when the odds are in our favor (just war theory). And yet Isaiah's language is that of a visionary; his poetic words are eminently memorable, graphic words to fire the imagination and spark visionary possibilities, words to evoke the conviction that "another world is possible," a world for which to yearn and strive. The liturgical refrain "O house of Jacob, come, let us walk in the light of the Lord!" invites us to take part in this future both personally and as a community.[138] This vision, then, drives forward on the road to international justice and peace those who are convinced that the future is in God's hands, those who experience God's Word (rule) breaking into daily life, and those who sense God as teacher and mediator, a God who settles disputes among nations.

How does Isaiah's text relate to the theme of ethnic and cultural diversity? Isaiah centers his international vision on Mount Zion and Jerusalem (city of *salām*). There is a world of difference between peaceful intercourse between nations brought about through the hegemony of one nation over the others (imperial power) and peace obtained through a commonly recognized international authority (negotiation by legal equals). In the first case ethnic, cultural and religious differences antagonize and divide; in the second they can mutually enrich and unite. By raising up Mount Zion spiritually, by replacing the temple priests by God's own self, by envisioning Judah on pilgrimage together with the other nations, and by insisting on the primacy of God's Word and leaving aside any notion of submission to human authority whether from the Jerusalem palace or temple, Isaiah has created a vision open to an egalitarian reading. "Nations" come on pilgrimage; therefore they presumably come in their ethnic groups and according to their living cultural traditions.

Jesus of Nazareth went to the temple on Mount Zion and prayed there. However, his attitude toward the temple was closer to the sharp critique of prophets such as Amos and Jeremiah rather than to the enthusiastic prospects of Isaiah. For although Isaiah is often quoted in the Gospels, it is not Isaiah of Jerusalem but rather Isaiah of the exile (586–539 BCE), in particular the songs of the suffering servant.[139] Jesus's strategy is based in Galilee rather than Jerusalem, his "mountain" is not the hill of Zion but the "mountain" of Galilee from where he proclaims God's Word.[140]

Jesus recasts the imagery of Isaiah 2:2–3. He does not picture the nations of the world coming to the temple in Jerusalem to learn to walk in God's ways; instead the Messianic people encounter God's Word wherever they go. The disciples are to "go into all the world and proclaim the good news to the whole creation."[141] The fourth Gospel is quite explicit: "The hour is coming when you will worship the Father neither on this mountain nor in Jerusalem . . . the hour is coming, and is now here, when the true worshipers will worship the Father in spirit and truth. . . . God is spirit, and those who worship him must worship in spirit and truth."[142]

Isaiah 2:1–5 envisages a future when the nations will rally to Jerusalem and listen to God's Word. When in New Testament times the first Christian communities expanded among the nations as a new religious movement rather than remaining a renewal movement within Judaism, the apostle Paul reversed Isaiah's prophecy; no longer will the nations go to Jerusalem, but rather Jerusalem will join the believing nations.[143]

For Isaiah, as for the whole of the Hebrew Bible, our fundamental identity is found in our common humanity, our creation in God's image.[144] In today's globalizing world, embattled local communities tend to seek security in their ethnic and cultural identities rather than in their common humanity. In Southeast Asia ethnic, cultural, and religious identities are closely interwoven. Under repressive regimes where the majority are politically silenced, economically exploited, culturally repressed, and socially disrupted, religious or ethnic identity is often the final bastion of human dignity and identity.

Some multireligious and multicultural countries have developed a political philosophy (for Indonesia it is the *Pancasila*) that underlines all national law. In religious societies this political philosophy is rooted in moral principles drawn from each of their cultural and religious traditions. More secular societies develop a "global ethic" upon which is built international law. Human rights law (personal, social, minorities, and environmental) is gradually creating a legal framework that can nurture a humanitarian culture between nations.

Galatians 3:28–29

The apostle Paul wrote the Letter to the Galatians most likely between 49–56 CE. It is a controversial letter written with great passion, quite possibly because of conflicts within churches recently founded by Paul. These disputes arose when people of different ethnic and religious origins attempted to live together as a single congregation. These congregations were mainly drawn from the lower strata of society but also from the periphery of the local upper classes. Deeply rooted in the popular classes, the Christian movement tried to live out an egalitarian ethic. Social equality, once the privilege of peer groups (among the elite or indeed among groups of slaves), now embraced the socially excluded: foreigners, slaves, and women. This new ethic was articulated primarily in creed, ritual, and community life; eventually, in much later times, it came to impact on the wider society.

Galatia was in central Asia Minor (modern Turkey). It was a heterogeneous society of many cultural and religious backgrounds. Celts settled in Galatia in the third century BCE, followed by various Hellenist and Roman migrations.

Paul himself was born in Tarsus in Cilicia but brought up in Jerusalem.[145] He was comfortably bicultural, with Jewish roots and a Hellenist education; thus, in his person and his ministry, Paul bridges the Aramaic–Hebraic and Greek religious environments. According to Lucien Legrand, Paul, in his letter to the Galatians, integrated both Greek and Hebraic cultural components, which work together in synergy.[146] Hebrew covenantal egalitarianism and Stoic or Cynic disregard of social, and ethnic discriminations coalesce in his argument.

A key concept in Paul's letter is the contrast between freedom and slavery, an apt image in a slave-based imperial economy. He castigates two forms of slavery: giving in to the imperial ideology of the Roman Empire and imprisoning oneself within (defining one's identity by) ethnic or religious laws. We can be enslaved by narrow ethnic values or by imperial global ideology; either would break a multicultural faith community apart.

Minority communities in mixed environments tend to maintain their identity through regular rituals, laws, and conventions. For Paul, however, life is not secured by law or ritual but by what is priceless: God's grace. Paul shows the problems that arise when churches try to preserve their identity through a legalism that crushes life out of a community, destroying its solidarity.[147] He addresses the absurdity of forgoing Christian liberty by favoring exclusionary laws that reduce life to ideologies that enslave.[148] Building loving relationships across racial, social and gender boundaries is the way of Christian liberty.[149]

The members of the multicultural communities in Galatia are all Abraham's children not by ethnic origin or adherence to religious laws and conventions but by faith in God and in God's Word. God's original blessing included Gentile believers.[150] The Galatians, through their baptism, are already Abraham's rightful heirs.[151] The abolition of social distinctions fulfills the promise to Abraham. Subsequent history informs us that this utopian vision has only very gradually permeated harsh social reality.

The issue was, do Christians who are not Jews have to become Jews to become Christians? That is, do they have to be circumcised and so follow the whole of Mosaic law? Paul's response is that Christ's death and resurrection inaugurated a new age in which the old laws and norms no longer apply: "Christ has set us free."[152] For Paul, the Christian community is no longer simply a reform movement within Judaism; it was in the process of becoming a new religious movement with its own separate identity.

3:28—"No longer Jew or Greek, no longer salve or free, no longer male and female."

Paul is probably quoting an early Christian baptismal formula—words, therefore, pronounced over each believer in Galatia at the time of their baptism, words that declared the end of exclusionary boundaries.[153] For Paul, our root identity and human dignity is no longer decided by our ethnic and religious background (Jew or Greek), nor by our legal status (slave or free citizen), nor by our gender (male or female); all who believe have the grace, the status, and the freedom of Abraham's children.

3:28—"No longer Jew or Greek."

"No longer Jew or Greek" sums up the central thrust of the apostle Paul's ministry in both West Asia and Southern Europe. Faith is no longer tied to a particular people but is available to every people that places its faith in God and joins a faith community (*umat/jemaat*). Circumcision, and thus the Mosaic law, protected the religious and cultural separateness of the Jewish people; everyone else was collectively categorized as "the nations" (Gentiles). In Christ, this separateness is abolished because Jews and Gentiles are reconstituted as one new people of God.[154] Consequently, circumcision as a boundary marker separating Jews from Gentiles is no longer significant.[155]

"No longer Jew or Greek" is a creedal statement that maintains the absolute impartiality of God, for "God shows no partiality."[156] This is a theological statement rather than a cultural ideal, a statement that does not demand cultural homogeneity but does reject exclusion. There is no indication that Paul discouraged Jewish Christians from remaining Jews or continuing to be part of their local synagogue. Just as Greek Christians do not have to become Jews to be Christian, so Jews can similarly maintain their Jewish identity. "No longer Jew or Greek" does not annihilate cultural distinctiveness but rather allows and affirms the continued existence of cultural pluralism within the faith community. It does, however, deny ultimate significance to ethnic distinctions.

In the parallel passage from Colossians, the terms "barbarian" and "Scythian" are added while "male and female" are omitted: "There is no longer Greek and Jew, circumcised and uncircumcised, barbarian, Scythian, slave and free; but Christ is all and in all!"[157] "Barbarian" and "Scythian" represent stigmatized groups. Thus, old designations referring to the cultural inferiority or superiority of nations are no longer relevant. This baptismal creed helped give cohesion to fragile multiethnic communities in Galatia, Corinth, and Colossae.

3:28—"No longer slave or free."

In the faith community, social distinctions are secondary. In baptism everyone, whatever their social position, becomes a child of God and is therefore related to the others as a brother or sister. Among siblings there are no masters or slaves, there is no rigid social hierarchy because brotherly and sisterly attitudes break through social class and power distinctions, at least within the faith community.[158] Christians are to form an alternative community that lives by an "ethic of compassion" that softened legal distinctions within the community and eventually in the wider society. Paul never drew this creedal statement to its logical conclusion—the abolition of slavery—possibly because he thought the last times were at hand. In Paul's day, a movement that turned slaves rebellious would have been crushed. It took around eighteen hundred years before "no longer slave or free" became not only a matter of interpersonal relationships within the believing community but also a statement of political and legal rights and duties for everyone as co-citizens. All the same, the apostolic movement gave slaves greater scope within their faith communities within a social order where life without slaves was inconceivable.

3:28—"No longer male and female."

The term "male and female" echoes the book of Genesis: "male and female God created them."[159] If this distinction no longer counts, then a new creation has taken place. Gender roles and distinctions are no longer decisive, initially within the Christian community (before the gender norms of the wider society reasserted themselves), and centuries later in wider society.

The baptismal formula quoted by Paul does not assert that there are no longer men and women, but that male-centered gender relations in the wider patriarchal society are no longer normative for Christians who are to form a contrast community with a rough equality between the sexes. The male is no longer normative, as perhaps he might tend to be where male circumcision is a religious marker. In principle, gender identity is no longer a ground for status, exclusion, privilege, or power.

In Paul's letters and other apostolic writings, all distinctions between men and women were not disregarded within the faith community. This baptismal formula helped shape the "symbolic universe" of the community. In turn, the symbols of faith enacted in worship impacted upon social interrelationships and the structures of the community itself.

Perhaps slaves and women took the baptismal creed into everyday social life and so raised troubling questions. This is perhaps the background to post-Pauline teaching that reasserts the old Aristotelian rule: "Wives, be subject to your husbands, as is fitting in the Lord. . . . Slaves, obey in everything those who are your earthly masters."[160] The Christian movement was not yet ready to live out its creed fully.

In his ministry, Paul does not focus on gender justice; the phrase "no longer male and female" is not only missing from the parallel formula in Corinthians, it is also not decisive in his theological argument.[161] Paul worked tirelessly breaking down barriers between Jew and Gentile; this parallel statement has had to wait almost two thousand years before it became a vital issue, first in secular society and then in the church. Nonetheless, Paul's emphasis on mutuality in marital sexual relations and his acknowledgement of prophetic women have been steadily undermining male supremacy within most churches.

3:28—"For you are all one in Christ Jesus."

Here is the decisive argument: the most salient feature in the identity of the Galatians is their unity in Christ. Our ethnic, cultural, and social identity has value insofar as it is rooted in faith; that is, we have become a new creation incorporated into a new body through baptism (dying and rising again) and eucharist (table fellowship). Ritual confronts the social group with its underlying ethos, values, and worldview through powerful, imaginative language and so reinforces them in social life.[162] In ritual, communities experience *communitas*, where social distinctions are temporarily collapsed or inverted.[163] In ritual enactment, hierarchical distinctions are eliminated; in worship and in table fellowship, all have equal dignity. "For neither circumcision nor uncircumcision is anything; but a new creation is everything!"[164] In principle these impartial statements qualify social differences. This egalitarian ethos was nurtured through regular ritual, weekly meals together, mutual help in daily life, mutual concern in sickness and death, care for children and the old, mutual assistance in travel and business, in short through a practical love, a "solidarity of compassion." Unity in Christ transforms social relationships; no cultural marker must diminish this primary identity.

Nothing is absolute, not even one's cultural, legal, or gender identity. The only ultimate is the new creation. Nonetheless, ethnic distinctions are not to be disregarded; the ideal is not a monochrome, monocultural community but rather pluralism without pressure to conform. The grace of God is made visible precisely in the reconciliation of Jews, Gentiles, barbarians, and Scythians. Reconciliation consists not in eliminating but in overcoming discrepancies. The goal is the eradication of hostility that springs from difference.

Consequently, Christians should not engage in "cultural imperialism" and try to impose one set of cultural norms, rituals, and traditions on another people, as some Jewish Christians in Galatia insisted on the circumcision of Gentile Christians. Paul passionately rejects this kind of ethnic or religious "identity politics." Experience shows that where ethnic markers do not generally coincide with religious boundaries, multicultural and multireligious societies help to prevent our faith from enhancing narrow class, ethnic, or national ambitions. But even where ethnic and religious boundaries coincide, as long as faith identity is primary, then ethnic, social, and gender distinctions will be subservient to our faith commitment. Local ethnic, social, and gender divisions should never decide the shape of the faith community. Christ's death frees us from such ethnic, social, economic, and gender captivity.[165]

In Paul's letters a certain ambiguity remains: if in Christ there is no longer male nor female, what roles should women have in the faith community, and how should Philemon treat his slave Onesimus?[166] In apostolic times, social and gender distinctions are maintained and yet softened by an ethic of compassion. In creedal statements, ritual enactment, and community living, class distinctions and hierarchies no longer matter. We are no longer to distinguish Jews from non-Jews, no longer to discriminate between those called slaves from those called free, and no longer to make hierarchy according to gender. Paul is not talking about a change of masters in a continuing structure of domination; he is talking about restructuring the relations of domination for you "have clothed yourselves with Christ."[167]

"For all of you are one in Christ Jesus." Composed of both Jew and Greek, the communities of Galatia were, in an important way, already distinct from either Jew or

Greek, for they did not meet in the local synagogue and were developing their own ethic, so they were already becoming a distinct religious movement in their own right.

The law that seems to determine life today is the so-called (imperial, global) free market, which is not free at all. In a commercialized world, everything and everyone is treated as a commodity, is defined by its price. 'The law of the market' is treated like a "natural law," a normal way of behaving, as though there is no alternative. The global market forces non-equals to compete; it suppresses the weak and enslaves those who lose. As such, the law of the market brings death, not life. For Paul what is truly free comes from God: divine grace, the divine Spirit, faith, absolute trust in God, rather than obedience to the law.

Revelation 7:9–10

Unique among the twenty-seven books of the apostolic scriptures, the final book in the Christian Bible is written in an apocalyptic idiom, a coded language of allegory and myth, of dreams and visions. Traditionally this book has been ascribed to John the Divine, a mystic who lived his last days on the isle of Patmos in Greece. By their vivid imagery and apparent incongruity, John's metaphors provoke the reader to look at the world with new eyes. Much of the imagery is violent, as is the language of many oppressed peoples; victims of violence rarely find such images offensive.

Apocalyptic speech seeks to "reveal" the deeper dimensions of our existence into which is breaking "the salvation and the power and the kingdom of our God and the authority of his Messiah."[168] Apocalyptic code is the choice of harassed minorities suppressed by imperial tyrants, who alone wish to determine truth in the public sphere. Born in the vivid imagination of John the Divine, the coded speech allows a subversive minority to opt out of the empire's public truth, to maintain its integrity, to recall God's Word and stubbornly sustain a flicker of hope: a word of optimism for an embattled minority, encouragement to the weak and vulnerable, a challenge to the rich and powerful. The images stimulate rather than prescribe while exciting the imagination. Its meaning is revealed to those who remain faithful.

The book of Revelation was written in tumultuous times when the empire of Rome ("the Beast") seemed to have history under its heel, when the ideal human was the male warrior, and the ideal task was "service" of the divine emperor. In such times, the Word of God appeared to have as much impact as dust scattered by the wind. The survival of the faithful few appeared to demand both silence and amnesia. What price a sustaining witness to hope?

The book was crafted to encourage small faith communities scattered throughout Asia Minor (roughly modern Turkey) who were being harassed and martyred during the final decade of the first century CE. The embattled minorities are urged to resist "the beast of Babylon," a symbol of oppressive social, political, and religious power. God's people are encouraged to create contrast communities over against the culture of the Roman Empire. Worship of the Beast is a cult of power, the decadent culture of an autocratic regime. The Beast of absolute political power replaces God (idolatry) and enslaves humans. The crime of "Babylon" is to persecute those who reject unlimited political power and who unmask the ideological propaganda that ensnares those not vigilant enough to see through it.

Apocalyptic discourse of picture and symbol refuses to accept that the dominant powers are the ultimate point of reference, and asks the reader to participate in another way of speaking about God and the world. Among grassroots communities in the Third World, the book of Revelation both offers hope and stimulates resistance, motivating Christians in their struggle for a more justly liberating world. Today images used in Revelation to castigate the oppressive Roman Empire at the end of the first century have been applied to the repressive economic, political, and cultural neocolonialism of globalization. Such communal reading at the grass roots helps to maintain hope that another world is possible.

The book contains two cycles of visions: 1:10b–11:19 and 12:1–22:5. The first cycle has three sections, namely the seven messages, the scroll with seven seals, and the seven trumpets (1:10b–3:22; 4:1–8:5; and 8:2–11:19, respectively). The text under consideration here has been inserted among the opening of the seven seals, immediately before the breaking of the last. The first four speak of war, dissension, famine, and pestilence; suffering is the lot of the faithful, neither as punishment nor judgment but as social injustice. Our text is a hymn of hope inserted in the midst of this world in turmoil. It proclaims a vision of political utopia: all nations unite in praising God. The hymn will be clarified by John in the verses that immediately follow (7:13–17).

> 7:9—"A great multitude that no one could count, from every nation, from all tribes and peoples and languages."

The hymn welcomes every ethnic and national grouping in a single, inclusive act of adoration that in its variety ("from all tribes and peoples and languages") manifests a remarkable range of praise. "From every nation" denotes both variety and universality; each joins in, without impediments, in the universal chorus of praise. Although earlier 144,000 children of Israel are marked out, here ethnic distinctions no longer decide.[169] This vision prefigures the future symphony of Iranians and Iraqis; Palestinians and Israelis; Malaysians, Singaporeans, and Indonesians; North Americans and British; and every other nation. In this vision, no one group is set over against another; God is sovereign over the history of the nations.

Unlike earlier in this chapter, here the great multitude does not bear a seal and hence is beyond calculation.[170] Their number "that no one could count" goes beyond all numerical limits and so breaks through all ethnic and cultural boundaries, indeed, bursts through the restrictions of organized religion, beyond the visible limits of God's people on earth.[171] The universal multitude, whatever their ethnic, cultural, or religious background, could include all those who have suffered the violence of the "great ordeal" of the ongoing oppression of the empire; the economic, political, social, cultural, and religious oppression endured by those not willing to be integrated into the *imperium* and take part in its oppressive and idolatrous structures; and those who willingly suffer the effects of war, hunger, pestilence, and persecution.[172] Identified with the Lamb, they are both dignified and defiant.

7:9—"robed in white with palm branches in their hands."

White is the color of the ceremonial dress of martyrs, those not stained with the idolatry of the empire, and palm branches are a token of the victory of the weak over the strong, of the slaughtered Lamb over the Beast. Such a victory demands the "revaluation of all values."

7:10—"Salvation belongs to our God."

Sōtēria (salvation) means total well-being. The official source of welfare, peace, and salvation, according to the political ideology of the time, was the Roman emperor. However, those who stand before the throne acknowledge not the emperor but God and the Lamb (Christ) as the ultimate source of well-being, security, and salvation. In this understanding, salvation involves radical transformation, bringing to birth a new world of justice and equality.

Salvation entails the abolition of all dehumanization and the restoration of the fullness of human well-being. This vision responds to the outcry of those seeking justice for the destruction of their lives. The central meaning of history lies not with the apparent success of empires imposing their might, wealth, and ideology on the nations of the world but in "Jesus Christ the faithful witness, the firstborn of the dead, and the ruler of the kings of the earth."[173]

For the author of Revelation, "the earth" is in the control of the idolatrous and the oppressors, while "heaven" is the transcendent world of God within history; it is the world of the holy ones, of those who do not oppress or idolize; it is the world carved out by communities of hope. "Heaven," then, is at the heart of human experience and is already here in an anticipatory and fragmentary way in fragments that encourage human action in the present. "Heaven" is not fully possible without a radical changing of the present order.

7:14—"Having washed their robes in the blood of the Lamb."

The multitude from every nation identifies with "the Lamb," Jesus the Nazarene, who was also a victim of injustice and condemned to death.[174] Jesus continues to suffer among those who, like him, are the victims of the injustices of our world. There is no guarantee of security and well-being for God's people on earth. "Washed . . . in the blood of the Lamb" could allude to the readers' present experience of suffering and violence, to the faithful who do not conform to the oppressive aspects of the dominant culture but doggedly hold on to a distinct way of life. The faithful martyrs who endure are singing a liturgy of praise in heaven. The faithful themselves wash their robes in the blood of the Lamb, that is, they are active participants in "God's project."

This text of Revelation has some clear implications for a Christian attitude toward ethnic and cultural diversity. Those who refuse to rely on the means deemed sufficient for assuring national survival—that is of economic, political, and military power—shall endure to the end. A person of faith identifies not first with the dominant culture or the nation but with God's people.

God's faithful, wherever they may be, prefigure the coming unity of humankind. Nations must be liberated from their own entrapments and brought into the global symphony praising God. Meanwhile, the faithful of each nation form an alternative community with their own reading of history. The well-known churches of Sardis and Laodicea had given in to the ethos, values, and principles of the empire while the least affluent churches of Smyrna and Philadelphia remained faithful.[175]

The vision of 7:9–12 is completely inclusive; it is an image of everyone anywhere, each with their own language, culture, and identity—those who resist the Beast, who refuse to compromise, and who are following the Lamb.

Four Concluding Questions

On Isaiah 2: Daniel Berrigan describes the vision of forging swords into ploughshares and spears into pruning hooks as the fusing of "the necessary with the impossible." Do we find in this passage an image of utopia, a pragmatic political project, or the fusing of the two? What would such a fusion of the idealistic and the necessary say about ethnic or cultural diversity today?

On Galatians 3: There were a number of options open to Paul as he sought to end disputes among the multiethnic and multicultural communities of Galatia. He could, for instance, have demarcated clear boundaries and insisted upon strong leadership. In fact, Paul deemed it sufficient to propose a transparently egalitarian faith that softened ethnic, social, and gender distinctions so that they no longer discriminate nor divide. Paul apparently left any implications regarding ethnic or cultural plurality for the Galatians to work out for themselves. Would such an approach make sense today?

On Revelation 7: John the Divine encouraged small, scattered faith communities to live as a creative minority over against the hegemonic military culture of the Roman Empire. As a contrast culture, they are urged to witness to other values and to another ethos. A distinct minority, they are to avoid becoming fanatic or exclusive by openly engaging with the world around them. What does this "creative minority" option say to us in a world where global hegemonic power is being opposed by extremist networks, each encapsulated within its individual ethnic, cultural, or religious self?

On all three texts: Each of these has been explained in an all-inclusive manner. Many texts in the Hebrew and Christian scriptures cannot be elucidated so all-embracingly. How should we engage discordant voices in the Bible? Do we simply focus on texts that confirm our contemporary agenda? Or are we discovering that such ecumenical texts are a key to reinterpreting the entire scriptures?

Isaiah 2:1–5
[1]The word that Isaiah son of Amoz saw concerning Judah and Jerusalem.
[2]In days to come
the mountain of the Lord's house
shall be established as the highest of the mountains,
and shall be raised above the hills;
all the nations shall stream to it.
[3]Many peoples shall come and say,
"Come, let us go up to the mountain of the Lord,
to the house of the God of Jacob;
that he may teach us his ways
and that we may walk in his paths."
For out of Zion shall go forth instruction,
and the word of the Lord from Jerusalem.
[4]He shall judge between the nations,
and shall arbitrate for many peoples;
they shall beat their swords into ploughshares,
and their spears into pruning-hooks;
nation shall not lift up sword against nation,
neither shall they learn war any more.
[5]O house of Jacob,
come, let us walk
in the light of the Lord!

Galatians 3:28–29
[28]There is no longer Jew or Greek, there is no longer slave or free, there is no
longer male and female; for all of you are one in Christ Jesus. [29]And if you
belong to Christ, then you are Abraham's offspring, heirs according to the
promise.

Revelation 7:9–10
[9]After this I looked, and there was a great multitude that no one could count,
from every nation, from all tribes and peoples and languages, standing before
the throne and before the Lamb, robed in white, with palm branches in their
hands. [10]They cried out in a loud voice, saying, "Salvation belongs to our God
who is seated on the throne, and to the Lamb!"

8.2 *Hūd* 11:118; *al-Rūm* 30:20–22; *al-Fāṭir* 35:27–28; *al-Ḥujurāt* 49:13

Osman Bakar

All of the Qur'ānic texts selected for discussion in this section shed light in various ways on the Qur'ānic perspective on diversity within the human race. But these texts are not the only ones dealing with this theme. Another text worth quoting by virtue of its clarity in stating the Qur'ānic position on human diversity is the following: "For each of you We have appointed a Law and a way of life. And had God so willed He would surely have made you one single community; but (His Plan) is to test you in what He had given you."[176]

Taken together, these texts suggest that this diversity is given by God and is to be embraced as a sign of the divine wisdom and as a blessing for human beings. The Qur'ānic perspective is that the ethnic and cultural diversity of humankind should not serve as a basis for divisive claims to superiority between different human groups but rather should provide opportunities for mutual knowledge and cooperation.

Diversity as treated in the selected texts pertains to both the natural world and the human world. Diversity in the natural world of minerals, plants, and animals—now popularly known as biodiversity—is entirely the product of natural forces and processes that are beyond human choice and determination. While the coming into being of this biodiversity is not determined by human beings, its future survival can be adversely affected by destructive human acts. The great tragedy in our own times is that biodiversity is under such increasing threat from human greed that many living species are on the brink of extinction, not to mention those that are already obliterated from the face of the earth as a result of unwise and excessive development.

Diversity in the human world is somewhat different. It is partly the product of natural forces and processes, and partly the product of human cultural development. This means that human diversity has two dimensions. One is the natural dimension, which refers to the physical and biological traits and characteristics of human beings such as skin color and gender; the other is the cultural dimension, which refers to such things as language and belief system or religion.

In what follows I note particularly relevant features of the different texts in turn.

Hūd 11:118

The wording of this verse is partly paralleled in other verses of the Qur'ān, all of which contain the phrase "*umma wāḥida*" (one nation, people, or community).[177] The interesting exegetical questions raised by this range of texts would take us beyond our present purposes; for now I simply note that in this verse (in contrast to the other passages considered below) differences between human beings are presented in a negative light.

The protracted differences or disagreements mentioned here (*wa lā yazālūna mukhtalifīna*) suggest religious disputation and division (cf. *akhtulifa*, shortly before this verse, referring to disputes over the revelation given to Moses[178]). According to the following verse, it is only those on whom God has mercy who are delivered from this ceaseless disputation.[179]

In contrast to this kind of human disunity apparently bound up with tensions between belief and unbelief, the other Qur'ānic passages considered here focus on positive examples of diversity at the level of ethnic and cultural diversity.

al-Rūm 30:20–22

This passage is about the natural dimension (physical and biological) of human diversity, which is to serve as a substratum or vehicle of cultural diversity. It is part of a longer sequence of verses (20–25) all beginning with "And of his signs" (*wa min āyātihi*), listing various manifestations in the created order of God's mercy and power, which should be recognized and acknowledged by human beings. Verse 20 refers to the sign of the creation of human beings from dust and their dispersion through the world. Verse 21 mentions the creation of human beings as male and female and refers to blessings associated with this.[180] Our chief interest is in verse 22.[181] Most striking here is the juxtaposition of "the creation of the heavens and the earth" with the diversity of human "tongues and hues" or, updating the translation, languages and skin colors. Here we have a significant reference to human diversity both in ethnic and in cultural terms, for language is a central marker of cultural identity. It is hard to imagine how the Qur'ān could accord greater dignity to these aspects of human diversity than to mention them in the same breath as the creation of the heavens and the earth and to say of all these together that they are signs of God. So we are encouraged to consider the cultural diversity of the human race as being as "natural" and as good as all the other signs of God in the heavens and the earth. As well as affirming that ethnic and cultural diversity are given by God, this passage is also making the point that such diversity does not exist just for its own sake but as a "sign" of the mercy, wisdom, and power of God. The diverse phenomena within God's creation thus point back to the unity from which they all derive. This interplay between affirmation of both plurality in the created order and the underlying reality of *tawḥīd* is a central feature of the Qur'ānic *Weltanschauung*.

al-Fāṭir 35:27–28

These two verses again set human diversity in the context of the wider created order. Here, however, there are slight differences from the last passage considered. In this case the focus is just on ethnic diversity or, more precisely, its natural dimension, which is again mentioned in terms of color. The distinctive way in which this passage suggests the God-given nature of ethnic diversity is to link it with the rich range of colors lavished on other parts of God's creation. Just as fruits and animals occur in various colors, and as a range of colors are to be seen in natural phenomena such as mountains, so also there is a diversity of colors in human beings. It follows that just as we appreciate the biodiversity evident throughout the earth, so also we should gratefully accept the ethnic differences among human beings. The second half of verse 28 suggests that to do so is to demonstrate piety (or fear of God) and the resulting true knowledge.

al-Ḥujurāt 49:13

In his essay in this volume, Vincent Cornell comments at some length on this much-cited verse. He points out that there are questions to be asked about the frequent use made of it in discussions of Islam and religious pluralism, and he alerts us to the danger of assuming too easy an equivalence between what the Qur'ān here calls "races" (*shu'ūb*) and "tribes" (*qabā'il*) and contemporary understandings of "nations," "ethnicities," "cultures," and so on. He also refers to the traditional explanation of the occasion of the revelation (*sabab al-nuzūl*) of this verse. It is reported that when Bilal, a black African, gave the call to prayer at Mecca, some newly converted Arabs were surprised at this.

In response to such a negative and arrogant attitude toward a person of a supposedly inferior race, the Qur'ān first affirms the common origin of all human beings and the positive place of ethnic difference (as well as sexual difference) in God's purposes. The branching out of the human family tree into numerous tribal and ethnic branches is a natural process that is in accordance with the divine cosmic plan. The aim of this diversity is that people should "know one another," suggesting respectful mutual understanding and recognition. Second, this verse insists that, in God's sight, what is of the greatest significance and value in human beings is not their race but the piety, or fear of God (*taqwā*), that they demonstrate. Thus the Qur'ān both provides a basis for valuing ethnic difference, as part of the richly diverse reality created by God, and relativizes ethnic difference by pointing to the religious virtue of *taqwā* as being ultimately more important. Once again, affirmation of the diversity within God's creation leads us back to *tawḥīd*, for the person who displays true *taqwā* is the one whose life is truly oriented to the divine unity from which all things come.

Hūd 11:118

118Had thy Lord willed, He would have made mankind one nation; but they continue in their differences.

al-Rūm 30:20–22

20And of His signs is that He created you of dust; then lo, you are mortals, all scattered abroad.

21And of His signs is that He created for you, of yourselves, spouses, that you might repose in them, and He has set between you love and mercy. Surely in that are signs for a people who consider.

22 And of His signs is the creation of the heavens and earth and the variety of your tongues and hues. Surely in that are signs for all living beings.

al-Fāṭir 35:27–28

27 Hast thou not seen how that God sends down out of heaven water, and therewith We bring forth fruits of diverse hues? And in the mountains are streaks
white and red, of diverse hues, and pitchy black;
28 men too, and beasts and
cattle—diverse are their hues. Even so only those of His servants fear God who have knowledge; surely God is All-mighty, All-forgiving.

al-Ḥujurāt 49:13

13 O mankind, We have created you male and female, and appointed you races and tribes, that you may know one another. Surely the noblest among you in the sight of God is the most godfearing of you. God is All-knowing, All-aware.

CHAPTER NINE

Humanity and the Environment

9.1 Jeremiah 5:20–25; 18:13–17; Romans 8:18–23

Michael Northcott

Jeremiah 5 suggests a continuing confrontation between the chaotic powers of the primordial earth and the continuing ordering power of God. It also suggests a certain precariousness in the orders of creation. Creation is sustained in its beneficence by right relations between God and creatures, especially humans. It is threatened by abandonment of right relations, by injustice and idolatry.

This relational conception of humans and other creatures is covenantal in the books of Jeremiah and Genesis. Jeremiah uses the Hebrew word for covenant to describe God's ordering of night and day, and for God's blessing of the line of David and the Levites: "If you could annul my covenant of the day and my covenant of the night, so that daytime and night would not come at their due times, then might my covenant with David my servant be annulled."[182]

The ordering of time and seasons, of oceans and rivers, of deserts and fertile plains, all belong to the matter of the covenant and to the human mandate of governance. The cosmic nature of covenant involves the duty to preserve the creation from chaos by practicing cosmic justice and the other virtues. When humans respect these covenantal relations of justice, then God will not again abandon the creation to destruction and flood as God did in the days of Noah: "While the earth lasts seedtime and harvest, cold and heat, summer and winter, day and night, shall never cease."[183]

The cosmic covenant links the orders of creation with the worship and governance of the people of God. Thus, true worship sustains the order of creation whereas idolatry threatens the return of chaos. This relation between human social order and cosmic order is substantiated in the ritual texts in the Hebrew Bible, particularly the royal psalms.[184]

True worship is performative and exemplary, and it sustains respect for created order. This is why the first commandment given to Moses is that the people of God are not to turn creatures into idols but to worship the true God. When the Creator is worshipped rightly, the creation is known and experienced as divine benison and is not used idolatrously or instrumentally. From true worship issue both moral order in human life and peace in creation. Analogously idolatry not only sustains injustice in divine and human relations but it produces disharmony and disorder in the land. Hence Jeremiah clearly links ecological devastation and the abandonment of the worship and commands of the Lord. Because the people of Israel had turned from the Lord to worship other gods, their land, its mountains and streams, animals and crops, had been laid waste, polluted, and destroyed.[185]

The prophetic reading of ecological breakdown recalls a conflict between the grand projects and large cities and large-scale farms of the late Hebrew monarchy. The pride of idolatrous kings denuded the valleys of great cedars for their massive building projects, and the wealthy grew rich while the poor went hungry. The land suffers and shares in the alienation that human corruption produces. The ecological devastation of the land is the consequence of the human rebellion against God and of the idolatry of other creatures. The prophet Jeremiah finds biological, moral, and spiritual significance in created order, and he identifies the pivotal moral responsibility of humans to tend and conserve the stability of the land and the cosmos and the welfare of creatures.

Moral responsibility of all life, including human life, is identified with the calling of all life forms to respond to God in praise and worship. This response of gratitude is a fundamental feature of creaturely being that is shared by all the creatures of the earth, humans and animals, landscapes, seas and mountains, earth, wind, fire, and rain. The psalmist charges all things with the first moral duty of the creation, to worship and praise the Creator, thereby establishing in as radical a fashion as any deep ecologist the moral agency of animals, and of nonsentient life forms and habitats. This moral responsibility to worship the Lord and reflect his glory may be said to be inherent in the beauty, fecundity, and order of the natural world. This response of worship and gratitude on the part of humans involves the active taking of initiatives in relation to the created order and to the Creator. Thus Adam and Eve are called upon not merely to be in the garden but to steward the earth and to replenish it, and not merely to observe the animals but to name them.

Jeremiah argued that the peoples of Israel and Judah had been exiled because they failed to worship the Lord, and to respect his justice in relation to the land and their neighbors. According to Isaiah, the restoration of the land will involve the recovery by every household of the means to livelihood and mutual sufficiency, for God's justice confers on every household the means to meet the basic needs of life and to provide for the flourishing of children and for security in old age.[186]

The restoration of true worship, and of justice in human society, also contributes to the restoration of nature as the peaceable kingdom of shalom and ecological harmony. This is why Saint Paul suggests in Romans that humans play a role in frustrating the *telos* of the cosmos to freely worship God, and that the salvation of humans in Christ involves the restoration of freedom to all creatures in their relation to God.[187]

In this way the original shalom of the first creation, which was despoiled by human rebellion, is restored. From the hope of shalom flow the themes of cosmic restoration and redemption as well as the ideals of the law tradition concerning the treatment of domestic and wild animals, the tending of the land, the care of the poor and widows, and restraints on economic power and oppression by which Israel in exile was to aspire to the goodness and grace of the original creation, and in response to which Yahweh would restore the fortunes of Israel and the fertility of the land. Hence Isaiah envisages a recovery of the original peace between all creatures so that

> The wolf and the lamb shall feed together
> The lion shall eat straw like the ox,
> But the serpent—its food shall be dust.
> They shall not hurt or destroy
> On all my holy mountain says the Lord.[188]

In the new creation described in the book of Revelation, creation is restored in such a way that the forces of chaos—in particular the sea and the ships that use the sea to trade and to enslave the land and its creatures—are finally bound, and the orientation of creation to the worship and vision of God is realized by all creatures.[189]

Jeremiah 5:20–25
20Declare this in the house of Jacob,
proclaim it in Judah:
21Hear this, O foolish and senseless people,
who have eyes, but do not see,
who have ears, but do not hear.
22Do you not fear me? says the Lord;
Do you not tremble before me?
I placed the sand as a boundary for the sea,
a perpetual barrier that it cannot pass;
though the waves toss, they cannot prevail,
though they roar, they cannot pass over it.
23But this people has a stubborn and rebellious heart;
they have turned aside and gone away.
24They do not say in their hearts,
"Let us fear the Lord our God,
who gives the rain in its season,
the autumn rain and the spring rain,
and keeps for us
the weeks appointed for the harvest."
25Your iniquities have turned these away,
and your sins have deprived you of good.

Jeremiah 18:13–17
13Therefore, thus says the Lord:
Ask among the nations:
Who has heard the like of this?
The virgin Israel has done
a most horrible thing.
14Does the snow of Lebanon leave
the crags of Sirion?

Do the mountain waters run dry,
the cold flowing streams?
15But my people have forgotten me,
they burn offerings to a delusion;
they have stumbled in their ways,
in the ancient roads,
and have gone into bypaths,
not the highway,
16making their land a horror,
a thing to be hissed at forever.
All who pass by it are horrified
and shake their heads.
17Like the wind from the east,
I will scatter them before the enemy.
I will show them my back, not my face,
on the day of their calamity.

Romans 8:18–23

18I consider that the sufferings of this present time are not worth comparing
with the glory about to be revealed to us. 19For the creation waits with eager
longing for the revealing of the children of God; 20for the creation was subjected
to futility, not of its own will but by the will of the one who subjected it, in
hope 21that the creation itself will be set free from its bondage to decay and will
obtain the freedom of the glory of the children of God. 22We know that the
whole creation has been groaning in labor pains until now; 23and not only the
creation, but we ourselves, who have the first fruits of the Spirit, groan inwardly
while we wait for adoption, the redemption of our bodies.

9.2 *al-An'ām* 6:141–42; 6:38; *al-Rūm* 30:41, *al-Naḥl* 16:112

Mohamed Yunus Yasin

"Gardens of diversity": *al-An'ām* 6:141–42

Ecology (from the word meaning "household" in Greek) is the study of the relationships of plants and animals to their physical (e.g., heat, light, water, atmosphere) and biological environment, forming a complex interlocking chain or web crucial for life on the planet. Thus, the environment is not merely one component but complex interlocking relationships between all components. For example, sugar is sweet, yet its components—carbon, hydrogen, and oxygen atoms—are tasteless. As another analogy, coal is made of carbon, and water is made of hydrogen and oxygen, yet coal and water together do not produce sugar. Thus, the environment that we sense with our five senses is a complex web of combinations of all its components and their set of multifaceted relationships.

Modern humans are destroying these systems by breaking the linkages that make up this web; in modern times, the frequency of these "breaks" in the web is alarming. The breaking and mending of these complex links is a natural system of disintegration and regeneration happening in perfect balance. However, this balance is being lost due to our own greed, hastened by modern innovations in science and technology: the breaks in the web are happening faster than nature's ability to mend them. The solution to this problem would require a complete shift in the paradigm of our modern perception and translation of reality and the sciences.

Traditional sciences used to revolve around the life sciences, for life is the central motive in the story of Creation. Modern sciences, conversely, revolve around physics and have relegated life sciences to be a substudy of physics. Descartes maintained that all philosophy was like a tree, with metaphysics the roots, physics the trunk, and all other sciences the branches. While traditional life sciences are more intuitive, holistic, and cyclical, and they emphasize cooperation, physical sciences are more rational, reductionist, and linear, and they emphasize dominion and control. Furthermore, traditional life sciences focus more on interactions, patterns, and relations between components that make up the whole: the sum is often more than, and different from, the parts. Physical sciences, conversely, focus on the components as a means to understand the whole. However, with the discovery of DNA, life sciences have become more like physical sciences in their method of inquiry. This method has thus seeped into all forms of knowledge in one way or the other. Although reductionist thinking is useful for some purposes, it is not suitable for thinking of our relationship with the environment because the environment is a living, self-generating system.

"Nations like unto yourself": *al-An'ām* 6:38

The study of ecology focuses mostly on biodiversity, which can be defined as the variation of life forms within a given natural system. The term "diversity" includes the totality of genes, species, and ecosystems of a region, embracing genetic diversity (genes within a species), species diversity (diversity among species), and ecosystem diversity (diversity within the ecosystem). Each can be viewed as a nation unto itself, surviving, self-regulating, and living with each other.

Because Islam recognizes that each species "is of its own nation," if each nation has a right to exist, do not the many nations of the animals and plants have a right to existence beside us? Do these "other types" of nations also praise the Almighty and worship their Creator each in their own way? If God has created humanity in tribes so we may know and respect each other, why should we not get to know and respect other nations of species that He has created too, as Solomon did?[190]

Biodiversity is the Creator's scheme for one diverse group aiding another, a sort of cooperation of nations for the continuation of life on the planet. Higher biodiversity also helps control the spread of certain diseases—for example, a virus will have to adapt itself to every new species it invades. Modern intensive monoculture, which destroys biodiversity as a result of linear and reductionist thinking, has contributed to several agricultural disasters in history, as, for example, the Irish potato famine shows. In 1847, when hundreds of thousands were dying, food worth seventeen million pounds was exported from Ireland under the protection of British troops. Thus, the Irish died not just because of monoculture, but as a result of extortionate rent, the pursuit of profit, and an economic theory focused on domination: this was indeed corruption created by humanity.

"Corruption has appeared in the land": *al-Rūm* 30:41

There have been at least five mass extinctions in the history of the planet, the most recent of which, occurring about sixty five million years ago, wiped out the nonavian dinosaurs. The emergence of humans has now sparked a new wave of extinction caused primarily by the impact of humans on the environment. The last century, with the Industrial Revolution coming into full force, saw an erosion of biodiversity at an alarming rate. Some scientists estimate that there is a loss of up to 140,000 species per year, indicating our current unsustainable practices. A species becomes extinct when the last existing member of that species dies. Extinction is imminent when there are not enough individuals in a specified area able to reproduce. Some of the factors contributing to the loss of biodiversity are overpopulation, deforestation, pollution (air pollution, water pollution, soil contamination), and climate change. We essentially "destroy the tillage and the stock" because we are not pleased with what God has created, but in the long term, we are only digging our own grave: "And some men there are whose saying upon the present world pleases thee, and such a one calls on God to witness what is in his heart, yet he is most stubborn in altercation, and when he turns his back, he hastens about the earth, to do corruption there and to destroy the tillage and the stock; and God loves not corruption; and when it is said to him, 'Fear God,' vainglory seizes him in his sin. So Gehenna shall be enough for him—how evil a cradling!"[191]

Biodiversity provides for variety in foods, shelter, and clothing for humans. Although about 80 percent of our food supply comes from just twenty kinds of plants, humans "use" and need at least forty thousand species of plants and animals a day. Biodiversity is also a source of medicine for people, especially traditional societies. A large proportion of modern drugs (about 40 percent) are directly or indirectly derived from biological sources; in most cases these medicines cannot presently be synthesized in a laboratory. Biodiversity also provides the ecosystem with its own "maintenance services" for regulating the chemistry of our atmosphere and water supply, recycling nutrients, and providing fertile soils. The Gaia theory, promoted by James Lovelock, maintains that life on the planet actually helps regulate its temperature and its atmospheric makeup. Do we not give thanks to Him who has subjugated so much of His creation on earth for us?[192]

Many traditional cultural groups view themselves as an integral part of the natural world, show it respect, and recognize the services provided by other living and nonliving entities in the environment. A conservation ethic is an ethic of resource use, allocation, exploitation, and protection. Its primary focus is upon maintaining the health of the natural world: its forests, habitats, fisheries and biological diversity. The consumer conservation ethic is sometimes expressed by the so-called four Rs: rethink, reduce, reuse, and recycle. The principal value underlying most expressions of conservation ethics is that the natural world has intrinsic and intangible worth along with its utilitarian value.

However, the origins of biological conservation can be traced to philosophical and religious beliefs that see humanity as a part of nature, not as above it. Conserving natural resources and the environment is not a recent concern but has deep cultural roots with the protection of nature. The Torah proposes the concept of the "Sabbatical Year," a period whereby the fields are left fallow, presumably to rejuvenate the soil, an ancient form of the ecological practice of crop rotation. Taoist and Shinto philosophies likewise encourage recognition of special sites, and Jainism, Hinduism, and Buddhism grant sacred values to animals and places. Primal religions also ascribe sacred values to sites such as forests, lakes, and mountains.

"A city with its provision allocated": *al-Naḥl* 16:112

The earth is like a large city, secure and in a complex interactive balance. God has created provision for all its inhabitants and has connected them with one another in the web of life. However, did He create enough to feed humanity's unending hunger and greed? It is this very greed that motivates humans to create death when there was once life, and that will result in us tasting hunger one day when we diminish the earth's capacity to produce enough food, clean air, drinkable water, and the energy that keeps us warm at night.[193] If we have experienced the Irish potato famine, may we not experience a world food famine as well?

The recognition of humanity as part of nature and as its "vicegerent" is in line with the oneness and unity of God, which recognizes the unity of nature and gives us a unity of meaning, and thus a unity of direction, which ultimately should lead us to our unity in action. God does not create in parts but in a whole, complete, and in perfect balance.

A Muslim has an obligation to practice *khilāfa* ("stewardship") over nature. This can be seen from the Arabic *ḥima*, meaning "inviolate zones" set aside solely for the conservation of their natural habitat—typically, fields, wildlife, and forests. This word has a different meaning from *ḥarām*, the purpose of which is to protect areas for more immediate human purposes. The selection of *ḥima* in traditional Islam was a religious rather than a community obligation, and was often the responsibility of religious scholars. There were traditionally five types of *ḥima* reserves: areas where grazing of domestic animals was prohibited; areas where grazing was restricted to certain seasons; beekeeping reserves where grazing was restricted during flowering; forest areas where cutting of trees was forbidden; and reserves managed for the welfare of a particular village, town, or tribe.

Have these concepts been forgotten by modern Muslims? Is there a need to revive and expand this concept, or have we forgotten God's laws, like many before us? Is there a sense of *hima* relevant to our times? For example, instead of beekeeping reserves, we might prioritize animal sanctuaries over housing developments, or protect water reserves from factory spill off. Who will select such new areas: would it be scholars, as in the past, or bankers and politicians, as in the present?

How does a wounded organism regenerate to exactly the same structure as before? How does an egg turn into a living being? God has created each species alike, and yet each individual within them is unique. Has He not created gardens and filled them with diverse crops and in abundance? Do we treat these cohabitants with care, or are we wasteful with His creation?

al-Anʿām 6:141–42

141It is He who produces gardens trellised, and untrellised, palm-trees, and crops diverse in produce, olives, pomegranates, like each to each, and each unlike to each. Eat of their fruits when they fructify, and pay the due thereof on the day of its harvest; and be not prodigal; God loves not the prodigal. 142And of the cattle, for burthen and for slaughter, eat of what God has provided you; and follow not the steps of Satan; he is a manifest foe to you.

al-Anʿām 6:38

38No creature is there crawling on the earth, no bird flying with its wings, but they are nations like unto yourselves. We have neglected nothing in the Book; then to their Lord they shall be mustered.

al-Rūm 30:41

41Corruption has appeared in the land and sea, for that men's own hands have earned, that He may let them taste some part of that which they have done, that haply so they may return.

al-Naḥl 16:112

112God has struck a similitude: a city that was secure, at rest, its provision coming to it easefully from every place, then it was unthankful for the blessings of God; so God let it taste the garment of hunger and of fear, for the things that they were working.

NOTES

1. In the texts that follow in part 2, translations of the Qur'ān are from Arthur J. Arberry, *The Koran Interpreted* (Oxford: Oxford University Press, 1964, reprinted by permission of Harper-Collins Publishers Ltd, copyright 1955, Arthur J. Arberry), but the numbering of verses has been brought in line with the more normal system used in the Egyptian standard edition. Translations of the Bible are from the New Revised Standard Version (copyright 1989, Division of Christian Education of the National Council of the Churches of Christ in the United States of America. Used by permission. All rights reserved.)

2. On the Sumerian king as the "bridge to the gods," see Tikva Frymer-Kensky, *In the Wake of the Goddesses: Women, Culture and the Biblical Transformation of Pagan Myth* (New York: Fawcett Columbine, 1992), 58–69.

3. Psalms 2, 72, 110.

4. 1 Timothy 2:2.

5. Exodus 19:5.

6. Colossians 1:15–20.

7. Romans 8:19–21.

8. Romans 8:20.

9. Psalm 8:8; see also Genesis 1:28.

10. James Gustave Speth, *Red Sky at Morning: America and the Crisis of the Global Environment* (New Haven, CT: Yale University Press, 2004), 15, 34.

11. Genesis 1:3, 7, 9, 11, 15, 24. The seventh, climactic iteration of the formula of completion, "And it was so" (v. 30), applies not to human dominion but to God's provision of food for all creatures.

12. *Hūd* 11:61; and *al-An'ām* 6:165.

13. *Ṣād* 38:26.

14. E.g., *al-Baqara* 2:251; and *al-Ḥajj* 22:40.

15. *al-Furqān* 25:70.

16. *al-'Alaq* 96:4–5.

17. *al Raḥmān* 55:3.

18. *al-Shūrā* 42:11; and *al-Infiṭār* 82:7–8.

19. *al-Taghābun* 64:3.

20. *Āl-'Imrān* 3:6.

21. *al-Isrā'* 17:70.

22. Professor Abdel Haleem here uses Arberry's translation, which had been distributed to seminar participants, but Abdel Haleem differs from Arberry in the translation of some important words.

23. Notably, *al-Baqara* 2:35–39; *al-A'rāf* 7:16–25; and *Ṭā' Hā'* 20:115–23.
24. Genesis 3:1–5, 6, 13, 16.
25. *al-A'rāf* 7:23.
26. Genesis 3:12.
27. *Ṭā' Hā'* 20:121.
28. Genesis 3:16.
29. 1 Timothy 2:11–15, especially v. 14.
30. Galatians 3:28.
31. See Jane Dammen McAuliffe's discussion of some relevant Qur'ānic texts in chapter 7.
32. In the ancient world the gods jealously guarded their superiority over humankind. For example, in the Greek myth Prometheus was condemned to torture for stealing fire from the gods to benefit humanity.
33. *Ṭā' Hā'* 20:115; and *al-A'rāf* 7:23.
34. *al-Baqara* 2:38.
35. Clare Amos, *The Book of Genesis* (Peterborough: Epworth Press, 2004), 43.
36. Romans 7:25; and Romans 7:17, 20.
37. Isma'il al-Faruqi, *Christian Ethics* (Toronto: McGill University Press, 1967). A compilation of al-Faruqi's works is published as *Islam and Other Faiths* (Leicester, U.K.: Islamic Foundation, 1998).
38. The word used for "devil" in Greek is *diabolos*, with which the name Iblīs is surely cognate. The Hellenistic Jewish work is *The Biography of Adam and Eve*, dating at latest to the fourth century CE and perhaps even to the first century. The apocryphal *Gospel (or Questions) of Bartholomew* seems to date to the fifth or late fourth century CE. See Peter J. Awn, *Satan's Tragedy and Redemption: Iblis in Sufi Psychology* (Leiden: Brill, 1983), 20–22.
39. Awn, *Satan's Tragedy*, 46.
40. Whitney S. Bodman, "Stalking Iblīs: In Search of an Islamic Theodicy," in *Myths, Historical Archetypes, and Symbolic Figures in Arabic Literature: Towards a New Hermeneutic Approach*, ed. Angelika Neuwirth (Beirut: Franz Steiner Verlag, 1999), 247–69. It should also be noted that the word "Satan" is Hebrew, meaning "accuser"—readers of the biblical text will notice in the Qur'ān echoes of the figure in the book of Job. With God's permission, Satan reveals by his trials the truth about human beings, and reveals who are the true servants (*al-Isrā'* 17:65).
41. *al-A'rāf* 7:12.
42. Ibid.
43. *al-Baqara* 2:37.
44. *al-A'rāf* 7:23.
45. Ṭabarī, *Jāmi' al-Bayān 'an Ta'wīl Ay al-Qur'ān* ad loc.
46. Isaiah 65:17, 66:22.
47. Revelation 21:1–22:5.
48. In the Western Church, Kingdomtide is the period in the Christian calendar that begins on the day after Pentecost and ends on Christ the King Sunday, the last day of the liturgical year. Known also as Dominiontide or Ordinary Time, this season celebrates the coming of the Kingdom of God and Christ's kingship. Eastertide begins with Easter and continues for seven weeks until Pentecost in the Christian liturgical calendar. The church during this period celebrates the resurrection of Jesus Christ and reflects on its significance for the salvation of humankind.
49. Although these chapters form a thematic unity, there are certain noticeable inner shifts in emphasis as God presents his vision. The final scene captured in Isaiah 65–66 may be presented in three episodes. In the first episode (65:1–16), Yahweh deals with his adversaries in his court, where his opponents are on stage, as it were, as they are being addressed. Verses 65:17–66:5

describe the second episode in which Yahweh directs his attention at completing the New Jerusalem. In the third episode (66:6–24), Yahweh completes the building of the New City and confirms his servants in it. People from different nations are gathered to Jerusalem to worship before him. This section brings the vision to completion. John Watts, *Isaiah 34–66*. Word Biblical Commentary (Waco, Texas: Word Books Publishers, 1987), 338.

50. Isaiah 65:17.

51. So stark is this break that many commentators designate this vision as apocalyptic. This term refers both to a specific genre of Jewish and Christian literature and to the characteristic ideas that literature presents. Chiefly, apocalyptic literature portrays the eschatological future as the result of direct divine intervention, universal judgment, and a new age of salvation in which the entire creation will be radically transformed.

52. Joseph Blenkinsopp, *Isaiah 56–66*, The Anchor Bible, vol. 19B (New York: Doubleday, 2003), 286. It is common to begin this passage with verse 16b. In this connection, the new creation is seen to be the reason for forgetting former troubles. See ibid., 285.

53. Isaiah 65:17–18a; 18b–24.

54. See Isaiah 42:5; 45:7, 12, 18, and so on. While there is certainly a connection between Isaiah 65:17–25 and the creation recital of Genesis 1:1–2:4a, which was composed around the same time and probably shares the same *Weltanschauung*, it is unlikely that the former is entirely dependent on the latter. Isaiah 40–66 generally has much to say about creation but often in terms quite different from Genesis 1. The passage under consideration refers not to the return to the Garden of the primordial creation but to the fulfilment of that creation, its *telos* in the new heavens and the new earth.

55. See Isaiah 42:5–6.

56. The new heavens and the new earth must be seen as the transformation or transfiguration of the present created order, not its destruction. As Claus Westermann has rightly noted, "The words, 'I create anew the heavens and the earth,' do not imply that heaven and earth are to be destroyed and in their place a new heaven and a new earth created. . . . Instead, the world, designated as 'heaven and earth,' is to be miraculously renewed." Claus Westermann, *Isaiah 40–66*, Old Testament Library (London: SCM, 1969), 408.

57. Isaiah 65:18b–24. A more detailed discussion on the significance of the New Jerusalem is presented in our introduction of the New Testament passage in Revelation following.

58. Alec Motyer, *The Prophecy of Isaiah* (Leicester: IVP, 1993), 529. Although the theme of rejoicing is also found in a number of other passages (66:10, 14; and 35:1–2), it is central to the Trito-Isaian core (60:15; 61:10; and 62:5).

59. Ibid., 530.

60. Isaiah 65:18a.

61. Isaiah 65:19b.

62. Isaiah 65:19a. Cf. Isaiah 62:5, "so will your God rejoice over you." Westermann, *Isaiah 40–66*, 409.

63. Isaiah 65:19cd, 22–23, 24–25, respectively. A series of contrasts between the present age and the age to come is clearly delineated in 19b–25 (see Watts, *Isaiah 34–66*, 354):

"Not any more"	*"But"*
Crying, distress	Rejoicing
An infant dying at a young age	A child lives to be a hundred
An elderly person dying prematurely	One hundred years of age is deemed an early age to die
Someone else living in the house you built	Build houses and live in them
Plant for another to eat	Plant and eat the fruits
Work for nothing	Enduring like a tree

Bear children in terror	Wear out their own things
(Build houses for others to take)	Build for children to live in
(Receive answers to prayer)	Before they call, God answers
(Constant violence)	No harm or destruction in all God's mountain

64. Isaiah 65:20. Life expectancy very clearly has a moral dimension in the Old Testament: a long life is correlative with a morally upright life while sickness and premature death is the result of immorality. In the postdiluvian world, life expectancy is at the maximum of 120 years (Gen. 6:3). The moral correlation has therefore resulted in problems when the righteous die at a young age (e.g., Josiah at 39) and the wicked live to a ripe old age (e.g., Manasseh at 67).

65. See Isaiah 25:7–8.

66. See Isaiah 65:6–7, 12, 15c. Alec Motyer explains: "Once more metaphor is being used, but the reality is that even if, *per impossibile*, a sinner were to escape detection for a century the curse would still search him out and destroy him. Thus verse 20 expresses a double thought: death will have no more power and sin no more presence." Motyer, *The Prophecy of Isaiah*, 530.

67. Isaiah 65:21–23. References to home (houses) and farm (vineyards) suggest that the blessing is to be seen everywhere, in every aspect of the lives of the elect. In addition, vineyards are mentioned here because they take a long time to cultivate and bring into production. In verses 21–22 there are two positive statements (21) and their negative counterparts (22ab). The negative statements in verse 22 relate to the fate of the disobedient (cf. Deut. 28:30). The fact that this is completely cancelled implies that only the righteous will inhabit the New Jerusalem. The metaphor of the tree, which suggests durability, longevity, and security, is used to describe the longevity and fruitfulness of the elect (22bc). The thought that nothing will mar the enjoyment of the elect is further elaborated in verse 23. The fear and insecurity that plagues life in the old order will be totally absent in the new heavens and earth. Thus, the elect are assured that they will not toil in vain (Deut. 28.33; and Jer. 3:24) and that their children will not have to live through disastrous and tragic events (Lev. 26:16; Ps. 78:33; and Jer. 15:8).

68. Isaiah 65:24.

69. Westermann, *Isaiah 40–66*, 410.

70. The expression "but dust will be the serpent's food" surely recalls the curse that Yahweh has placed upon it in Genesis 3:14. But as John Watts has pointed out, "the context of the verse calls for understanding this, not as a parallel to enmity with humankind, but as a peaceful element of the newly created order," Watts, *Isaiah 34–66*, 355.

71. Cf. Isaiah 11:9a.

72. Isaiah 65:25b, 25d. Cf. Isaiah 11:7 and Isaiah 11:9. "Holy Mountain" is a phrase used by Isaiah to refer to the place where the presence, peace, and joy of Yahweh may be experienced (see Isa. 11:9, 27:13, 65:11, 25, and 66:20). This expression is also used elsewhere in the Old Testament (Jer. 31:23; Joel 2:1; 4:17; Zech. 8:3; Ps. 3:5, 43:3, 48:2, and Dan. 9:16, 20).

73. It is important to note the function of the appeal to intertextuality in this passage by its inclusion of the terminology of "my holy mountain" found in 11:9. The inclusion of this terminology in 65:25 aims to incorporate the heavenly Zion into the portrayal of the transformation of Jerusalem in 11:9. The new creation of chapter 65 is therefore identified with the messianic hope in First Isaiah (chapters 1–39), together with the promises in Second Isaiah (chapters 40–55). In this way, the beginning, middle, and end of the book of Isaiah are redactionally linked. As Brevard Childs has so pertinently remarked, "The promise in chapter 65 is not an apocalyptic flight into an imaginative world of fantasy, but the fulfilment of God's will taking shape throughout the entire book of Isaiah." See Brevard S. Childs, *Isaiah: A Commentary* (Louisville, KY: Westminster John Knox Press, 2001), 538–39.

74. Quoted in G. R. Beasley-Murray, *The Book of Revelation*, New Century Bible (London: Marshall, Morgan & Scott, 1974), 305.

75. Some theologians have understandably concluded that the present created order will be annihilated and replaced by the "new heavens and a new earth." This conclusion is based on a number of passages in both the Old Testament and the New. The prophets of the Old Testament spoke of the dissolution of the heaven and earth (see Ps. 102:26; Isa. 34:4, 51:6) while Jesus himself declared that "heaven and earth will pass away, but my words will not pass away" (Matt. 24:35). While this interpretation is understandable when considered in light of the earlier passages, other passages seem to suggest that more nuanced interpretation is necessary. Paul describes the present creation as waiting "in eager expectation for the sons of God to be revealed" and that it will be "liberated from its bondage to decay and brought into the glorious freedom of the children of God" (Rom. 8:19–22). This shows that the new creation will be a renewal of the old. This view corresponds with Paul's statement regarding the renewal and rebirth of the person in Christ (2 Cor. 5:17). To destroy the present creation and to bring about another entirely new order of creation would mean that God has failed in his purpose to bring the original creation to fulfilment. Such an understanding of God would be incongruent with the general biblical portrayal. In addition, the annihilation of the present world and the creation of another *ex nihilo* would sever the link between creation and redemption. This is also incompatible with the account of the Bible taken as a whole, which does not speak of the redemption *from* the world (which is more akin to Gnostic soteriology) but rather the redemption *of* the world. The "new heavens and the new earth" therefore refer neither to the restoration of the original state (*restitutio in integrum*) nor to the destruction of the existing created order (*reductio in nihilum*). Rather it points to its transformation (*transfiguratio mundi*). For more detailed discussion, see Roland Chia, "Creation and Eschatology," in *Theodicy and Eschatology*, ed. Bruce Barber and David Neville (Adelaide: ATF Press, 2005), 173–92.

76. The "sea" must be understood figuratively, not literally. Philip Hughes explains: "The disappearance of the sea does not imply that it was regarded as evil in itself, but rather that its aspect was one of hostility to man. It held in its depths the bodies of unnumbered persons who had perished in its waters (hence the concept of the sea giving up its dead at the last judgement, 20:13). Its claims were deceptive. Its restless turbulence was a picture of the instability of the wicked (Is 57:20f). And because its expanses separated men and peoples from each other, its removal may symbolise the harmonious unification as well as the security of all mankind in the renewed creation.'" Philip Edgcumbe Hughes, *The Book of Revelation: A Commentary* (Grand Rapids, MI: Eerdmans, 1990), 222. The connection between the sea and evil made throughout Revelation here reaches its climax. Just as Daniel's monstrous beasts rose from the sea (Dan. 7:3ff), so John's Antichrist comes from the sea (13:1ff). In the same way, the anti-Christian empire in the Revelation has an identical appearance of the devil, that is, the characteristics of a sea monster (Rev. 17:3, cf. 12:3).

77. Revelation 21:2a.

78. Beasley-Murray, *Book of Revelation*, 308.

79. See Hosea 2:16, 19; Isaiah 54:6; Ezekiel 16; 2 Corinthians 11:2; and Ephesians 5:25.

80. Revelation 21:9, 22:17.

81. As place, the New Jerusalem is at once paradise, holy city, and temple. Richard Bauckham explains: "As paradise it is the natural world in its ideal state rescued from the destroyers of the earth, reconciled with humanity, filled with the presence of God, and mediating the blessings of eschatological life to humanity. As holy city, it fulfils the ideal of the ancient city, as the place where heaven and earth meet at the centre of the earth, from which God rules his land and his people, to whose attraction the nations are drawn for enlightenment, and in which people live in

ideal theocentric community. As temple, it is the place of God's immediate presence, where his worshippers see his face." Richard Bauckham, *The Theology of the Book of Revelation* (Cambridge: Cambridge University Press, 1993), 132.

82. Revelation 21:3. The statement "I will be their God and they will be my people" is a covenant formula that ties in well with the picture of God dwelling with his covenant people. There are a number of Old Testament passages that deal with this theme. In Exodus 29:45, the covenant language is used in connection with the establishment of the tabernacle: "Then I will dwell among the Israelites and be their God. They will know that I am the Lord their God, who brought them out of Egypt so that I might dwell among them. I am the Lord their God." Leviticus 26:11–12 reads, "I will put my dwelling-place among you, and I will not abhor you. I will walk among you and be your God and you will be my people." The same correlation between the divine presence (indicated by the metaphor of "dwelling") and the covenant is found in Zechariah 2:10b–11, "'For I am coming, and I will live among you,' declares the Lord. 'Many nations will be joined with the Lord in that day and will become my people. I will live among you and you will know that the Lord Almighty has sent me to you.'" See David Aune, *Revelation 17–22*, Word Biblical Commentary (Nashville: Thomas Nelson Publishers, 1998), 1109.

83. Victory: Deuteronomy 7:21, 20:4, 23:14; 1 Chronicles 22:18; Isaiah 8:10, and Zephaniah 3:17. Providential grace: Genesis 21:20, 31:5, 48:21; Exodus 3:12; Numbers 23:21; Deuteronomy 20:1, 31:6; Joshua 1:5, 9; 1 Samuel 16:18; 1 Chronicles 17:2; 2 Chronicles 9:8, 15:9, 26:23; Nehemiah 3:8; Isaiah 8:10, 41:10, 43:5, 45:15; Jeremiah 42:11; Hosea 11:9; Amos 5:14; Zephaniah 2:7; Zechariah 8:23; Job 29:3–5; and Romans 15:33.

84. 1 Corinthians 15:26; Isaiah 65:19. The contrast is intended between the New Jerusalem and the Rome that the original readers of John's Revelation knew. In Revelation, Rome is presented as "the great whore" (17:9) and portrayed as Babylon the great city and harlot. Babylon is also described as the "mother of whores," which are the other cities in the Roman Empire that were corrupted by the influence of Rome and that share its luxury and evil. Babylon and the New Jerusalem are therefore contrasting pairs of women-cities that dominate the final chapters of the book of Revelation. Richard Bauckham provides a list that shows how the two cities are contrasted in John's Revelation: The chaste bride, the wife of the Lamb (21:2, 9) versus the harlot with whom the kings of the earth fornicate (17:2); her splendour is the glory of God (21:11–21) versus Babylon's splendour from exploiting her empire (17:4; 18:12–13, 16); the nations walk by her light, which is the glory of God (21:24) versus Babylon's corruption and deception of the nations (17:2; 18:3, 23; 19:2); the kings of the earth bring their glory into her (i.e., their worship and submission to God: 21:24) versus Babylon rules over the kings of the earth (17:18ff); they bring the glory and honor of the nations into her (i.e., glory of God: 21:26) versus Babylon's luxurious wealth extorted from all the world (18:12–17); uncleanness, abominations, and falsehoods are excluded (21:27) versus Babylon's abominations, impurities, deceptions (17:4, 5; 18:23); the water of life and the tree of life for the healing of the nations (21: 6; 22:1–2) versus Babylon's wine, which makes the nations drunk (14:8; 17:2; 18:3); life and healing (22:1–2) versus the blood of slaughter (17:6; 18:24); God's people are called to enter the New Jerusalem (22:14) versus God's people are called to come out of Babylon (18:4). Bauckham, *Theology of the Book of Revelation*, 131–32.

85. Revelation 22:1. The water that in Ezekiel flows from the sanctuary of God now flows from the throne of God because there is no temple in the New Jerusalem. The water of life from the throne has a parallel in John 7:38–39: "Whoever believes in me, as the Scripture has said, streams of living water will flow from within him." See also Genesis 2:9–10; Ezekiel 47:1, 6–7, 12; Joel 3:18; and Zechariah: 14:8.

86. Revelation 22:2; and Genesis 2:9f.

87. See Isaiah 12:3, 41:17–18, 43:3–4; Ezekiel 47; Zechariah 13:1, 14:8.

88. Revelation: 21:22.

89. Ezekiel calls the New Jerusalem "The Lord is There" (Ezek. 48:35) while Zechariah declares that the whole city is the temple of God (Zech. 14:20–21). Isaiah has excluded the ritually unclean from the New Jerusalem because they are excluded from the temple (Isa. 52:1; Ps. 24:304).

90. 1 Corinthians 15:28. In the Old Testament, the high priest wore the name of God on his forehead once a year and entered God's immediate presence in the holy of holies of the earthly temple. The eschatological Jerusalem, however, *is* God's eternal holy of holies in which all will enjoy the immediate presence of God without interruption. Bauckham, *Theology of the Book of Revelation*, 142.

91. Revelation 21:23. "In this context," Beasley-Murray writes, "the lamp is the Lamb recalls the saying, 'I am the Light of the world' (Jn 8:12), uttered at Tabernacles, and which implies that what the *Shekinah* was to Israel in the desert and shall be in the coming kingdom, so Christ is for the whole world, the source of salvation and the manifestation of the divine glory for all mankind." Beasley-Murray, *Book of Revelation*, 328.

92. Revelation 22:4.

93. Exodus 33:20–23; and Judges 6:22–23.

94. Bauckham, *Theology of the Book of Revelation*, 142.

95. Revelation 22:3. See also Revelation 1:4; 3:21; 4:2–6, 9–10; 5:1, 6, 11, 13; 6:10; 7:11, 15, 17; 8:3; 12:5; 14:3, 5; 16:17; 19:4, 5; 20:4, 11; 21:5; and 22:1, 3.

96. Revelation 11:15.

97. Richard Bauckham, *The Climax of Prophecy* (Edinburgh, U.K.: T & T Clark, 1993), 242.

98. Isaiah 60:3.

99. Cf. Revelation 22:15. Revelation does not present the view that in the end every human being will receive the salvation of God and be included in his holy city. Indeed, the entire tenor of the Bible—especially the New Testament—concerning salvation is the twofold outcome, namely, acceptance or rejection. This is seen in the parables of Jesus, such as the parable of the rich man and Lazarus (Luke 16:19–31) and the parable of the bridesmaid (Matt. 25:1–13). Universalists argue that although the Bible does speak of divine punishment, these punishments are temporary and have a purificatory function. Thus, the metaphor of God as Judge must be contrasted with that of God as King. The latter concept points to the eventual unity of the kingdom of God under divine kingship. But this interpretation fails to take into account the passages in scripture that explicitly speak of the double end of history (see 1 Cor. 1:18; cf. Phil. 1:18; and Rom. 9:22). Universalists often appeal to the love of God, and argue that divine justice must be understood as serving divine love. Friedrich Schleiermacher therefore maintains that "there are great difficulties in thinking that the finite issue of redemption is such that some thereby obtain the highest bliss, while others . . . are lost in irrevocable misery." He insists that the "milder view" should be embraced, that is, the view that "through the power of redemption there will one day be a universal restoration of all souls" Friedrich Schleiermacher, *The Christian Faith*, eds., H. R. Mackintosh and J. S. Stewart (Edinburgh: T&T Clark, 1948), 722, §163. The history of theology, however, has presented eloquent objections to the doctrine of universal reconciliation. As Helmut Thielicke has put it, "But how can it (universalism) be affirmed and how can one refrain from calling it an 'error' (however unwillingly) according to the venerable judgement of theological history?" *Apokatastasis* can therefore never be a dogma. "If we call it this," to cite Thielicke again, "then in view of its monistic basis we can hardly avoid the result of annulling the conditionality of the present hour of decision and letting things take their course in the name of the expected eschatological 'happy ending.'" Helmut Thielicke, *Evangelical Faith*, vol. 3 (Grand Rapids, MI: Eerdmans, 1982), 455. See also Roland Chia, *Hope for the World: A Christian Vision of the Last Things* (Downers Grove, IL: Inter-Varsity Press, 2006).

100. Cf. Revelation 2:11; 14:10; 18:8; 19:20; and 20:10, 14.
101. *al-Raḥmān* 55:39; and *al-Qiyāma* 75:24.
102. *al-Mu'minūn* 23:110.
103. E.g., *al-Nūr* 24:24; and *Yā' Sīn* 36:65.
104. *al-Wāqi'a* 56:7–11.
105. E.g., *al-Baqara* 2:25; *Āl-'Imrān* 3:15; and *al-Nisā'* 4:57.
106. E.g., *al-Dukhān* 44:54.
107. *al-Wāqi'a* 56:17; and *al-Insān* 76:19.
108. *al-Qiyāma* 75:22–23.
109. Joseph Soloveitchik, *The Lonely Man of Faith* (New York: Doubleday, 1992).
110. I have developed this further in my article "Jesus and Muhammad: New Convergences," *The Muslim World* 99 (2009): 21–38.
111. St. John Chrysostom, *On Marriage and Family Life*, tr. Catherine Roth and David Anderson (Crestwood, NY: St. Vladimir's Seminary Press, repr. 1997), 51.
112. Fr. Alexei Young, "Authority and Obedience in Marriage," *Orthodox America* 3 (September 1984): 32.
113. Pius XI, *Casti connubii* (December 31, 1930), §74. See also Pius XII, speaking to wives: "You are equal in dignity, but this equality does not preclude a hierarchy that establishes the husband as head, and the wife as subject to him. Catholic men and women have the duty to combat the changing social conditions that undermine hierarchy in the family." Pius XII, "Allocution to Newlyweds," September 10, 1941, in *The Woman in the Modern World*, ed. The Monks of Solesmes (Boston: St. Paul Editions, 1959), 65.
114. "Father Cantalamessa on Marital Submission," August 27, 2006. www.catholiconline.net/featured/headline.php?ID = 3582.
115. Shabbir Akhtar, *The Light in the Enlightenment: Christianity and the Secular Heritage* (London: Grey Seal, 1990); and Muhammad Suheyl Umar, "'Voltaire's Bastards': A Response to Koshul," in *Scripture, Reason and the Contemporary Islam-West Encounter: Studying the "Other," Understanding the "Self,"* ed. Basit Bilal Koshul and Steven Kepnes (New York and Basingstoke: Palgrave Macmillan, 2007), 39–68.
116. Useful introductory treatments are Kecia Ali, *Sexual Ethics and Islam: Feminist Reflections on Qur'an, Hadith and Jurisprudence* (Oxford: Oneworld, 2006); and Sa'diyya Shaikh, "Transforming Feminisms: Islam, Women, and Gender Justice," in *Progressive Muslims: On Justice, Gender and Pluralism*, ed. Omid Safi (Oxford: Oneworld, 2003).
117. As an exegetical source, I have drawn primarily on the compact Sunnī commentary of Abū l-Faraj 'Abd al-Raḥmān b. al-Jawzī (d. 1200), *Zād al-masīr fī 'ilm al-tafsīr*, 9 vols. (Damascus, 1984).
118. Muhammad Asad's translation: "Men shall take care of women with the bounties which God has bestowed more abundantly on the former than on the latter."
119. For a survey of English translation of this verse see Obaidullah Fahad, "Equality of Sex in Islam: An Analysis of English Translations of the Quran," in *Aspects of Islam and Muslim Societies*, ed. Nadeem Hasnain (New Delhi: Serials Publications, 2006), 289–91.
120. The majority of the commentators (*mufassirūn*) make *Allāh* nominative, which gives three meanings: (1) God is guarding them; (2) God is guarding their dowries for them and requiring expenditures on them; (3) protectors in the [husband's] absence of something that the command of God protects. Abū Ja'far puts it in the accusative (i.e., by what protects God), and it means by their protecting God with their obedience. Ibn al-Jawzī, *Zād*.
121. Ibn al-Jawzī, *Zād*.
122. Ibid.

123. Ibid. But he also admits that some *madhāhib* do not require that admonishment follow this sequence. On this verse, particularly the terms "*qawwamūna*" and "*nushūz*," see Ali, *Sexual Ethics*, 117–26; and Sa'diyya Shaikh, "Exegetical Violence: *Nushūz* in Qur'ānic and Gender Ideology," *Journal for Islamic Studies* 17 (1997): 49–73.

124. Farid Esack, "Islam and Gender Justice: Beyond Simplistic Apologia," *What Men Owe to Women: Men's Voices from World Religions*, eds. John C. Raines and Daniel C. Maguire (Albany: State University Of New York, 2001), 187–210; and Amina Wadud, *Inside the Gender Jihad: Women's Reform in Islam* (Oxford: Oneworld, 2006), 200.

125. *al-Aḥzāb* 33:35; *al-Rūm* 30:21. Fazlur Rahman, *Islam* (New York, 1966), 39; Amina Wadud, *Qur'ān and Woman: Rereading the Sacred Text from a Woman's Perspective* (Oxford: Oneworld, 1999), 9; and Asma Barlas, *Believing Women in Islam: Unreading Patriarchal Interpretations of the Qur'an* (Austin: University of Texas Press, 2002), 23.

126. Al-Jawzi, *Zād*.

127. Muhammad Asad's translation: "Men have precedence over them."

128. A final concern of the classical exegetes is whether this verse was abrogated either in whole or in part. Al-Jawzi, *Zād*: "The scholars disagree about whether this verse is abrogated or not. (1) Some say it is abrogated but disagree about what part of it is. One group says it is the phrase 'divorced women shall wait by themselves for three periods.' They say that it used to be incumbent on every divorced woman that she wait for three periods but the judgment about the woman who is pregnant was abrogated by *al-Ṭalāq* 65:4, 'And for those with child, their period shall be until they bring forth their burden.' The judgment about the woman divorced before consummation is abrogated by *al-Aḥzāb* 33:49, 'If you marry believing women and divorce them before you have touched them, then there is no period that you should count.' This is reported on the authority of Ibn 'Abbās. Another group said that the first part of it is *muḥkam* and the abrogated section is 'their mates have better right to restore them.' They say that when a man divorces his wife, the better right to her return is as though it were the third divorce or beyond that. So it was abrogated by *al-Baqara* 2:230, 'If he has divorced her [the third time] she is not afterwards lawful to him until she has wed another husband.' (2) Others say that the entire verse is *muḥkam*. The beginning of it is of general applicability (*'āmm*)."

129. Fazlur Rahman, *Major Themes of the Qur'ān* (Minneapolis: Bibliotheca Islamica, 1980), 49.

130. Barlas, *Believing Women*, 196.

131. Isaiah 3:1–5.

132. Isaiah 1:12–17; 3:13–15; 5:1–7, 8–10.

133. Isaiah 2:5.

134. Daniel Berrigan, *Isaiah: Spirit of Courage, Gift of Tears* (Minneapolis: Fortress Press, 1996), 12–14, 18–19.

135. Proverbs 29:18; or NRSV, "Where there is no prophecy, the people cast off restraint."

136. Micah 4:4.

137. Joel 3:10.

138. Isaiah 2:5.

139. Isaiah 42:1–4 is quoted in Matthew 12:18–21; Isaiah 53:4, in Matthew 8:17; and Isaiah 61:1 ff, in Luke 4:18 ff.

140. Matthew 5:1; 17:1; 28:16.

141. Mark 16:15.

142. John 4:21–24.

143. Romans 11:11f, 15f, 25f.

144. Genesis 1:26–28.

145. Acts 22:3.

146. Lucien Legrand, *The Bible on Culture* (Bangalore: Theological Publications in India, 2001), 84–85, 120–21.
147. Galatians 2.
148. Galatians 3–4.
149. Galatians 2:10; 5–6.
150. Galatians 3:6–9.
151. Galatians 3:26–29.
152. Galatians 5:1.
153. See 1 Corinthians 12:13; and Colossians 3:11.
154. Galatians 6:16; and Romans 3:29–30; 15:7–13.
155. Galatians 5:6.
156. Romans 2:11.
157. Colossians 3:11.
158. Philemon 15–16.
159. Genesis 1:27.
160. Colossians 3:18–4:1; Ephesians 5:22–6:9; and 1 Peter 2:18–3:7.
161. 1 Corinthians 12:13.
162. Clifford Geertz, "Ritual and Social Change: A Javanese Example," *American Anthropologist* 59 (1957): 32–54.
163. Victor Turner, *The Ritual Process: Structure and Anti-Structure* (New York: de Gruyter, 1969).
164. Galatians 6:15.
165. Galatians 3:1.
166. See 1 Corinthians and Philemon, respectively.
167. Galatians 3:27.
168. Revelation 12:10.
169. See Revelation 7:4.
170. See Revelation 7:1–8.
171. See Revelation 7:9, and 7:4.
172. See Revelation 7:14.
173. Revelation 1:5.
174. John 18:38–19:2.
175. Revelation 3:1–6, 14–22; and Revelation 2:8–11; 3:7–13, respectively.
176. *al-Mā'ida* 5:48.
177. *al-Baqara* 2:213; *al-Mā'ida* 5:48; and *Yūnus* 10:19.
178. *Hūd* 11:110.
179. *Hūd* 11:119.
180. This verse is discussed in the essay by Jane McAuliffe, "al-Aḥzāb 33:35; al-Rūm 30:21; al-Nisā' 4:34; al-Bugara 2:228," chapter 7.2.
181. This verse is discussed in the essay by Vincent Cornell, "Islam and Human Diversity," chapter 2.2.
182. Jeremiah 33:20–21.
183. Genesis 8:22
184. E.g., Psalm 72:1–6.
185. Jeremiah 18:14–16.
186. Isaiah 65:20–22.
187. Romans 8:19–21.
188. Isaiah 65:25.

189. Revelation 22:1–4.
190. *al-Ḥujurāt* 49:13.
191. *al-Baqara* 2:204–6.
192. *al-Naḥl* 16:14–17.
193. *al-Rūm* 30:41.

AFTERWORD

Reflections on Humanity in Text and Context

Rowan Williams

THE GREAT ISSUES of our century are all, in one way or another, about what human beings believe about themselves. At the most pronounced extreme, some people talk as though humanity were essentially identical with its own will to domination, as though to be human was to be involved in a struggle to become more and more completely emancipated from "nature" and free to exercise the choice to be whatever we will. The effects of this are obvious over a range of contexts. Most dramatically, this mindset stands behind our environmental crisis, but it is also visible in some of our mythology about technology and its capacity to free us from humiliating limits, a mythology that operates in the medical world as well as the world of management of what lies around us. We can manipulate what the "natural" world presents us with, and there is no constraint on that manipulation other than what we decide.

All the great religious traditions begin from somewhere else; that is why they are all, in one degree or another, committed to a critique of this image of a dominant humanity emancipated from the limits imposed by the material environment. For Christians and Muslims alike, the human self is from the very first involved and implicated in relations that it did not itself create. It is, first and foremost, constituted by relation with the Creator: the human self *is* because God has spoken, and it lives because God has spoken *to* it. Consciously or not, it depends second by second on a will not its own, and it has such solidity as it has because it is endowed with the capacity to respond to what God says and gives. What is more, the human self exists in relation to the rest of the world. Some of the contributors to this book note in passing that the way modern people talk about "nature" cannot be translated back into the language of Bible or Qur'ān or classical theology and commentary: there is no clear separation between what is human and what is (merely) natural. Humanity is what it is as belonging to an ordered whole, the balance and welfare of which it is called to serve and sustain. When we get into the habit of thinking of ourselves as outside the "natural" world, we are taking a first step into an unreal universe and the dissolution of our real identity as human.

Exactly what it means to say that we are called to serve the order of the world needs some spelling out. But several of the contributions to this book rightly insist that the cliché about how the Abrahamic faiths have contributed to environmental degradation by underlining the authority or dominion of humanity in creation is a serious misreading of scripture and tradition. The language about human responsibility in the world is grounded firmly in the assumption that human care for creation has to mirror God's own care, God's "delight" in what he has made, to pick up one powerful strand in the Judaeo-Christian world. It is a check on any human temptation to flatten out the diversity of the natural order, let alone of the human world itself—a strong theme in some of the Qur'ānic texts discussed here. In both Christianity and Islam there is, in a whole assortment of ways, a clear vision of humanity being answerable for the rest of the world—not as possessing proprietorial rights over it, with sole disposition of its resources. This vision is expressed vividly in the biblical and Qur'ānic picture of Adam naming the animals and of the covenant recorded in Genesis with "all living things" at the end of the story of Noah. It is also expressed in the Qur'ānic idea of Adam as created by God to communicate or manifest the divine will in the midst of the created order. One of these essays reflects the debate about the exact meaning of *khalīfa* as a term for the dignity of human beings in creation, and questions the common translation as "viceroy." Whatever the conclusion to this particular debate, there is no doubt at all that God is believed to have conferred on humanity a unique dignity that, in both Islamic texts and some Christian traditions, establishes that even the angels owe a kind of homage to human beings.

Humanity is itself, therefore, in this twofold relation: with its maker, whose image (in Christian and Jewish thinking) it bears or whose authority (in a more obviously Islamic idiom) it in some sense holds; and with the creation, the care of which is the distinctive vocation of men and women—the particular way in which image or authority is exercised. If humanity is thought of simply in terms of its innate dignity in relation to God, it is misconceived: that dignity has to be fleshed out in a human life that is answerable for creation. And if it is answerable for creation, it is in a very special sense answerable also for its own corporate life: it has to realize in its intrahuman relations the same intensity of divine care. All the social ethic of Christianity and Islam rests on this. For Christians, there is a further dimension in that humanity is made specifically in the Trinitarian image: its irreducible relatedness is seen as mirroring the self-relatedness of God as eternally a threefold interweaving of agencies, Father, Son, and Holy Spirit. This is one of the areas of Christian thought least accessible or sympathetic to the Muslim, but it is also an affirmation of one thing that is common to both faiths: the clear repudiation of any idea that the essential moral unit of humanity is the isolated individual as opposed to the individual in relation.

To say this about the essential moral unit is not, of course, to deny the ethical centrality of personal liberty, and this too is significant for both religions. Christianity has laid a good deal more stress than Islam on the consequence of the first destructive choice made by human agents, the Fall of Adam, with its consequences for every subsequent human being. Christianity has tended to think of humanity as limited in its freedom because of the wrong perceptions that this primordial choice created: we cannot simply choose the good because our vision is obscured. Islam is skeptical about this inherited defect and more inclined to affirm strongly the continuing liberty of human beings to say yes or no to the divine command. But both Christianity and Islam regard liberty as an inherent defining characteristic of human identity; and both would agree that it is in self-denying harmony with the eternal will of God that liberty finds its fulfillment. Both also face formidable philosophical problems in holding that there is a real human liberty of consent or refusal and that God foreknows or even foreordains human action. But the sense in which we can attribute this foreknowledge to God does not, in either faith, take away the clear conviction that we are held responsible for what we decide for or against God—and thus that the response of faith is not something to be coerced by human power. Both Islam and Christianity have, historically, a mixed record in this area, but the understanding of religious liberty as something that a just social order entails is now enshrined in most of the weightiest statements from leaders of the two faiths.

Mention of religious liberty leads in to the issue that a couple of contributions in this volume touch upon—the connection between contemporary Christian and Muslim views of humanity and the Enlightenment legacy represented in the discourse of human rights. It is a highly complex area. On the one hand, Christians and Muslims agree in defending an exalted notion of human dignity and personal responsibility, and a robust doctrine of what social justice demands for all. They are both, very importantly, universalist in their vision: neither faith can tolerate any suggestion that the good for human beings is divisible, that certain benefits or liberties are restricted only to some of the human race. This is why, among other things, they are both missionary religions: the missionary impulse is not to be written off as aggressive bigotry and exclusivism, but is to be understood as rooted in this conviction that all must have access to the same goods, spiritual no less than material. As universalist discourses, they have something in common with Enlightenment principles. On the other hand, they are suspicious of that kind of Enlightenment language that seeks a universal basis for religious knowledge independent of any authority or tradition, and that sees the ideal human condition as one that is emancipated from various forms of dependence, social or material. We have already noted the difficulties of this from a position of Christian or Muslim faith.

As argued in places in this book, the result is a certain complexity about issues such as equality as understood in religious terms. This may appear in the assertion from strongly traditionalist Christians or Muslims that an acceptance of a kind of hierarchy as between the sexes or even in the social order is not incompatible with a clear commitment to spiritual equality and equal dignity. Others would say that the history of religious communities shows too many examples of this principle being abused for the contemporary believer to be confident that it is now defensible in this form. But to share anxieties about this does not mean a capitulation to Enlightenment values as the natural and obvious view of the world; it is more to suggest, as do some of the authors here, that history and social change do help us draw out into full daylight, so to speak, aspects of our fundamental beliefs that will make us look again at certain historical practices or conventions long thought to be authoritative or revealed. The essays here do not offer a simple and rapid answer to this set of problems but indicate more work to be done on all sides around the question of faith and modernity. Some of this work the Building Bridges seminar has continued to undertake.

What emerges from all this discussion is a real convergence around the belief that humanity has a distinctive calling from its maker; we do not have the liberty to invent ourselves, to relocate the limits of what it is to be human, to accord with our own unfettered wills. That distinctive calling is manifest in three ways: in devotion to the Creator expressed in prayer and adoration and holy life; in responsibility for justice and generosity in the social order; and in being answerable for the care and nurture of the rest of the created order. In the contemporary world, none of these is a belief that can be taken for granted; the outworking of each is likely to bring the believer into conflict with many aspects of our social, economic, political, and technological life. To recognize this in the ways that this book does is not to summon Christians and Muslims into a sort of cobelligerence against the spirit of the age. That can be a form of self-righteous obscurantism. But it is important to see that part of the singular importance of religious belief in our era is its capacity to challenge limited and impoverished versions of human identity. To return to where we started, what we believe about humanity is bound up with what we believe about the context of humanity—hence the title of this book. That context, for the person of faith, is specified by the reality that is the context of all particular things and is itself no particular thing, no item in a list, no object to be given a label or a definition by the finite mind. Humanity is fully human in relation with God, and in that relatedness, humanity discovers how to exercise its glorious and extraordinary dignity. In our world, the service of that dignity may bring us into conflict with cultures of paranoia, violence, and indiscriminate slaughter; cultures of trivial entertainment; or cultures of exclusive privilege and hard-hearted selfishness. These essays seek to provide resources for some of that service, in a spirit of openness and mutual gratitude—a spirit, indeed, of relatedness and a recognition that we need one another to make sense of ourselves. To demonstrate such a spirit is, we believe, a sign to the world not only of critique but also of positive hope.

INDEX TO BIBLICAL CITATIONS

INDEX TO QUR'ĀNIC CITATIONS

GENERAL INDEX

Abdel, Haleem, Muhammad, 75–77
Abu Madyan, 36
affinity, image of God and, 27–29
Ahaz, king, 106–7
'Ajamī term, 39
Akrami, Seyed Amir, 93–96
alienation
  Christian viewpoint on, 78–83
  Muslim viewpoint on, 84–86
  Siddiqui on, 15, 18–19
  Soloveitchik on, 97
Anan, Kofi, 58
anger, 6
apocalypticism
  Prior on, 115
  term, 135n51
Arab, term, 38
Aratus, 28
al-Attas, S. M. N., 44
Augustine, 79–80
avarice, 6
āyātology, 22

Babel, tower of
  Ipgrave on, 31
  Northcott on, 58
Baharuddin, Azizan, 41–49
Bakar, Osman, 120–23
Barlas, Asma, 104
Barth, Karl, 57–58
barzakh, term, 93
Bauckham, Richard, 137n81, 138n84
Bellah, Robert, 4
Berkouwer, G. C., 9, 61n5, 62n15, 63n31
Berman, Marshall, 4
Berrigan, Daniel, 108
Berry, R. J., 56
Berry, Wendell, 58
Bilal the Ethiopian, 35, 37, 122
biodiversity
  Bakar on, 120
  Yasin on, 128–30
bride image, Chia on, 89
Building Bridges seminar, xv–xvii
Burridge, Richard, 24–26

Calvin, John, 5, 8, 62n30
Cantalamessa, Raniero, 99
Chapra, Umer, 48–49
Chesterton, G. K., 6
Chia, Roland, 87–92
Childs, Brevard, 136n73
city
  Baharuddin on, 42
  Bauckham on, 137n81, 138n84
  Chia on, 87–90
  Prior on, 109, 115–16
  Yasin on, 130–31
civil society
  Earth Charter on, 43
  Malaysian, 44
color distinctions
  Bakar on, 121–22
  Cornell on, 37–38
communication, mission and, Ipgrave on, 30–32
community of interpretation, extension of, 24–25, 29–30
conservation ethic, Yasin on, 130
Cornell, Vincent, 33–40, 100, 122
cosmopolitanism, Islam and, Cornell on, 33–34
covenant
  Ng on, 12–14
  Northcott on, 124